Making Common Cause

Also by Vasilis Vourkoutiotis

PRISONERS OF WAR AND THE GERMAN HIGH COMMAND: The British and American Experience

REGIONAL ECONOMICS AND INTERNATIONAL RELATIONS, Volume 3 (*Co-edited with Dimitrii Doronitchev*)

REGIONAL IDENTITIES IN SIBERIA AND THE RUSSIAN FAR EAST (*Co-edited with Julia Oulianovka*)

Making Common Cause
German–Soviet Secret Relations, 1919–22

Vasilis Vourkoutiotis

© Vasilis Vourkoutiotis 2007

All rights reserved. No reproduction, copy or transmission of this publication may be made without written permission.

No paragraph of this publication may be reproduced, copied or transmitted save with written permission or in accordance with the provisions of the Copyright, Designs and Patents Act 1988, or under the terms of any licence permitting limited copying issued by the Copyright Licensing Agency, 90 Tottenham Court Road, London W1T 4LP.

Any person who does any unauthorised act in relation to this publication may be liable to criminal prosecution and civil claims for damages.

The author has asserted his right to be identified as the author of this work in accordance with the Copyright, Designs and Patents Act 1988.

First published 2007 by
PALGRAVE MACMILLAN
Houndmills, Basingstoke, Hampshire RG21 6XS and
175 Fifth Avenue, New York, N.Y. 10010
Companies and representatives throughout the world

PALGRAVE MACMILLAN is the global academic imprint of the Palgrave Macmillan division of St. Martin's Press, LLC and of Palgrave Macmillan Ltd. Macmillan® is a registered trademark in the United States, United Kingdom and other countries. Palgrave is a registered trademark in the European Union and other countries.

ISBN-13: 978–0–230–00644–7 hardback

This book is printed on paper suitable for recycling and made from fully managed and sustained forest sources. Logging, pulping and manufacturing processes are expected to conform to the environmental regulations of the country of origin.

A catalogue record for this book is available from the British Library.

Library of Congress Cataloging-in-Publication Data
Vourkoutiotis, Vasilis, 1970–
   Making common cause:German–Soviet relations, 1919–1922/by Vasilis Vourkoutiotis.
     p. cm.
   Includes bibliographical references and index.
   ISBN-13: 978–0–230–00644–7
   1. Germany—Foreign relations—Soviet Union. 2. Soviet Union—Foreign relations—Germany. 3. Germany—Politics and government—1918–1933. 4. Soviet Union—Politics and government—1917–1936. I. Title.
DD120.R8V68 2007
327.4304709′042—dc22
                                          2006050355

10 9 8 7 6 5 4 3 2 1
16 15 14 13 12 11 10 09 08 07

Contents

Acknowledgements	vi
1 Introduction	1
2 Historical Background: End of War and Start of "Peace"	8
3 Exploring the Options: 1919	35
4 Opening the Door Wider, Amid Rumours and Chaos	62
5 Confirming the Contacts, Building a Framework	106
6 Under the Umbrella of Rapallo	137
7 Conclusion	169
Notes	174
Bibliography	185
Index	196

Acknowledgements

My interest in this era and topic first came as a result of contact with colleagues at the institutions where I lectured for three years, in Russia: the Faculty of International Relations of Ural State University (led by Prof. Valeri Mikhailenko), and Smolny College of Liberal Arts and Sciences, St Petersburg State University (led by Director Valeri Monakhov). The latter, especially, greatly facilitated my access to the Russian archives. My current colleagues and students at the University of Ottawa provide me with a stimulating environment in which to work.

Early encouragement of the viability and necessity of this study came from Prof. Dr Hans-Heinrich Nolte of the University of Hannover (editor of *Zeitschrift fuer Weltgeschichte* and Chair of the Verein fuer Geschichte des Weltsystems). Academic support was also kindly offered, in part, by Prof. Georges-Henri Soutou (of the Centre d'histoire de l'Europe et des Relations internationals, Université de Paris IV—Sorbonne) and Prof. Masayuki Yamauchi (of the University of Tokyo, and expert on Enver Pasha). Financial support for this project came from the German Academic Exchange Service (DAAD), the University of Ottawa, and Queen's University at Kingston. I wish to thank, as well, the archivists and staff in Germany, where researching has always been unhindered (the Foreign Office and Federal archives in Berlin, and the Federal Military archives in Freiburg im Breisgau), and Russia, where the reputation for obstruction proved far worse than my actual experiences there (the State Archive of the Russian Federation, the State Socio-Political Archive (former-Comintern archive), the State Military Archives, and Ministry of Foreign Affairs/Historical Documents Department).

And lastly, I am grateful to my family: Taka-chan, Sia-chan, and Sifis.

1
Introduction

> [If Russia] turned to Germany, and these two powers made common cause, a most gravely dangerous situation would be created.[1]
> —Signor Nitti, the Italian Prime Minister, on 23 February 1920

> The Italian stand is dictated by opportunism, subsequently vacillating, unclear and anyway not of crucial influence.[2]
> —Count Brockdorff-Rantzau, former German Foreign Minister and the first post-Treaty of Rapallo Ambassador to Moscow, on 24 April 1921

No one listened to the Italians. Although Brockdorff-Rantzau's comments were produced in a different context, they nonetheless summarize the totality of the impact made by Prime Minister Nitti upon the leaders of Britain, America, and France. But be that as it may, the Italian warning had come well after the first steps had already been taken in exploring a German–Soviet clandestine relationship which would have important consequences for Europe, and the world.

With the open hostilities ended in November 1918, the German military and the Soviet Russian leadership began to wonder about what kind of a relationship each would eventually be able to develop with the rest of the international community of nations. In Moscow, it was clear that there was a shared hostility towards the communist revolution in every quarter of capitalist Europe—regardless of which side of the First World War one happened to have been on. Germany's troops, despite their loss, continued to occupy large swathes of former Russian imperial territory, thanks not only to the generous terms of the Treaty of Brest-Litovsk, but also to the terms of the Entente's armistice with Germany. And although the Allied powers had made clear that Brest-Litovsk would be relegated to posterity, their own desire to see the eradication of the Soviet regime meant that the new Soviet state faced a front of common hostility, in which former enemies—Germany and the Entente—could pose a menace to the existence of the communist experiment.

The Soviet foreign commissar Chicherin noted this directly on 15 November 1918, when he warned Hugo Haase, the newly appointed member of the German Council of People's Commissioners responsible for foreign affairs (and ostensibly a socialist leader), that the "German occupation troops" were building a convenient cover and bridge for the eventual arrival of Entente soldiers in Russia.[3] The full level of Allied participation on the side of the counter-revolutionary Whites during the Russian Civil War was still not fixed, but the Soviet need for splitting the capitalist ranks was clear, and became a strategic necessity well before the final terms of the Treaty of Versailles would clarify the future shape of Europe. The Soviet interest in resurrecting a relationship cultivated by Bismarck in the 19th century, but then abandoned by Kaiser Wilhelm II, was obvious, while the events of the years that would follow would demonstrate the need for this special relationship to the Germans.

The Soviet side was by no means unified. Ideologically, if anything else, there remained the purists' belief that what had transpired in Russia—however unlikely by traditional Marxist interpretations of the inevitable paths of historical evolution towards a worker's communist paradise—was simply the first step in global revolution. The Communist International (Comintern) was the vehicle through which Soviet Russian leadership and guidance could be transmitted to fellow communists across Europe, and eventually across the world, and the Comintern saw no reason why it should not take as much advantage as possible of the ferment in post-armistice Germany to further this goal. Although formally created in March 1919, its Russian militants had been actively supporting the cause before that point, throughout Europe. That this might work against the interests of the Soviet Russian *state* in its attempt to develop a mutually advantage economic and military relationship with the German government was not of their concern. The split within the Soviet hierarchy would prove to have a continuing impact upon the nature of contact between Germany and Soviet Russia, and the relationship between the two would not be able to develop until the Comintern was reigned in.

On the German side, the matter was complicated as well. The collapse of the German imperial system, and the arrival of the Weimar Republic thanks to the midwifery of the German Social Democrats, ensured that within the mythology of nationalist circles (both extreme and traditional) the democratic state would be viewed as the product of socialist treachery and complicity for the defeat of the Fatherland. That the republic was born amid complete and utter domestic, social, and political chaos did not improve matters, nor did the proclamation of a "socialist" state in Bavaria under the leadership of Kurt Eisner. These were, however, German socialists, not communists—and certainly not the same breed of radicals as the Bolsheviks in Moscow. These were the socialists who voted for the flag instead of ideological convictions in 1914, when they supported the final military budget of the government before the outbreak of the First World War with a solemn declaration not to abandon the Fatherland in its hour of need. And, as the Soviet leadership would dumbfoundedly find out, these were the sort of socialists who would prefer to forgo an offer of food from the Soviet Russia in the midst of the Allied blockade, with the sheepish explanation that the Entente powers had already promised to ensure that the country would not starve in the immediate chaotic aftermath of the armistice.

Although the Social Democrats had nominal control of the civilian apparatus of the German state at the time of the armistice, the German military continued to exercise a mind of its own. The generals who had spirited Lenin and his entourage through Germany in a sealed railway car to assist with the destabilization of Imperial Russia, and who then imposed a peace-treaty upon the resulting regime whose harshness would make the later conditions of Versailles seem magnanimous, had even before the war's end begun to realize that it might be a good idea to not antagonize Soviet Russia too much. Under the terms of the Berlin negotiations between the Soviets and the Germans in August 1918, some of the harsher terms of Brest-Litovsk were clawed back. And Ludendorff himself would at one point in his post-war political vacillations veer towards "National Bolshevism"—an alliance of the officer-class and workers—before returning to his natural inclinations to advocate an invasion of Soviet Russia.[4] The German army, the only true power in the state despite its apparent disarming by the Allies, was at times confused, but not blind. Given the fluidity of the immediate post-war scene, it simply tried to keep its options open, and as 1919 wore on and the terms of the "peace" became known, it grew increasingly convinced that ultimately the Entente powers of the West were the greater enemy and threat to the political and military rehabilitation of Germany: Versailles imposed limits, reparations, and—perhaps most unforgivable of all—gave away much German territory to Poland. West Prussia and Posen were lost, but the territories and citizens would not be forgotten. And so the army looked further east, for an ally who shared a common hostility to Warsaw, and by extension, the victorious powers of the First World War.

That the roots of the German–Soviet relationship formed the subject of significant historical enquiry after the Second World War is understandable. The Molotov–Ribbentrop Pact of 1939, given the war it unchained, is the perfect example of totalitarian diplomacy at its most infamous. Given, as well, the simple reality that many of the tools used by Hitler had technological and doctrinal origins that could be traced to the 1920s collaboration between the two countries, it is natural that the Treaty of Rapallo of 1922 became viewed as a precursor to 1939, and hence to the Second World War.

The Treaty of Rapallo's significance for the two pariah states of the early post-First World War era is rarely underestimated, but often overstated. The actual treaty simply allowed for the reestablishment of diplomatic relations and the establishment of commercial ties, and dealt with the issue of debts. But the secret military agreements concluded both before and in its aftermath were of greater importance to global security as a whole: they allowed for the Luftwaffe to develop in terms of technology and pilot-training, for the principles of Blitzkrieg to be established and confirmed in practice away from prying Allied eyes at the tank centres near Kazan, while the Red Army, drained by the Civil War and the conflict with Poland, received the right to expert (i.e. German) military training and financial benefits of which they were desperately in need.

A German–Soviet private firm ("Bersol") in Samara was established to explore the production of poison gas under German management. The Soviets also received "technical assistance" from German industrial and military specialists in munitions at Zlatoust, Tula, and Petrograd (St Petersburg/Leningrad). The German side received a share of the profits and of the product, from these works. The financial underpinings for the projects came from what later economists might refer to as "German government-supported junk-bonds", issued by the Gesellschaft zur Foerderung gewerblicher Unternehmungen (GEFU) (Company for the Development of Trade Enterprises), based in Moscow and Berlin with (in 1923) 75 million marks (18 million dollars). The German army's special group dedicated to Russia (Sondergruppe R) had already, well before Rapallo, established Zentrale Moskau in the Soviet capital, under the leadership of the colourful Major Oskar Ritter von Niedermayer (alias Herr Neumann); he had been the head of a German expedition to Afghanistan in the First World War, evaded British capture there, and liked to refer to himself as the German "Lawrence" [i.e. of Arabia].[5]

The German military wished to take active steps to prepare for rearmament, and to have a functional base from which it could stay on the leading edge of technology and doctrine. This could only be done in hiding from the victors of the First World War (and, once the terms of the Treaty of Versailles became known, in violation of it). Soviet Russia, physically vast and politically a leper, was the only real option. The Red Army, and Soviet industry as a whole, was bound to benefit from the cooperation, but in the hard view of Realpolitik, the only significant point of potential contact and conflict between the two countries—Poland—could be dealt with the way Germany and Russia had traditionally dealt with it in centuries past: dismemberment and division. The German army would have provided training for the Red Army, and would have assisted it to achieve a level of efficiency and organization that might have given Hitler pause for concern in 1941, had Stalin not already done him the favour of "purging" most Soviet commanders before the war even began. The War Academy in Berlin, with expertise developed over hundreds of years, had been made available to Soviet officers. The main irritant on both sides was the pestering attempts of the Comintern to destabilize Germany internally. Lenin and the majority of the Soviet leadership would, in weighing the likelihood of a successful German revolution to occur against the benefits of dealing with the Prussian officer class, see soon enough (and before Rapallo) that cooperation had greater advantages. One might observe that the German socialists were not the only ones who sacrificed ideological purity in the early part of the century.[6]

* * *

The collapse of the Soviet Union and the opening of its previously closed archives for historical researchers from all countries have made possible a reexamination of the interwar period which was previously unimaginable, as one can finally see most records from all sides of the events. But with so much terrain open to revision, it is not surprising that no lengthy effort has been made since then to see what new light may be shed specifically on the earliest secret relations between Germany and Russia by examining the records of Russian archives, and comparing the findings with the German archival material. The major works which have appeared in Russian, German, English, or French have all tended to focus on the immediate implications of the Treaty of Rapallo and the relationship in the mid- to late-1920s, rather than the process by which the military agreements were made in the first place.[7]

Thus, a gap in the historiography of the post-First World War relations between Germany and the Soviet Union exists; this study is an attempt to, in part, bridge that gap, from the armistice to Rapallo. Specifically, it seeks to learn when and how the first steps towards sounding each other out were taken, in both military and economic terms. The traditional interpretation, such as that offered by Carsten, was that "Although the first tentative moves between Berlin and Moscow were made as early as [August] 1920, it does not seem likely that any direct negotiations between the German and Russian military authorities took place in that year; or, if they took place, they had no immediate result."[8]

This work aims to demonstrate that significant contacts began before this point, and that (more importantly) concrete steps indicative of a desire for such contacts had begun even before the Allies had presented the terms of Versailles to the German delegation, in May 1919; it then will flesh out the contacts, as they evolved up to the signing of the Treaty of Rapallo, in April 1922. It hopes to do so in a manner which will be accessible to general readers as well as to those with a firmer grounding in modern European history. Thus, the work also intends, especially in the early chapters, to offer a narrative history of the chaotic first post-war years, to provide a sense of greater context for the reader into which the developments of the subsequent events leading to Rapallo (and the archival findings of both past and present research) will make sense.[9]

The work wishes to build upon the existing work of other historians of the field. For the more general narrative portions, reference has been given to the most current, thorough authors on various subjects. With regard to the precise focus of the study, this work seeks to build upon the work of Horst Guenther Linke and Sergei Gorlov. Linke pioneered the field from the German side, and made the first exhaustive studies based on the fully accessible German archival perspective. Gorlov, in Moscow, has led the post-Soviet-era investigations into the Soviet archival mass, but has focused more extensively on the post-Rapallo era rather than the negotiations which preceded it—and it is in this earlier period that the majority of Soviet archival material was found to be under-explored.[10] This work is intended as a complement to the pre-existing historiography of these two historians. It is based on archival research conducted in Germany (Foreign Office Archives, Federal Archives, and Federal Military Archives) and Russia (State Socio-Political Archive [former-Comintern archive], State Military Archives, Ministry of Foreign Affairs/Historical Documents Department, and the State Archive of the Russian Federation).[11]

2
Historical Background: End of War and Start of "Peace"

Although there was little sympathy for the Tsarist regime of Russia in the West, at the very least it was an ally against Germany during the Great War. The February 1917 Revolution did not necessarily threaten the status of Russia's participation in the war, and so was considered not directly threatening to the interests of the Allies. The Bolshevik Revolution later that year, however, with its declared aim of ending Russia's involvement in the war, compounded the anxiety caused by the declared ideological goals of the incoming regime. To three competing visions for the post-war scene (the German desire for continental dominance, the Allied desire for the opposite, and Wilson's anti-imperial and liberal agenda) was added a fourth, in the form of global revolution.

Although there may have been some support for the Bolsheviks among some components of the left in the West, the overall Allied response was to try to figure out how best to deal with such a fractured political scene as was Russia's, while still keeping it committed to the war against the Kaiser. The Allies kept their diplomatic representatives in St Petersburg through the first months of 1918, during the ongoing discussions and negotiations between Soviet Russia and Germany, and maintained hope that they might break down, and that Russia could be persuaded (or coerced) into continuing to fight. The peace between the two states brought by March 1918's Treaty of Brest-Litovsk did more to cement the new Soviet regime's status as an international outsider vis-à-vis the Allies, than their professed devotion to the principles of Marx.

For Lenin, the matter was clear from the beginning. What had caused the February Revolution in the first place was the burning desire of the Russian people to end the war—the food shortages in the cities combined with the mismanagement of the war at the front served to highlight the overall decay of the Tsarist regime. The primary failure of the Provisional Government of Kerensky was to ignore the strongest desire of the people, for a way out of the conflict.[1] The soldiers at the front, as well, were understandably deserting in ever greater numbers, and the Soviet hierarchy was concerned at the destabilizing role they could play once they found their way to their homes—or, worse, to the cities. Thus, the pressing priority of Lenin upon seizing power was to negotiate an end to the war, and to then consolidate the domestic scene. Further, there was the hope that the Russian Revolution would still be the spark to a general revolution which would wash across Europe, and that an armistice in the East would lead to rebellion in the armies of the West, and general strikes in their home industries. For these reasons, it was clear that negotiations needed to be opened, and an invitation was offered to Germany and Austria immediately upon the Bolshevik assumption of power, on 8 November 1917. The initial negotiations led to the armistice of December 1917, with discussions beginning shortly thereafter.

The Allies were rightfully concerned that the potential military implications of a German–Russian peace would be to free greater numbers of Germans to be placed against their soldiers in the West. The Allied governments responded initially with attempts to both reassure their own populations that the situation was under control and highlight the contrast between their own countries and Germany; they hoped to perhaps entice the Soviets to remain in the field to participate in the construction of a post-war world more amenable to their interests, than one dominated by Germany. Thus, the British Prime Minister David Lloyd George declared in a speech to trade unionists at the start of January 1918 that the war was not directed against the German people *per se,* but against the imperialist system of government under which they suffered. Wilson went further and, on 8 January 1918, offered his Fourteen Points as a vision of the future: (1) open covenants of peace, openly arrived at, with subsequent diplomacy proceeding in the public view; (2) absolute freedom of navigation upon the seas; (3) the removal of all economic barriers and equality of trade conditions; (4) the reduction of armaments; (5) the impartial adjustment of colonial claims, respecting the will of the local population; (6) the evacuation of Russian territory and right of Russians to determine their own fate; (7) the restoration of Belgium; (8) the restoration to France of Alsace-Lorraine; (9) the fixing of Italy's borders along clearly recognized lines of nationality; (10) autonomy for the nationalities in Austria–Hungary; (11) settlement and restoration of the Balkan states, including access to the sea for Serbia; (12) autonomy for the nationalities within the Ottoman Empire and freedom of the Dardanelles; (13) an independent Poland with access to the sea; and (14) the creation of a "general association of nations" offering "mutual guarantees of political independence and territorial integrity".[2]

Point 6 was something of an olive branch offered to the Bolshevik leadership in Moscow, an attempt to convince them that the best guarantee of their future lay with the Allies:

> VI. The evacuation of all Russian territory and such a settlement of all questions affecting Russia as will secure the best and freest cooperation of the other nations of the world in obtaining for her an unhampered and unembarrassed opportunity for the independent determination of her own political development and national policy and assure her of a sincere welcome into the society of free nations under institutions of her own choosing; and, more than a welcome, assistance also of every kind that she may need and may herself desire. The treatment accorded Russia by her sister nations in the months to come will be the acid test of their good will, of their comprehension of her needs as distinguished from their own interests, and of their intelligent and unselfish sympathy.

But the self-interested promises of a far-away American president were less compelling than "Peace, Bread, and Land", and the first part of the slogan was a clear prerequisite to the obtainment of the latter two. Thus, the Soviet negotiations with the German army facing them continued, despite the public attempts of the Allies to influence or perhaps win over the hearts of the Bolsheviks.[3] The basic Soviet tactic in dealing with the Germans was to simply stall and delay, while issuing inflammatory propaganda statements designed to encourage the German soldiers and workers to rise against their Prussian overlords.

Trotsky, the relative newcomer to the Bolshevik ranks who nonetheless organized many of the details of the successful October Revolution, took over as head of the Soviet negotiating team after the first week of January 1918. He continued the delays which had begun before his arrival, sometimes lecturing his opponents (in German) on the finer points of Marxist theory. The German delegation, under General Max Hoffmann, grew increasingly impatient, and by 18 January formally and firmly presented their government's demands, which foresaw the creation of independent countries (Poland, Estonia, Latvia, and Lithuania) in the territory of the former Russian empire.[4] Trotsky's request for a fortnight pause in the negotiations to allow him to consult with his government was accepted.

The most obvious options open to the Soviets were to continue to fight and risk being defeated (and hence overthrown), or to see the loss of over half of the former European territory of the Russian empire. Trotsky, firmly committed to the hope for international revolution, was perhaps encouraged by some murmurs of social discontent within the Central Powers; but both a call for a general strike in Berlin and a mutiny in the Austrian fleet during this time were, in the end, easily controlled by the respective authorities. A third and final option, "neither war nor peace", involved the simple withdrawal without a treaty from the war, and it was this which Trotsky managed to convince sceptical colleagues in the Soviet leadership to adopt.

Upon the resumption of talks, Trotsky initially continued the previous delaying tactics, but upon the signature of a separate peace between the Germans and nationalist Ukrainians on 9 February, the Soviet delegation formally announced their new policy, and attempted to withdraw from the war; Soviet forces advanced, however, into the Ukraine. The Germans, underwhelmed by the Soviet diplomatic tactics, renewed their military campaign with spectacular advances on 18 February. In response to the Soviet request for the reopening of negotiations, Germany offered an ultimatum in which the Soviets were allowed less than one week to agree to the terms: the Soviet state was essentially to lose all of its non-ethnic

Russian territories: the Ukraine, Poland, Finland, Latvia, Lithuania, and Estonia.

Such significant losses were deemed unacceptable to many of the higher-ranking Bolsheviks, and the signing of an onerous peace treaty—instead of continuing to press for the inevitable global revolution—was also considered by many among them to be an abandonment of the German (and European) working class. But given the military impossibility of continuing to fight, and the menace to the regime's very existence which a German victory would pose, Lenin persuaded the others to accept the terms, under the threat of his personal resignation.

With the Treaty of Brest-Litovsk, signed between Soviet Russia and Germany on 3 March 1918, Russia lost approximately one third of its population and agricultural production, half of its industrial base, and most of its coal mines. Germany, in addition to these gains (via the friendly regimes in the newly independent states carved out of the Russian empire), freed potentially hundreds of thousands of soldiers for use in the West, and thus revived the hope that a victory of sorts (either outright, or a peace negotiated from a position of relative strength) would still be possible before the United States managed to fully mobilize and send more soldiers to Europe.

The willingness of the Soviet government to accept such desperate terms made it clear to the Western powers that the new state was lost forever as an ally, and the Allies' attention turned to reviving the Eastern Front by any means possible. As the success of the Bolsheviks had seen Russia withdraw from the war, so the defeat of the Bolsheviks might see a new government re-enter the war. This was especially likely if the new government was "White"—that is counter-revolutionary and patriotic enough to be outraged by the willing dismemberment of the Tsarist empire by the Bolsheviks.

The Allied intervention in the Russian Civil War would have far-reaching consequences.[5] If, as Wilson had said in Fourteen Points, the treatment accorded to Russia by the other nations would be an "acid test" of their intentions, then the conclusions were plain to see: Germany was willing to slice portions of the state away, but still left it to survive; the Allies first supported the Whites, and later sent military contingents in support of the enemies of the regime. Among these was the Czech Legion of former prisoners-of-war which had been released by the Kerensky government in 1917 after promising neutrality, but which Trotsky would attempt to disarm (with disastrous result) in May 1918. There was also the fear of the Allies that the previously shipped war material (over one hundred and fifty thousand tons alone in Archangel) might find its way into the hands of the German military. The German attacks against the Allied forces in the West, beginning in March, increased the sense of desperation of the Allies for a reopening of the Eastern Front; consequently, their commitment to involvement in combatting the Bolsheviks became, in their eyes, a strategic necessity. Although the numbers of foreign troops involved in the Russian Civil War were less than thirty thousand, they did serve their purpose of encouraging White Russian forces to form and fight the Bolsheviks. Japan, with Far Eastern ambitions of its own, landed its troops in Vladivostok, encouraging American participation in Siberia as well, if simply to keep an eye on the Japanese.

With the murder by the Bolsheviks of the Russian imperial family in Ekaterinburg in July 1918, and Soviet military successes in European Russia against the Whites, an invitation by President Wilson to Japan to support the Czech Legion meant that the possibility of finding an understanding between the Bolsheviks and the Western powers was slight. Japanese military advances in early August 1918, coupled with increased Allied intervention in Siberia and the direct combat between the Bolsheviks and the Allied troops, made possible rapprochement even less likely, either then or in the post-Armistice period, and served only to push Soviet Russia closer towards Germany.

The fact that the British recognition of Czechoslovakia came at the heels of the Czech Legion's declaration of war against the Central Powers, in mid-August 1918, also led to the drawing closer together of Germany and Russia (the American recognition of Czechoslovakia, for the same reasons, would come a few weeks later, at the beginning of September 1918). The creation of the state of Czechoslovakia, in name if not deed, was born out of combat against both Soviet Russia and Germany—allowing for another mutual interest to develop between them. It was hardly surprising, then, that conversations between the Bolsheviks and the Germans were opened in August, that supplementary agreements to Brest-Litovsk were signed on 27 August 1918.

At first glance, the supplementary treaties appeared to be in the same punitive direction as the original Treaty of Brest-Litovsk: the Bolsheviks renounced formal claim to the territories of Estonia and Livonia, and recognized the independence of Georgia; Germany would withdraw from Belorussia, but at a cost of 25 per cent of Baku's oil output; Soviet expropriations of German property were to be compensated by the payment of six billion marks.[6] In return, Germany assured Soviet Russia that there would be no further territorial occupation and no support for counter-revolutionary schemes. A secret military appendix, however, provided the most important promise for the Soviets: Germany pledged to offer its own and Finnish troops to help combat Allied intervention troops from northern Russia and Baku.

In an eleven-point official communique to the German foreign ministry clarifying the Soviet interpretation of the supplementary treaties, the Soviet Ambassador to Berlin took note of: Germany's "readiness to use its influence" to ensure that Ukraine did not support the other independence movements within Russia; Germany's obligation, in the event of Russian failure to drive out Entente forces in north Russia, to undertake such action, if necessary with the help of Finnish troops (with it being "understood that any Russian territory occupied in the course of such action will be again evacuated by the German and Finnish troops after the expulsion of the Allied forces [...]"); and the German use of its influence to ensure the procurement of one-fourth of Georgian manganese ore exports.

The supplementary treaties were the first clear indication that the German army was willing to do more than simply impose onerous conditions for peace, with regard to Russia. Rather, it actively committed Germany to direct military collaboration, and hence should be considered a wartime precursor to the trends which would develop in the immediate post-war scene. The reception of the treaty in Germany also gave an indication of the domestic differences of opinions between the military command and various civilian leaders, including the future President of the Weimar Republic, Friedrich Ebert. The government (under the influence of the German High Command) ratified the treaty without the consent of the Reichstag; in return, the Socialists attacked the apparent unconstitutionality of the process, and Ebert further declared that it would always remain a misfortune for Germany, as it would strengthen Bolshevik rule in

Russia. The Center Party deputy Matthias Erzberger argued (correctly, as the Soviets saw it) that the secret military agreement could serve as a legal invitation for a German intervention force.

By early October 1918, the military situation had deteriorated for Germany to the extent that the newly appointed German Chancellor, Prince Maximilian of Baden, sent an appeal to the American President Woodrow Wilson for an armistice, to be based on the Fourteen Points. The negotiations for the precise terms were conducted over the following weeks. Among the President's demands were the evacuation of all occupied territories and the insistence that negotiations be conducted only with a democratic government. The German government accepted the requirements, but in the meanwhile, the domestic situation was proving more precarious.[7]

The day after the initial appeal of the Chancellor to the Americans, the Independent Socialists of Germany made an appeal for a "socialist republic" to be created, and a committee of Revolutionary Shop Stewards began the process of collecting arms for a coming struggle. As the Kaiser's reforms of the German constitution (announced on 28 October 1918) were considered too moderate and too late, a general strike was planned for 6 November; it failed to materialize due to internal divisions among the Independent Socialist leadership, and the arrest of some of its prominent leaders by the police. The Revolutionary Shop Stewards decided to go forward anyway, and planned a general strike for 9 November.

Germany's internal military situation had also begun to deteriorate by this time, with disturbances aboard the warship SMS Markgraf soon to spread to other ships in the German navy. Upon receiving word that one last raid was planned in defence of the honour of the German navy, the sailors at Kiel mutinied and refused to go to sea. Their leaders were arrested, and demonstrations in their support were fired upon by the authorities, resulting in several deaths and dozens wounded. Despite the appointment of Gustav Noske, a socialist of significant stature, to become Kiel's new governor, the mutiny continued to spread; the base commander Prince Heinrich of Prussia fled in disguise, and Workers' and Sailors' Councils were formed (in imitation of the councils, or *soviets*, which had formed in revolutionary Russia), actions which soon spread to industrial workers nearby. The simple demands were for both immediate peace and reform, and the message was carried in revolts in several other cities during the subsequent days. The newly formed councils, however, were rarely under the control of the most radical elements of the German socialist movements.

The outbreak of revolutionary activity in Germany was clearly of interest to the Soviet Russian leadership, but of greater concern were the apparent territorial changes which occurred around them as well, at the start of November. Taking advantage of the overall chaos, the Poles announced, on 3 November, the creation of a Polish Republic in Warsaw. General Pilsudski, released from a German prison on 10 November, assumed command of the new government, and assumed full military power a few days later. At the same time, the Austro-Hungarian government saw its military forces collapse, and negotiated an armistice with the Allied powers which saw the complete demobilization of their armed forces, the withdrawal of their soldiers from service in the German armed forces, the surrender of half of the country's war material, the evacuation of territories which their soldiers occupied, and the surrender of their fleet.

By this time, Wilson's Fourteen Points were appearing far too generous in the eyes of the British and the French, who proved unwilling to negotiate with the Germans on their basis. The President, angry with his Allies, threatened to negotiate a separate peace with Germany. The resulting British and French acceptance was made with two significant reservations: that the question of freedom of the seas be open for discussion in the coming peace conference; and that damage to civilians be included in the reparations to be demanded of Germany. Rather than risk a full rupture, Wilson accepted these two conditions and passed them along to the German government, thus giving the impression to the Germans that the remainder of the Fourteen Points would be the basis for the negotiations.

But before this could occur, the German state itself appeared to be on the verge of disintegrating. One year after the successful 1917 Bolshevik Revolution in Russia, the Independent Socialist leader Kurt Eisner, at the head of a Constituent Soldiers' Workers' and Peasants' Council in Munich, declared Bavaria to be a "free state", the Bavarian Democratic and Social Republic.[8] He assumed the position of Minister-President, and though the symbolic allusions to Soviet Russia were clear, Eisner was still careful not to want to scare the German public too much with fears of a radical communist takeover. Property rights were among the first to be guaranteed by the new government, and in addition to his Independent socialists, some respected academics were solicited for service within the new cabinet, along with a few members of the Majority (i.e. moderate) Socialists. The local population was nevertheless taken somewhat by surprise at the turn of events, but the seizure of power was accomplished calmly, and without significant incident; by the end of the first day, a sense of normalcy appeared to have returned to the streets of the Bavarian capital. At least some level of popular support existed for the new regime and its promise for peace, given the military collapse of Austria and the subsequent threat of invasion from the south which this allowed. The peace movement was tied up with local Bavarian regional pride (if not to say nationalism). The basic demands of the protesters in the days before the assumption of power were similar to those made by Lenin: bread and peace, and better working conditions.

Little of Eisner's declared programme for the future was particularly threatening. He promised the public: personal security and property rights, a new constitution to be decided upon by a popular assembly, the retention of all civil servants, the maintenance of public order, and, most importantly of all, peace. The new government foresaw a loose federation of German states coming into existence, including Austria. With regard, however, to the implementation of economic socialism, Eisner demurred, arguing that it seemed impossible to socialize when there was hardly anything to socialize.

Unlike the cause-specific rebellion of the sailors in the north, the events in Munich, and the subsequent declarations of Eisner, held importance for all of Germany. Bavaria was a large and populous state, with a significant separatist tradition. Despite Eisner's attempts to be reassuring on the question of the potential Bolshevization of the new state, the German military leadership in Berlin saw instead the potential dangers which Eisner posed to the Germany they knew. While willing to deal with Bolsheviks in Soviet Russia for pragmatic and utilitarian reasons, on a state-to-state basis, there was a clear distinction between the international relations and the domestic threat posed by the ideology it espoused. The cooperation demonstrated in Bavaria between the Majority and the Independent Socialists (between "moderates" and "extremists") served only to taint the former with the latter's reputation in the eyes of the army, rather than the reverse. The Majority Socialists were therefore regarded as being as untrustworthy as the Independents, contributing to the military's unwillingness to accept Ebert and the Majority Socialists as true leaders of the Weimar Republic. There was also fear in Berlin that the Bavarian revolution, as mild as it attempted to give the appearance of being, was merely the precursor to a Spartacist, or truly radical, coup. Radical agitation, including the distribution of illegal pamphlets, had become ever more prevalent in the final months of the war, and there was little doubt in the military minds that much if not all of it was directed by Moscow.

Compounding the sense of growing desperation within the army ranks were the terms of the armistice, given by Ferdinand Foch to the leader of the Center Party, Mathias Erzberger, on 8 November, near Compiegne, France. The purpose of the terms was to establish conditions which would make it impossible for Germany to resume the fight, and hence force Germany to accept whatever peace terms would be decided upon by the Allies; in this, it succeeded admirably. Germany had to evacuate all occupied territories and all land west of the Rhine, which would be taken over by the Allied soldiers; the Allies as well would control the bridgeheads at Coblenz, Mainz, and Cologne. The Treaties of Brest-Litovsk and Bucharest were to be renounced by Germany; but the Allies decided to allow Germany to continue to occupy, temporarily, the lands under its control in the East: a clear indication that the Allies were not prepared to simply withdraw from their participation in the Russian Civil War and leave the field to the Soviets, now that the initial reason for their intervention (reopening the Eastern Front) had been rendered moot by the ending of hostilities with Germany. The material conditions placed on Germany were predictably severe as well: the surrender of one hundred and fifty thousand freight cars, five thousand locomotives, five thousand trucks, most of the German fleet, and the destruction of tanks, heavy artillery, and aircraft. Given the shortages facing all of Germany, the continuation of the Allied naval blockade ensured (thanks to the earlier British reservation concerning the Fourteen Points) the future atttention of the German government despite the assurances of the Allies, described below, that Germany would not starve.[9] The armistice terms, including the reservation of the right to assign reparations later, were not open to discussion, and the German government had one month to either accept them or face renewed hostilities.

That the Kaiser's continued position was untenable was clear to most observers but himself. He was at the army's headquarters at Spa, and was under the impression that the army would be able to prop up the monarchy in this time of trouble. There was enough dissent in the ranks, however, to cause even the head of the army, Hindenburg, to recognize that the overall loyalty of the army could no longer be depended upon, and the Kaiser simply had no further support. The unfavourable task of informing the Kaiser of the state of affairs was delegated to Hindenburg's adjutant, General Groener, and the Kaiser finally agreed to leave shortly after Prince Maximilian had made an announcement that an abdication had occurred. The last emperor of Germany headed into exile to the Netherlands on 10 November 1918.

The Chancellor then handed control of the government to the leaders of the Majority Socialists, Friedrich Ebert and Philip Scheidemann, who made the announcement of the establishment of a republic. Though unplanned, the proclamation was, in Scheidemann's words, "the logical conclusion of a lost war of unmatched privation and of loathing of the war mongers [. . . it was a] protest against the continuation of an utterly hopeless slaughter [. . .] the day on which it was impossible to carry on any longer".[10]

Though Ebert was suspected of harbouring desires of perhaps re-establishing the monarchy within a constitutional context, Scheidemann's proclamation of a republic forced the matters to a head. Scheidemann wished to avoid a potential coup attempt by the Independent Socialists and the Spartacists, and a subsequent Bolshevik-style revolution. The Majority Socialists goal was "freedom, not terror [. . .] not dictatorship but democracy: Not callous experimentation on the living body of society, but a planned construction of a new socialist economic order based upon scientific knowledge and practical experience".

Ebert's first public announcement as "Reich Chancellor" stated that the new government—which would be composed equally of Majority and Independent Socialists—wished "[. . .] to bring peace to the German people as soon as possible, and to establish firmly the freedom which it has achieved". It was a 'legal" transfer of power from Prince Maximilian to Ebert, on the basis of constitutionality, rather than a Bolshevik-styled revolution. The actions in Berlin were influenced by concern with what was developing in Bavaria and the mutinies in the north.

The difficulties facing Ebert and the new government are difficult to overestimate. He was forced to come to an arrangement with the more radical socialists in the hopes of staving off open attempts at the revolution led by the even more radical Spartacists. He had even agreed to rename the provisional government as the Council of Peoples' Commissars, in order to gain the support of what he viewed was the lesser of the two evils to his left. Councils of Workers and Soldiers were rapidly appearing across the country—especially along the northern seaboard, influenced, as the port towns were, by the activities of the Kiel sailors. The radical leader Karl Liebknecht hoped and believed that the coming month would see the election of Workers' and Soldiers' Councils across the country, which would in turn elect a national Council, and thus lay the foundation for a truly socialist state. In mid-November 1918, there was little reason to believe that this was far-fetched: the German public itself was still bewildered with the apparently sudden swing in military and political fortunes, and seemed ready, given the hardships it was facing due to the continued blockade and the Spanish influenza (which claimed almost two thousand lives in Berlin in one day, in mid-October).

The German army was discredited (but not in their own eyes, "defeated"), and on its way to being disarmed and demobilized; it nonetheless refused to accept responsibility for the war. Despite the Allied advances in the final stages of the war, the Germans had managed to effect a somewhat orderly retreat before them, destroying the communications infrastructure as they went. The effect was to slow down the Allies, and to give the German army a little space in which to attempt to regroup. Although the Allies had almost 30 divisions with over 600 tanks ready to attack, the Armistice came at a most propitious time for the Germans. The fighting stopped on 11 November, while the next Allied attack was planned for 14 November; thus, before the Allies had actually moved into Germany proper, and even before the British were able to carry out a planned bombing of Berlin, the fighting was at an end. Responsibility was also evaded by the German decision to have Erzberger, of the Center Party, lead the German armistice delegation, rather than a German General. His collusion with Ebert ensured that the "stab in the back" myth would gain credence: the German army, undefeated in Germany, had been abandoned at its most critical moment by defeatist, socialist, civilians. The idea was promoted by General Ludendorff among others—his high-strung personality had not yet grown into the obviously visible flakiness which retirement would bring, and his name as a war-hero carried weight. The support and propagation of the myth by the German army neatly allowed them to avoid responsibility, and still maintain that the honour of the army was unsullied.

The German army began its final withdrawal from still-occupied territories soon after the Armistice was announced, and their last troops had departed from France and Belgium by 18 and 26 November, respectively. The city of Strasbourg was occupied by the French on 25 November, and American and British soldiers began arriving in Germany on 1 December 1918.

Although Germany had already been forced to renounce the gains made under Brest-Litovsk as part of the armistice agreement, the Soviets followed suit with their own official cancellation of the treaty, and of the supplementary agreements of August, on 13 November 1918. Germany seemed to hardly be in a position to offer military support (with or without the Finns), and the cancellation allowed the Soviets to begin an active policy of attempting to recover the lands lost since March 1918. It also allowed the Soviet government to ignore the debts incurred as part of the peace process. In addition to the 260 million marks already sent in the form of gold rubles, another 203 million marks in Tsarist banknotes had been sent as well. Additionally, the Soviet state had compensated individual Germans and firms from a special fund created after the August accords had been signed, to a total of another 121 million marks (paid mostly in gold). In total then, from March to December 1918, the Soviet state had paid Germany 584 million marks in gold and paper money, but would have to pay no more. The payments were, however, not forgotten by the Soviets, and were used in the calculations and preparations before the Genoa conference, and subsequently Rapallo.[11]

The German defeat also had an impact on the Baltic borderlands with Soviet Russia, in addition to the creation of the state of Poland as announced by Pilsudski.[12] The German-friendly King William of Lithuania abdicated, and as Germany withdrew from parts of the country, Bolshevik forces invaded from the other direction, leading to the start of the Russian military adventures in the Baltics, and thus a potential source of contact (though whether of conflict or cooperation was not yet written in stone) with Germany. The same occurred shortly thereafter in Latvia, with the declaration of independence coming on 18 November, while Estonia—supported by the British Royal Navy—combatted Soviet Russian forces after the withdrawal of German troops from 22 November. The Estonians would only repulse the Soviets by February 1919 with more assistance from the British, as well as other Scandinavian volunteers. Most of Siberia and parts of eastern European Russia were by this time under the control of Admiral Kolchak's White Russian forces; through the month of December they continued to advance eastward, with the effect that by the end of 1918 the Soviet state was fighting no longer to regain lost territories, but for its very survival.

While the representatives of the individual German states met in Berlin, on 25 November, to plan for the election of a National Constituent Assembly, the foreseen American and British occupation of parts of the country was under preparation as well, and began on 1 December. They began by taking control of bridgeheads on the Rhine river, and occupied the major cities of Cologne on 6 December, and Mainz on 9 December. In the words of a *Daily Chronicle* reporter accompanying the advance,

> This morning the passing of the [British] cavalry over the Rhine was an impressive sight for all the people of Cologne, and for the British was another historical episode on the long journey of this war, which has led at last to this river flowing now behind the British lines. To the German people the Rhine is the very river of their life, and down its tide come drifting all the ghost memories of their race, and its water is sacred to them as the fount from which their national legends, their old folk songs, and the sentiment that lies deep in their hearts have come forth in abundance. In military history the Rhine has been their last line of defence, the moat around the keep of German strength; so today when British troops rode across the bridge and passed beyond the Rhine to further outposts it was the supreme sign of victory for them and of German defeat.[13]

Not all Germans were as ideologically mild as Ebert and the leadership of the SPD. With the hopes and expectations of communist-inspired uprisings, the Soviet Russian leadership was determined to assist a second chance (the German "October" following their "February" of the previous November), with direct support of experienced agitators. Thus, Karl Radek was sent from Moscow to Germany in December 1918, an act of utmost importance for the evolution of the German–Soviet Russian relationship.[14]

Soviet Russia's main specialist on German affairs was a one-time citizen of the Austrian empire—a polyglot, talented journalist and propagandist, with access to Lenin and the highest circles of the Soviet leadership, and the right-hand man of Trotsky during the negotiations at Brest-Litovsk. Radek was a classical "internationalist" who spoke German with native proficiency. He would also prove to be the driving force on the Soviet side for the collaboration in the post-war years, with the Treaty of Rapallo (as well as the military agreements in place at the same time) serving as the high point in his influence; his familiarity with Trotsky would earn him Stalin's enmity, and eventual execution during the Great Purges of the 1930s.

In his memoirs, it is clear that Radek and the Soviet leadership viewed the "revolution" which was occurring in Germany in the autumn and early winter as being at best a bourgeois affair. Written with the events relatively fresh in mind, they offer an important insight into the mind-set of the Soviets at the time, and are thus worth citing at length:

> Another telegram from [the Soviet ambassador in Berlin] Yoffe. He was being expelled from Berlin. What was the meaning of this? Are the Social Democrats afraid of our propaganda? Ilyich [Lenin] interpreted the matter differently. Germany, capitulating before the Entente, was offering the latter her services in the struggle against the Russian revolution. This was his solution of the riddle. As we know, it was perfectly correct. Erzberger plainly offered the Allies, in return for more advantageous peace terms, to throw the German troops against Soviet Russia. Yoffe was put on the train within 24 hours. But he had not yet reached our frontier when the wireless station in Khodynka picked up a telegram sent from a warship in Kiel: "Today we are burying the first victims of the revolution. The Red Flag has been hoisted over the German fleet. May it be hoisted over the whole of Germany, and may our victims be the last." [. . .] within a few hours we had already intercepted from the Allied radio stations news of the revolution in Germany.

[... We told Yoffe] not to leave the territory occupied by German troops, for we were immediately going to propose to the new German revolutionary Government a revocation of the expulsion order made by the last Imperial Government. I began to call the Berlin Ministry of Foreign Affairs. The connections, which went through Kovno, had been cut by General Hoffmann. In the end the Ministry replied.

"Who is at the other end?"
"The telegraphist of the Ministry of Foreign Affairs in Berlin."
"Call Herr Haase, the People's Commissar." [...]
—"There is no one in the Ministry. Everyone has run away."
—"Then find some one to look for Haase or Liebknecht."
—"There is no one to send."
"I order you in the name of the All-Russian Central Executive Committee of Soviets and on your responsibility before the Soviet of Workers' and Soldiers' Deputies of Berlin."

Silence. But the connection had not been interrupted. The apparatus kept up the signal Berlin. Berlin. Berlin. Berlin. At last an answer.

"Very well. I shall go and look."

In the factories something which defies description was going on. I had never seen such elation. I spoke in the Prokhorov plant. I said that the German revolution was not only our greatest victory, but at the same time our supreme duty. Only this summer we had learned what hunger was. But they, the German workers, had lived for three years on two ounces of bread and turnips. I said that, out of our scanty means, we would have to help the German revolution with bread. I watched with greatest attention the faces of the audience. Always in meetings, at a difficult moment, my eyes look for the weakest link in the chain, I always select the most backward worker and I speak solely for him or her, and if that hearer is convinced one can be sure of having convinced them all. But now, in front of me, there were faces full of elation. I could not find anyone indifferent or tired. "Even if we starve, we shall help our German brothers!" This cry of mine was unanimously taken up by the masses of workers.

I returned to the Commissariat. The German Embassy informed me by phone that Berlin was calling us. I followed Chicherin to the Denezhny Lane. At first the Independent deputy Oskar Cohn came to the apparatus. He informed me briefly of the situation. He expressed the hope that Yoffe would soon be able to return to Berlin. He announced that the vice-president of the Government of the People's Commissars, the Commissar for Foreign Affairs, Georg [sic: Hugo] Haase, was going to speak to me, Haase, with a lawyer's politeness, conveyed to us the greetings of the Government of the People's Commissars, and their thanks for our offer of bread. He hesitated for a moment. There was an uneasy silence. I felt the beating of my heart. Comrade Chicherin and I stood without taking our eyes from the tape. Slowly the letters began to appear: "But as we are aware that there is hunger in Russia, we ask you to divert the bread which you are prepared to sacrifice for the German revolution to the benefit of the hungry in Russia. The President of the American Republic, Wilson, has guaranteed to Germany the supply of bread and fats required for feeding the population during the winter."

I saw the face of the old textile woman worker of the Prokhorov plant who, despite her hungry children at home, willingly sacrificed a piece of bread in order to help the German brothers. Her outstretched hand remained hanging in mid air. The leader of the German revolution, Haase, was prepared to take bread and fats from the leader of American plutocracy. He did not want help from the Russian revolution. A second August 4th; Judas Iscariot completed his betrayal.

We inquired whether Yoffe's expulsion remained in force. Haase replied that his Government would be glad to enter negotiations with us on the resumption of diplomatic relations, but he asked that, before negotiations began, the German consuls still remaining in Moscow should be permitted to leave for Berlin in order to report, while comrade Yoffe should proceed to Moscow; and afterwards both Governments could come to terms. Our worst expectations were confirmed. We stated that we had no intention of detaining the German consuls, but that we were notifying the Government of the People's Commissars that the General Staff of the German forces in the Baltic, Belorussia and Lithuania was arming the bourgeoisie, and suppressing the workers and peasants; this was liable to lead to clashes with our troops, for, having annulled the Treaty of Brest, we did not consider these territories as having seceded from the RSFSR. In our opinion, the population of these territories must determine its fate by a free vote, which was impossible in the presence of the armed forces of Germany, or under conditions where the bourgeoisie had arms and the workers and peasants had none. On these grounds, we should regard as indispensable negotiations with plenipotentiaries of the Government of the People's Commissars. We were suggesting that for this purpose Yoffe or someone else should go to Berlin, or that a German plenipotentiary should come to Moscow. Haase replied wearily and briefly that he would convey our offer to his Government. We pointed out that time was short. Any day could lead to a clash. He answered that he could not on his own responsibility fix the time limit for the reply. Then we replied:

"We are informing you that, unless we receive from you within three days a definite answer to the questions raised by us, the Red Army will have freedom of action, and the responsibility for complications in the evacuation of your forces will be entirely yours." "I shall endeavour to accelerate the reply", announced Haase and, after some conventional courtesies, discontinued the conversation.

The position was quite clear. The same night a long radio telegram was sent to the Berlin Soviet, defining the policy of Ebert and Haase as the policy of a deal with the Allied bourgeoisie against the Russian and German revolution. We informed the Berlin Soviet of the desire [...] to send a delegation to the projected congress of German Soviets. The very same night, I wrote a pamphlet for distribution among the German soldiers entitled "Trau, Schau, Wem?" ("Know Thine Enemy!") We received an invitation to the Congress of German Soviets, signed by Brutus Molkenbuhr. A delegation was formed consisting of comrades Yoffe, Rakovsky, Bukharin, myself and Ignatov. We had a meeting with Lenin and Sverdlov in order to discuss our line of conduct at the Congress. After the talk, Ilyich stopped me. His face was as worried as it had been on the balcony of the Moscow Soviet.

"The gravest moment has arrived. Germany is beaten. The Entente's road to Russia is cleared. Even if Germany does not take part in the campaign against us, the hands of the Allies are free.

Franchet d'Esperet can move with the whole Balkan army of the Allies through Hungary and Rumania against the Ukraine. They can throw troops across the Dardanelles. The Straits are in their hands!"

[...] He began to instruct me on my work, in the event of my remaining in Germany. "Remember that you will act in the rear of the enemy. Intervention is inevitable, and much will depend on the situation in Germany."

"The German revolution", I answered intently, "is too great an event to be regarded as a diversion in the rear of the enemy."

"Yes," said Ilyich, "I don't suggest that you should force developments; they will proceed according to the internal laws of the German revolution."[15]

Despite Lenin's confident assertion, matters in December 1918 indicated that the situation was perhaps becoming riper for a second revolution sooner than he had anticipated. International events, as well, were indicating the common interests in cooperation between the Soviet state and Germany, regardless of the hue of government in power in Berlin.

Economically and socially, the situation of the German people continued to be difficult, but the decision of the Allies on 5 December, to extend their naval blockade of Germany to include the entire Baltic coastline, had direct repercussions for Russia as well. The winter of 1918–1919 saw continued food and fuel shortages in most German cities, and the weaker health of the general population continued to prove to be fertile ground for the ravages of the Spanish influenza as well. With the mass demobilization of the German army in the first month after the armistice, hundreds of thousands of veterans found themselves without jobs, food, or any sense of hope for the future.

Despite this, it was still clear that events in Germany might still need a helping hand, if a Soviet-style revolution was to come.[16] In mid-December, a Berlin Congress of Soldiers' and Workers' Soviets did not even bother to invite the radical leaders Karl Liebknecht and Rosa Luxemburg to their gathering. The Councils, which had been set up at the behest of the Independent Socialists in their negotiations with Ebert, had lost what revolutionary zeal may have existed a month earlier, and were more inclined to follow the Majority Socialists than the Spartacists, who opposed Ebert's plan for a National Assembly.

By the end of the month, with Germany weakened militarily, General Pilsudski of Poland sent troops to occupy the province of Posen (Pozenania), in order to stake an early favourable interpretation of Wilson's Point 13. The Soviets fared little better than the Germans in the Baltic region, having being driven out of Estonia by force, by January of 1919. A Soviet counter-offensive against White Russian forces in January began to show signs of military success, and led to an atmosphere of increasing confidence in Moscow. The city of Orenburg was retaken on 25 January, and Ekaterinburg two days later; Kolchak was subsequently pushed back into his firmer bases in Siberia.

The Allied interventionist forces continued to support the Whites, but in a half-hearted manner after the Armistice of 11 November. Only the British saw direct combat against the Red Army, and the French and the American forces trickled to almost symbolic numbers by the end of 1918. It was mainly due to the insistence of Winston Churchill that there was any continuation of a foreign presence in the conflict at all; he saw Bolshevism as a direct threat to civilization, and argued forcefully that the infant had to be strangled while still in its cradle. The White armies were further limited in their overall effectiveness by the fact that, in the end, they were outnumbered almost ten to one by the Red Army, saw their forces dispersed into too many parts to form an effective whole, and most importantly, had nothing to offer either the Russian worker or peasant in return for support, except for a return to the tsarist days. Approximately 80 per cent of peasants conscripted into the White armies ended up deserting. In the end, the Whites were too divided among themselves, had no popular support, and simply were not as ruthless as their Bolshevik enemies. The only factor in the Whites' favour was the relative disorganization of their enemy, in the early stages of the conflict. Once, however, the Red Army was formed and increasingly better trained (by the start of 1919), the tides turned.

The three main White Russian forces were led by Denikin in the south, Yudenich in the north-west, and Kolchak in the east. Their initial successes in making advances towards Moscow in late 1918 and then in 1919 seemed proof of their professional advantages. In fact, they were not the trained professional collection of former tsarist soldiers which many outside of Russia imagined them to be. While the leadership was undoubtedly professional, conscripts formed an integral (indeed, the most essential) bulk of the troops. Initial military success, not coupled with an alternative political message to captivate the masses, was impossible to maintain over time. The leaders of the three White forces did not ever effectively collaborate among each other; personality rivalries over the future shape of the post-Bolshevik Russia, as well as the need to maintain an outwardly positive face for the Allies, did not engender effective military cooperation. Furthermore, they had little to offer the people. Coming as they did from the aristocratic classes, they were certainly not in favour of agricultural (or any other kind of) land reform—the one issue which, in addition to stopping the participation in the First World War, did most to win support to the Bolsheviks. While the position of the White officers was understandable given their class and background, it was less understandable why any peasant would fight and perhaps die for a cause which would simply see a return to the feudal conditions existing before 1914.

Despite the fact that General Denikin's southern White army was able, from January through to March 1919, to launch an offensive in southern Russia, this did not effectively detract from Soviet policy towards helping a revolution along in Germany. The setbacks in the south were further countered by the successful Soviet attack on Latvia at the start of January 1919, which gave hope that Soviet influence might yet reach across westward, to the point where it could be of use in supporting communist uprisings in Germany. This was compounded by the successful capture of Vilna in neighbouring Lithuania, at the same time.

Radek, who had been sent with the initial brief of helping the Spartacists organize themselves, was not initially well received by the radical German communist leader, Rosa Luxemburg. She hated him, in fact, and thought that he arrived in Germany with the arrogance of a successful relation who was determined to offer unsolicited advice to less fortunate cousins. His talents were recognized as useful, however, and despite the abrasive impact he had upon Luxemburg, he played a significant role in the Spartacists' formal break from the Independent Socialists, and their reformation as the German Communist Party (KPD) on New Year's Day, 1919.

With the elections to the National Assembly due in early January 1919, a pre-emptive armed uprising was begun by more extreme radicals among the workers' movements in Berlin. Despite the fact that both Liebknecht and Luxemburg felt that the time was still not quite ripe for a successful revolution in Germany, the leadership of the KPD considered itself obliged to support the rebellion, and the Spartacist uprising was underway.[17] It lasted 10 days, in the course of which public and important private buildings (such as newspapers) were occupied; the initial successes and call for a socialist Germany led to smaller uprisings in other cities as well; from 10 January until 4 February, a Soviet republic had been declared in the city of Bremen, after a local KPD coup.

Ebert turned to the military and the Freikorps to suppress the rebellion, which they did with ferocity. The Freikorps were private, unofficial armies set up by the German army in December 1918 to help defend the Baltic region against Bolshevism, and staffed by recently demobilized soldiers and officers.[18] Although some units maintained a level of relatively military professionalism, many others (whose numbers would increase with time) degenerated to the level of mere adventurers and domestic mercenaries. Luxemburg and Liebknecht, who had been arrested in the course of the uprising, were murdered by the Freikorps on 15 January. The majority of workers in Berlin and the rest of Germany did not support the uprising, and Radek, who had encouraged the events, went into hiding after hearing of the murders.

The SPD had thus demonstrated clearly that it was an "evolutionary socialist" party, which would not prove a threat to the existing order. In turning to the Freikorps to restore order, it on the one hand acted to simply maintain the existence of the state in the only way it knew, while on the other hand it placed itself in the ranks of hated "collaborators" with the capitalists, as far as Moscow was concerned. The events in Berlin did not go unnoticed elsewhere in Europe, as most of the leaders of the Allied cause from the First World War opened the Paris peace conference just three days after the uprising was put down, on 18 January 1919.[19]

Seventy delegates from 27 countries were represented at the conference, but among those left out were the defeated parties of Germany, Austria, Hungary, Bulgaria, and Turkey; they were not invited except to receive the final results of the victors' deliberations, at the end of June. Despite the fact that, at the time of the armistice, Wilson's Fourteen Points were considered to form the basis of the coming peace terms, what developed instead in Paris was the time-honoured tradition of competition among the states for advantage against an enemy which had been effectively disarmed. And although the Russians as well were not invited to partake in the spoils of victory, the Allies nonetheless made some effort to negotiate a settlement to the Civil War (if for no other reason than to be able to extract their own soldiers from the conflict). The attempt to gather the two sides together on the Prinkipo Islands for talks failed, however; the Bolsheviks accepted the invitation, while the White generals, certain of their cause with the Allies behind them, refused.

Fresh upon the suppression of the communist uprising, and the day after the Paris peace conference opened, elections were conducted for the National Assembly in Germany, which would decide upon the new constitution of the republic. Given what had just happened to its founding leaders, the KPD understandably refused to participate, but the remainder of the political spectrum supported the process, giving it a claim to legitimacy. It proved a success for Ebert and the SPD, which came from the contest as the largest single party, and 163 of the 421 seats.

After the suppression of the Spartacists, then, there was a genuine sense of optimism in Germany that matters might finally take a turn for the better, and that the Paris peace conference would offer Germany a chance, after the domestic chaos of the preceding months, to become a normal member of the European community. The reservations to Wilson's Fourteen Points demanded by Britain and France, and agreed to by Wilson (on freedom of the seas, and the right for civilian damage to be included in the reparations), now appeared minor in nature, given the difficulties of the preceding months. Wilson's programme, at the very least, appeared to promise Germans as well the right to national self-determination and the genuine possibility that Germany could become a democratic state. The unheard of public popularity received by Wilson upon his arrival in Paris seemed to further indicate that this conference would be one in which his ideals would dominate. This impression was given further credence by the unanimous adoption, on 25 January 1919, of the delegates for a resolution which called for the creation of a League of Nations; although a committee was appointed to draft a constitution and others were to deal with territorial and reparations issues, international cooperation based on Wilsonian ideals seemed to be the direction of the future. The future of Polish–German and

Polish–Russian relations were complicated by the decision of the Polish Constituent Assembly, on 26 January 1919, to attempt to focus on the reconquest of all territories which had belonged to Poland in 1772.

In this context, the general public, let alone the authorities, took an even darker view of the recent communist attempts to alter the fundamental nature of the state, and thus drive Germany further into political obscurity. Thus, it was not surprising that when Radek was eventually found in early February, he was immediately arrested. The German authorities knew full well that while Radek had been ostensibly sent by Soviet Russia to assist in the creation of the KPD, he was in fact given freedom to assist in any revolutionary developments which might occur while he was in Germany. The police, however, lacked any direct evidence. They charged him anyway, and simply planted false evidence amid his possessions.

The Soviet reaction came in the form of a telegram to Berlin on 19 February 1919, while the Entente leaders were still organizing themselves in Paris. The disappointment with Haase had now given way to anger, as the "counter-revolutionary" SPD government of Ebert and Scheidemann was denounced in no uncertain terms for stooping to "the lowest and vilest of manoeuvres" in order to attempt to stop the "rising tide of the Revolution", and have Radek falsely arrested the previous week. The false papers claimed to provide proof that the Soviet government was planning to invade Germany in support of a successful German Bolshevik (i.e. Spartacist) uprising in the spring. The "absurdity of the children's fairy-tale" beggared the belief of anyone who was even superficially acquainted with the ideas of Soviet Russia, according to the telegram, and all German workers were exhorted to protest the infamy of the act.[20]

The Soviet claims might have carried more weight, had not more communist disturbances broken out immediately afterwards. From February through March 1919, uprisings were staged at various times and for varying durations, in Berlin, Munich, and other cities. Gustav Noske, the SPD military expert who had been called upon to deal with the Kiel mutiny in 1918, was asked by the provisional government of Ebert to suppress the newest revolts, as well.

They had begun as a result of another political murder. In Bavaria, after the loss of elections by the Independent Socialists, Kurt Eisner on 21 February was on his way to parliament to announce his resignation. He was murdered on his way by a right-wing fanatical student. The assassination was met with protest and widespread revulsion throughout the state, and lawlessness and unrest soon took root, through the month of March. This second wave of rebellion was encouraged, in part, by the success of Bela Kun in leading a communist coup in Hungary. On 6 April, a Bavarian Soviet Republic was declared to exist, led by a combination of Independent Socialists and Anarchists. The government was unable to restore order in Munich, and contributed to its own lack of credibility by making occasionally bizarre decisions (such as a declaration of war against Switzerland, after the latter refused a request from the new Soviet republic to be loaned 60 train locomotives). The leadership collapsed after being in power for less than a week, and was replaced by the Communists, under the direction of Eugen Levine—after Liebknecht, the most likely leader to be a potential German Lenin.

The reforms immediately implemented by Levine mirrored many of those put into place by the Bolsheviks in Russia, including giving direct ownership and control of the factories to the workers, confiscation and redistribution among the poor of large apartments, and plans for the reform of the educational and monetary systems of the state. The new state also promptly organized its own Red Army, whose ranks were swelled by unemployed factory workers, and quickly reached a strength of 20,000. Like the parent Red Army, the Rote Armee was also not above conducting a terror campaign, and in the course of a wave of arrests of suspected "counter-revolutionaries", eight men, including a Prince, were murdered, at the end of April 1919. These murders provided Noske with all the excuse he needed to call upon the Freikorps to restore order. A force of almost 40,000 entered into Bavaria to fight the communists, and after bitter fighting which saw more than 1000 people killed in street battles, the uprising was crushed, by early May 1919.

The German army was firmly convinced that a genuine danger to the security of the state existed, and that Radek was involved. In an Army high command conference held at the end of March 1919 (while the unrest was raging but just before the proclamation of a Bavarian Soviet Republic), an assessment of Germany's overall political situation was presented by the minister of war, General Groener.[21] In the section on the internal conditions of the state, the recent murder of the relatively moderate Bavarian socialist leader,

Eisner, was viewed as being the sign for the start of the "second" revolution; the details of how to execute the revolution to a successful conclusion were believed to be directed by Radek. The revolution was viewed as being in reaction to the tendencies of the right-wing Nationalist forces in Germany, and the potential for the revolutionary mentality to persist in Germany could last for years—unless the army ensured that the internal stability of Germany was secured. This was viewed as being a vital task, to which the training of a reliable corp of men in the Army had to be directed.

Given this, it is not surprising that Radek had been somewhat brusquely treated in the initial stages of his captivity. It might also be noted that, while negotiating and delaying with Trotsky before Brest-Litovsk, Radek was adept at blowing irritating pipe-smoke into the faces of his German officer counterparts. In prison, he apparently was faced by threats from a senior officer, but replied, "Now that the Entente is disarming you, why do you Germans want to make yourselves yet another enemy, Soviet Russia?" His fortunes would take a turn for the better, when after August 1919 he was transferred to more comfortable quarters in the prison, and was allowed visitors; the War Ministry controlled access, and issued the permits to see him.[22]

But even before that point, while the Bavarian Soviet State was still in existence (and hence threatening the existence of the German state as a potential base for a nation-wide communist revolution), at least some members of the German military were beginning to consider the possibility of using contact with Radek to somehow reach Soviet Russia, in an attempt to find a counter-balance to the victorious Entente powers.

3
Exploring the Options: 1919

General Hans von Seeckt was, in 1919, responsible for the northern command of the German army, based at Bartenstein in East Prussia, and was thus responsible for securing the border against the instability from the east. He would shortly become the head of the Personnel Department of the Army, as the General Staff was renamed—that is, the head of the German army. In keeping with a tradition of maintaining good relations with Russia which can be traced at least back to Bismarck, Seeckt came to the conclusion that in the post-war world, exploring the possibility of collaboration with the Soviets might prove a prudent course of action for the German state.

In 1939, before the world was shocked by the Molotov—Ribbentrop Pact of August, the official and authorized biography of General von Seeckt was prepared under the auspices of another general of the army, Rabenau. Seeckt's contemporaries of the time, in preparing notes for Rabenau, viewed the German–Soviet relationship as a successful exploitation of a difficult time by Seeckt, and were eager to give proper due to their former mentor. It was the German military that led the path to the establishment of a relationship which bore fruit being enjoyed in the present time, they wrote with pride in their various memoranda. General Seeckt was determined, on the one hand, that Germany should under almost no circumstances allow itself to get into a war with Russia—that the Eastern Policy (Ostpolitik, i.e. an understanding with Russia) be pursued. This was at the time that he was in command of the northern borders, and specifically with helping the newly independent Baltic states attempt to resist absorption into the Soviet experiment. Germany was being put to use by the Entente powers directly, to organize the Balts as buffer states against the potential advance of Bolshevism. In this, Seeckt was also fully in agreement—while he wanted to find an accommodation with Soviet Russia, he also mistrusted the Soviet leadership on ideological grounds, and did not doubt the infectious domestic potential of Bolshevism should it be allowed to enter Germany. By helping stabilize the Baltic states against Soviet Russia, he also clearly influenced the course of the Russo-Polish war.[1]

While stationed in Turkey during the First World War, Seeckt had developed a close relationship with Enver Pasha, one of the original Young Turk leaders alongside Kemal Ataturk, as well as one of the architects of the Turkish attacks against Armenians; Enver had been dismissed from his position of Minister of War by Sultan Mohammed VI in mid-October 1918 in the light of the collapse of the Ottomans against the Allies at the end of the war. In the post-war scene, Enver was in Germany avoiding the Entente powers, who wished to try him for war crimes. In the spring of 1919, Seeckt began the process of making discreet inquiries to the Soviets about sending Enver Pasha to Moscow. This was done by German officers visiting Radek in prison, as well as Enver himself—who also visited Radek.

Radek later described his quarters in prison as a "political salon". Among the many visitors he was allowed to receive were army officers coming to inquire about the possibility of establishing military cooperation of some sort between Germany and Soviet Russia. One of Radek's visitors was Colonel Max Bauer, who had links to both the General Staff and personal connections to General Ludendorff.[2] Towards the end of his term in prison, while awaiting the settlement of terms for his return to Russia, Radek was hosted in the appartment of another of these officers, Baron Eugen von Reibnitz. According to E. H. Carr, Reibnitz later claimed that he and Radek had discussed, among other things, arrangements for a new partition of Poland, to be effected by a Freikorps invasion once the Red Army had captured Warsaw. Radek's impression was that:

> Raivnitz [sic] was the first representative of the species labelled "National-Bolsheviks" with whom I had to deal. He was the champion, in officers' circles, not only of alliance with Soviet Russia, but of the so-called peaceful revolution. He was of the opinion that the central task of restoring the productive forces of

Germany was insoluble without the nationalization of industry and without factory committees. The factory committees must, even before nationalization, draw the proletariat into the problems of organizing industry. During that time, while the workers would be "drawn" into the organization of production, it would be necessary to bring about a moral revolution and, through the pressure of the organized proletariat and the intelligentsia, compel the propertied classes to consent to a deal which would include compensation. He begged me to write an article in this sense, referring to Lenin's April 1918 speech on the next tasks of Soviet power. The speech, which appeared in Germany at that time, made a tremendous impression on a section of bourgeois public opinion. I pointed out to him that Lenin had made that speech after the seizure of power, and I suggested to him that he should persuade the bourgeoisie to capitulate, whilst we Communists would organize the "pressure" of the working class.

The visits by military officials were not the best-kept secret in Europe—the Polish security services (and hence, France) were well informed of the identity of Radek's visitors, and noted eventually in December 1919 that visits to Radek had been made by representatives of various German governmental ministries, who were apparently interested in economic and general geo-political matters (i.e. Poland).[3]

That the Poles were more interested than most in Radek's German visitors was a natural consequence of the events occuring at the time. The Polish government had just signed an armistice with Czechoslovakia, to end the fight for control over Teschen; the territory would remain under Czech control, but at the very least Poland was now free to keep its focus on its greater two enemies, Germany and Russia. Russia, for its part, was also active: from the start of February, and lasting until the first week of April, the Red Army had launched a successful military offensive in the Ukraine, capturing Kiev on 3 February. The advance was so successful that they managed to force the evacuation of Odessa by the Allies, at the start of April.

Before that point, however, German forces were also actively engaging in combat in the east. From March 1919, Germany had been given approval by the Allied powers to mount an offensive alongside

Latvian forces, in order to drive the Red Army out of Latvia. Essential in this operation were the Freikorps. Specifically, General Ruediger von der Goltz's "Iron Division", parts of which would be employed by Noske to maintain order in Silesia, was tranferred in late January and early February 1919 to the south-western section of Latvia, the only part of the country left unoccupied by the Bolsheviks after the withdrawal of the German army in December 1918.[4] Goltz successfully organized the local Latvian forces alongside his own Freikorps units, and began the process of working across the country and pushing the Red Army back. By mid-March, Golz was ready to launch an attack to liberate Riga from Bolshevik control. The Allies, now nervous at the success of the German general and his private army, ordered the German government to reign Goltz in, and to refrain from, making further advances. The Germans circumvented this order by placing units of the Latvian defence forces in the lead, and then simply following behind them in apparent support; thus, the attack was by Latvians, and not by Goltz. Riga was taken from the Soviets in late May.

While this was occuring in the north, the Soviets, building upon the momentum of their success in the Ukraine (which, after 8 April, would become the Soviet Republic of the Ukraine), launched a further counter-offensive in southern Russia. Lasting from March through April, it stopped the advances made by the White General Denikin, and pushed his army down to the Black Sea coast, where they remained until they could regroup for further action later in the year.

But of exceptional significance to the domestic scene in Germany, and for the Soviet Russian state as well, was the formal establishment in March 1919 of the Third International. A supposedly independent international communist organization, the Comintern was founded by the Bolshevik leadership of Russia, including Lenin and Trotsky, with the aim of pushing "by all available means, including armed force, for the overthrow of the international bourgeoisie and for the creation of an international Soviet republic as a transition stage to the complete abolition of the State".[5] In practical terms, it was a fig-leaf of deniability for the Soviet government, which could thus pursue propaganda and agitation throughout the world, all the while claiming that the activities were the actions of a separate organization, and not Soviet Russia's official governmental policy. An early example of the strengths and weaknesses of such an approach came with Hungary.

On 22 March 1919, a Socialist-Communist government was formed in Hungary to deal with the ongoing border crises with virtually all of the country's neighbours. Bela Kun, a veteran Bolshevik with direct ties to Lenin, and founder of the Hungarian Communist Party, was released from prison where he had been for more than a month previously, and invited to become foreign minister. The primary claim he made which saw him brought into government was that he could obtain Soviet help to rid the country of Romanian forces who had already begun successful occupation of significant territory. Kun organized a Hungarian Red Army, and, riding a tide of nationalism, was able to make major military gains against both the Romanians and the Czechoslovakians. At the same time, Kun isolated and then pushed from power the moderate elements of the government, and moved to govern the country with a Bolshevik model of Red Terror.

The other major foreign event which affected the perceptions of the German military at the time was President Wilson's threat to leave the Paris Peace Conference, on 7 April 1919. After the initial glows of cooperation had worn down, and the true agendas of the major participants became clearer, President Wilson realized that the ultimate aim of many of the other leaders was not to follow his lead in building an idealized future, but rather was the pursuit of nakedly self-interested political agendas. The matter was made most clear with the case of France, when Georges Clemenceau demanded the right of France to annex the left bank of the Rhine, as well as the Saar industrial region, from Germany. The Americans and British were horrified if not entirely surprised, and opposed the demands. However, Lloyd George did agree with Clemenceau that their reservation concerning the civilian costs of war, made at the time of the Armistice, be interpreted to mean the total cost of the war for the British and the French. President Wilson also was irritated by the French support for Pilsudski's Polish claims—interpreting the phrase "access to the sea" to mean direct territorial annexation of more land than Wilson had originally had in mind. Wilson threatened, bluntly, to leave the conference and return to the United States, forcing Clemenceau to back down on his annexationist demands. The compromise grudgingly agreed to by Wilson (and probably what Clemenceau had wanted all along as a minimum) was for a temporary occupation of the industrially valuable German lands. In return, the President agreed to support a treaty of defence which would bind Great Britain and America to France, should the latter face an unprovoked German attack. With these events in mind, the turn of events in terms of the contacts between the German military and the Soviets becomes all the more noteworthy.

Amidst all this, Seeckt took more concrete steps to reach out to Soviets, to explore the possibility of some form of collusion and cooperation in the face of issues of joint concern. That Enver Pasha was the first conduit to the Soviet state from the military circles of Germany is alluded to—though without reference to specific dates—in Radek's memoir:

> Two of my first guests were the former Grand Vizier Talaat Pasha, the Head of the Young Turk Government, and his War Minister Enver Pasha, the hero of the defence of Tripoli. After the rout of Turkey, they lived semi-illegally in Berlin the Entente was demanding their extradition and they were planning how to conduct the further defence of Turkey. *Enver, having fled after the rout through Soviet Russia illegally to Germany, was the first to bring home to the German militarists that Soviet Russia was a new and growing world force with which they would have to count, if they in fact meant to struggle against the Entente* [emphasis added]. I knew Talaat from the time of Brest-Litovsk. There I had seen him at the victors' table. Here in the Berlin prison, a broken man, he recalled that he was the son of a telegraphist and himself a former telegraphist, and kept saying that the Moslem East could free itself from slavery only with the support of the popular masses and an alliance with Soviet Russia. They described their relations with Kemal Pasha, who was leading the defence of Turkey after her defeat in the world war, in such a way as to suggest that, while Kemal was allegedly compelled to dissociate himself from the fallen Young Turk regime, there were no essential divergences between them, and they were organizing help for him abroad. *I tried to persuade them to go to Russia, which in fact Enver Pasha did later on.* [emphasis added] [...] Talaat struck me as a man with great innate intelligence and will power; he spoke a mixture of broken German and French. Enver Pasha, expressing himself freely in French and German, nervous by temperament, gave the impression of an unstable man who had completely lost

his balance and was fighting more for his personal position than for his country.[6]

Despite Carr's interpretation that these visits came only after more comfortable quarters had been arranged for Radek by a well-connected and aristocratic Swiss socialist named Karl Moor in August 1919, it is clear from Radek's own words that it was he who had encouraged Enver to attempt to travel to Russia in the first place. That Enver's first attempt occurred in April (if not February) indicates that the earliest contact between the two came at the start of Radek's prison term.[7] The documentation concerning this early attempt at contact is scarce; the most complete version is a report written by a former aide of Seeckt, then-Major Tschunke, who was based at the time in Kowno, Lithuania. In the typed version of his report, the date given for this event was "the end of February" 1919; it was later corrected in pencil to read "April", though the author of the correction is not evident.[8] This is confirmed by reference to other reports made by Major Tschunke,[9] as well as Captain Humann's 12 July 1919 letter to Seeckt concerning some of Enver's later complaints (both described below).

Less than a month after Radek's arrest as an instigator of the communist disturbances in Germany, and before the Treaty of Versailles was presented to the German delegation on 7 May, the German military had already sent an envoy to see Radek while he still was under strict arrest in prison, received encouragement from Radek that Enver should go to Russia personally, and organized the first direct attempt at contact between Enver and the Soviet government, in order to explore the possibility of military cooperation between the two states. Aware that the coming peace might not be as benign as hoped, the German army took immediate steps to attempt to keep other options open.[10]

Enver had his own reasons for wishing to meet with the Soviets—specifically, to begin a pan-Turkic uprising again British influence in Central Asia (something to which the Soviets were more than willing to lend some support to, in principle at least). Enver made three attempts to reach Moscow by German aircraft, by arrangement of Seeckt, between April 1919 and March 1920.[11]

The first flight made by Enver met with almost disastrous results, from the German perspective. According to Tschunke,[12] who was stationed at the time as a liaison officer in Kowno, Lithuania, one day Enver Pasha simply appeared in his orderly room under the heavy armed guard of two Lithuanian soldiers. Tschunke, who had served with Seeckt in Turkey during the war, recognized Enver immediately, but it was clear to him that the Lithuanians did not know the Turk's true identity; he had been travelling with false documentation claiming to be a member of the Turkish Red Cross.[13] Enver had been aboard a Junkers Liselotte airplane, en route from Berlin to Moscow, which had to make a technical emergency landing in Kowno. Tschunke was keenly aware of the price on Enver's head by the Allies for war crimes, and the presence of an Entente military commission in Kowno itself prompted the German liaison officer (whose ostensible job was to offer defence advice to the Lithuanians) to place an immediate long-distance call to Seeckt. He did not inform the Lithuanian authorities of Enver's identity. Enver informed Tschunke that important maps and documents from the German General Staff were in fact hidden in the airplane, and Tschunke took it upon himself to organize a rescue of the situation. With the aid of a German pilot in Lithuanian military service, he retrieved the incriminating documentation at night, from the airplane. In the succeeding days, he used his influence to have Lithuanians grant the as-yet unrecognized prisoner the right to go for successively longer walks, rather than being kept in a cell, while the investigation was ongoing. Tschunke then coordinated an escape. The aforementioned German pilot was at the controls of a plane in the taxi position of the airbase Alexota, at the time Enver and his fellow prisoners were being taken on their walk through a meadow. The prisoners made a dash away from their guards, who subsequently opened fire. Covering machine-gun fire was returned, Enver made it to the plane, and the plane managed to take off and head back to Germany. The timing of the escape was fortuitous, as the higher headquarters of the Entente military commission had only just managed to piece together Enver's identity. Tschunke met Seeckt the evening of the escape in Tilsit, just across the border from Lithuania in East Prussia, where the General greeted him joyfully with "With you in Kowno, I didn't have any doubts that everything would turn out a success." Had the Entente found Enver with the incriminating German military documentation, the suspicions of the British may have had significant consequences. A later attempt by Enver to make it to Moscow, by rail, was conducted with a similar level of drama at the border.[14]

The entire region was in relative flux, given the recommencement of activity by the Freikorps under General Golz. While General Seeckt on the one hand was attempting to send an emissary to the Soviets, Goltz continued to use the Latvians as a front and have his forces push forwards into a position from which they could link with the White Russian armies in the north, and then continue the fight against the Bolsheviks. His forces were defeated by an Estonian led group at the end of June.

The matters, including Enver's travel plans, were complicated further by the arrival of an Allied military mission in the Baltic under the command of a British general, with orders to clear the Germans out of the region and to organize the Baltic states' own armies so that they could defend themselves without German assistance. The first step was an order for the Germans to evacuate Riga in the first week of July, and soon thereafter other cities. The Freikorps forces retreated to the interior and waited. The local Latvian forces, which had been close allies of Goltz to that point, were placed under the authority of British officers. Goltz stalled as much as he could, and would eventually transfer formal command of his forces to the authority of the White Russian Colonel Prince Avalov-Bermondt (of dubious morality and even more dubious aristocratic lineage) in late September 1919. Despite the obvious nature of the ruse, the German government, largely under the direct influence of the German army, agreed that it did not have authority over the private and now Russian controlled army, and informed the Allies of this fact. And while this had been going on, the Poles had in the interim taken Vilna from the Lithuanians, adding a further complication to the region.

The difficulties which Enver was having in making his way to Moscow caused him to complain of his troubles throughout the summer of 1919. In a mid-July 1919 response to an inquiry from Seeckt, a German military official named naval Captain Humann, who had been in touch with Enver, wrote to the general that Enver had not been able to offer much new information of late on the difficulties dealing with Russians; instead, Enver gave an overall evaluation of the political situation at hand, which indicated to Humann that he seemed to be listening "only to Turkish and Bolshevik" voices. Humann felt that Enver's reports and commentaries in general were superficial in nature; Enver's apparent pleas for letters of support from "friends" was best explained in this context.[15] Enver continued to visit Radek in prison, especially once he had been transferred to his more comfortable quarters and had begun to receive more guests, from August 1919.[16]

The wisdom, from Seeckt's perspective, in seeking an arrangement with the Soviets rather than hoping for the best from the Allies, had been proven on 7 May 1919, with the presentation of the terms of the Treaty of Versailles. The German delegation, led by Count Brockdorff-Rantzau, had been in Paris since the end of April.[17] They argued strenuously that demands placed upon Germany by the terms presented in the Treaty bore little resemblance, in the end, to Wilson's Fourteen Points, and that the Treaty was simply impossible to fulfill. The Allies, however, would brook no significant reopening of the terms which had taken them so long to finally agree to, after such detailed and multilateral negotiation. Although counter-proposals were made by the German delegation on 29 May, the Allied response was to accept only minor revision of some of the territory in dispute with Poland. Elsewise, the Germans had to accept the treaty, or accept the possibility of a renewed war.

After the hopes of the earlier part of the year, the bitterness of the moment was great. Brockdorff-Rantzau expressed the German sentiments, in his formal reply to Clemenceau:

> I have the honor to transmit herewith the observations of the German Delegation on the Draft of the Treaty of Peace. We had come to Versailles in the expectation of receiving a proposal of peace on the basis actually agreed upon... We hoped to get the Peace of Right which has been promised us. We were aghast when, in reading (the treaty), we learned what demands Might Triumphant has raised against us. The deeper we penetrated into the spirit of this Treaty, the more we became convinced of its impracticability. The demands raised go beyond the power of the German Nation. [...] In spite of such monstrous demands the rebuilding of our economic system is at the same time made impossible. We are to surrender our merchant fleet. We are to give up all foreign interests. We are to transfer to our opponents the property of all German undertakings abroad, even of those situated in countries allied to us. Even after the conclusion of peace

the enemy states are to be empowered to confiscate all German property. No German merchant will then, in their countries, be safe from such war measures. We are to completely renounce our colonies, not even in these are German missionaries to have the right of exercising their profession. We are, in other words, to renounce every kind of political, economic and moral activity. But more than this, we are also to resign the right of self-determination in domestic affairs. Dictatorial powers are conferred on the International Reparation Commission over our whole national life in economic and cultural matters, its power by far exceeding those ever enjoyed within the German Empire by the Emperor, the German Federal Council and the Reichstag put together. [...] Her principal rivers are placed under international administration, she is obliged to build on her own territory the canals and railways desired by the enemy, she must, without knowing the contents, assent to agreements which her adversaries intend concluding with the new states in the East [Poland and the Baltic states] and which affect Germany's own boundaries. The German people is excluded from the League of Nations to which all common work of the world is confided.

Thus a whole nation is called upon to sign its own proscription, yea, even its own death warrant.

Germany knows that she must make sacrifices in order to come to Peace. Germany knows that she has promised such sacrifices by agreement and wishes to carry them through to the utmost limit she can possibly go to.

1. Germany offers to take the lead before all other nations in disarming herself, in order to show that she is willing to help them in bringing forth the new era of the Peace of Right. [...] But she hereby acts on the assumption that she will be immediately admitted, as a state with equal rights, into the League of Nations. [...]
2. In territorial questions Germany unreservedly endorses the Wilson program. She renounces her sovereignty in Alsace-Lorraine, desiring, however, a free plebiscite to be carried through there. [...]

3. Germany is prepared to make the payments incumbent on her [...] up to the maximum amount of 100 billion marks gold, namely, 20 billion marks gold until May 1, 1926, and the remaining 80 billion marks gold afterwards, by annual installments bearing no interest [...]
4. Germany is ready to devote her entire economic power to the work of reparation. She is desirous of actively cooperating in the restoration of the devastated territories in Belgium and Northern France. [...]
9. The German Delegation again raise their demand for a neutral inquiry into the question of responsibility for the war and of guilt during the war. An impartial commission should have the right of inspecting the archives of all belligerent countries and examining, as in a court of law, all chief actors of the war. [...] The high aims which our adversaries were the first to establish for their warfare, the new era of a just and durable Peace, demand a Treaty of a different mind. Only a cooperation of all nations, a cooperation of hands and intellects, can bring about a permanent peace. We are not under a misapprehension as to the intensity of hatred and bitterness that is caused by this war; and yet the forces at work for the union of mankind are now stronger than ever. It is the historical task of the Peace Conference of Versailles to bring about this union.[18]

The German government could simply not bring itself to accept the treaty, at first. On 20 June 1919 the cabinet of Philipp Scheidemann resigned rather than accept responsibility for the treaty. This was followed one day later by an act of defiance by the German navy. Rather than see the fleet fall into the hands of the Allies, the crews of the German High Seas fleet, interned by the British at Scapa Flow, scuttled their ships on 22 June. But faced with the direct threat of a recommencement of the First World War, the newly formed cabinet of Gustav Bauer on 23 June unconditionally accepted the Treaty of Versailles, after the Assembly voted, 237 to 138, for conditional acceptance to forestall an Allied invasion.

The final terms of the Treaty, which was signed by the German delegation on 28 June 1919, caused a despair in Germany in marked contrast to the hopes of six months earlier. While the issue of reparations was bad (five billion marks to be paid immediately, and the total final amount—to be determined later—over the next 30 years), the moral implications of the war guilt clause were worse; to compound matters, the emperor and higher leadership were declared to be war criminals, and were to be placed on trial. The territorial concessions ensured the loss of both disputed lands as well as territory (and citizens) considered undeniably "German" as well: Alsace and Lorraine, Moresnet, Eupen, and Malmedy; the international administration of the Saar for 15 years, followed by a plebiscite; the potential losses (depending on plebiscites) of central and northern Schleswig, Upper Silesia, Allenstein, and Memel; and the outright loss of Memel, most of Posen and West Prussia, and the German colonies. What was left of the former German empire would have to make due for its defence against hostile neighbours with a lightly armed military capped at 100,000 men, with no heavy weaponry, submarines, or aircraft, and a navy with only six major warships. The Rhineland was to be demilitarized and occupied for 15 years. the Kiel canal was opened to the ships (merchant and military) of all nations, and the major German rivers were internationalized. All large merchant ships, half of those of medium size, and one quarter of the fishing fleet had to be transferred to the Allies; the Germans also had to build 200,000 tons of new shipping over the next five years, for the Allies. Large amounts of coal would be paid directly to Italy, Belgium, and France over the next decade, while the cost of maintaining the occupation armies was also to be born by Germany.

The same day, 28 June, President Wilson and Prime Minister Lloyd George signed a treaty of alliance with Clemenceau, committing the United States and Great Britain to come to France's aid in case of a future German attack. Thus, the promises made earlier in return for the French "compromises" on the question of direct annexation of German territory were fulfilled. Although there was much angst in Berlin about whether or not to ratify the signed Treaty, the Reichstag obliged on 7 July 1919; as much to end the continued naval blockade as to avoid futher military action.

The Allied naval blockade of Germany compounded the sense of frustration and anger—regardless of the justness of the emotions—directed at the West by the German military, and further cemented in Seeckt's mind the necessity of an Eastern Orientation in German policy. Although lifted formally on 11 July 1919, upon the formal ratification by Germany of the Treaty of Versailles, it had already left an indelible mark. It was a classic utilization of siege warfare—the forced and increased scarcity of food which resulted, in many instances, in famine and death for eight months after the cessation of hostilities on the land, and fully explained the British reservation against Wilson's proposed "absolute" freedom of the seas, at the time of the armistice. Although an Allied policy, it was essentially a British operation. Though the French bore the traditional enmity of the Germans for their plight and the harshness of the peace terms, there was no doubt in the German military that the British were at least as serious enforcers of their vision of the peace, with their command of the high seas; the British were simply more subtle than the French. That the Allies, in the armistice terms, "contemplated" relieving the blockade in no way obliged them to do so. American attempts, under the leadership of Herbert Hoover, to distribute humanitarian aid to German cities was met with refusal on the part of the French and British to allow the distribution even of food which had already been unloaded in Europe, let alone the shipment of any new supplies. German commercial fishing rights in the Baltic were even rescinded, preventing them from even feeding themselves. It was only after a violent outburst from Hoover, reminiscent of Wilson's threat to leave the Paris peace conference, that the British and French were persuaded, in early March 1919, to relax the conditions of the blockade slightly. The reasons for the continued blockade included the British desire to have an instrument with which to force German acceptance of the peace terms, but also French desire to gain access to German gold reserves rather than see them paid to America for food, and a general suspicion of Amercian motives in proposing humanitarian aid in the first place (a potential projection of soft power aimed at undermining European control of their own continent). The resulting malnutrition affected everything from basic health of most citizens, to the fact that the influenza epidemic had a far greater impact on mortality in Germany than in other western European countries. The impact upon the German military's outlook on the potential for true reintegration into the western community of nations was decisive. The existence of an Allied blockade against Soviet Russia this time was yet another point in common between the two countries.

Once the terms of the Treaty of Versailles were known, the reasoning behind the initial decision to open contacts between Germany and Soviet Russia was confirmed not only in German minds, but it was also feared by others, without knowing precisely the nature of the desired cooperation: the British Foreign Office took note, as early as 1 June 1919, that "Germans were still negotiating with the Soviets".[19] This seemed to confirm some of the suspicions expressed by Lloyd George on 25 March 1919, when he stated to the Americans and French that "The greatest danger that I can see in the present situation is that Germany may throw in her lot with Bolshevism and place her resources, her brains, her vast organising power at the disposal of the revolutionary fanatics whose dream it is to conquer the world for Bolshevism by forms of arms. The danger is no mere chimera."[20] The need for a prisoner-of-war exchange mechanism between Germany and Russia provided at least some semblance of necessity for contact, and justification for the sending of a delegation from Russia to Germany.[21] A few months later, in October, reports were filtering back to London that German financial interests were active in Russia (apparently behind the cover of Italians).[22]

The physical dismemberment of the German colonial empire was undertaken at this time: German East Africa was given to the British to administer as a mandate, New Guinea to Australia, and all Pacific islands north of the equator went to Japan. Though bad enough, it was at least somewhat expected. Less so was the attempt by France to circumvent their previous commitment to Wilson not to detach more German territory. On 1 June, a French-back separatist movement proclaimed the independence from Germany of a "Rhineland Republic". The French attempted to exploit religious differences between the local Catholic population, and the protestant Prussian-dominated government in Berlin. The hostility of the local population, however, ensured that even with (or perhaps because of) French support, the Rhenish republic collapsed of its own accord within a few months. Nonetheless, it was a serious indication for the German military of the true intentions of France and the Entente powers, towards Germany.

For its part, the Soviet government was also becoming increasingly aware of the benefits which an ally might bring, given the continuation of the Civil War, and the beginning of new conflicts: from June until October 1920, Finland went to war with the Soviets in an attempt to gain control of Karelia.

The potentials of a closer relationship with Russia were not limited to direct military benefits at this point in time. Although this was an important part of Seeckt's motivation from April onwards, even the civilian leadership of Germany was also aware of the potential commercial benefits which could come from gaining access to the now decayed Soviet market. Brockdorff-Rantzau, in a letter to the Reich economics minister, demonstrated this potential even before Versailles had been ratified, in mid-June 1919.[23] The need and desirability of "friendly" economic relations was promoted by German diplomats in Eastern Europe, even while maintaining the need for caution as regards fuller diplomatic relations.[24]

Given the physical inability of Enver to make it to Moscow on Seeckt's behalf during the first half of 1919, it is unsurprising that the German circles interested in closer cooperation with Soviet Russia turned to a source closer to them—Radek, who was still in prison in Berlin. But as the German Foreign Office noted in a report on his situation in mid-July 1919,[25] although Radek was certainly guilty of the charges against him, it was clear that a political solution of some sort would have to be found. To release him in Germany would simply be to complicate matters too much, whereas to return him to the Soviets would be to hand them a propaganda victory. As German hostages in Kiev and Odessa (conveniently, in "independent" Ukraine, thus allowing Moscow to distance itself from any claims of blackmail) had been taken, a way needed to be found to kick Radek back to Russia, but so that he did not easily return. His isolation in prison limited his utility in acting as a conduit, but at the very least he could, when eventually back in Moscow, bear witness to the German interest, and thus ensure that someone accredited to some degree to speak on behalf of the Soviets could perhaps be sent to Germany.

By the end of July, the Weimar Republic finally had a consitution, which should have gone some way to defining the lines of authority for the military with regard to the conduct of an independent foreign policy vis-à-vis Russia. Under the final draft which had been accepted by the National Assembly, there would be an elected president who would serve a seven-year term, and who would be responsible for choosing a Chancellor to form a cabinet which would have the support of the majority of the Reichstag. Articles 47 and 48 made clear where the loyalty of the army ostensibly lay:

Art. 47. The President [...] has supreme command over the whole of the defense force of the federation.

Art. 48. If a state fails to perform the duties imposed upon it by the federal constitution or by federal law, the President... may enforce performance with the aid of the armed forces.

If public order and security are seriously disturbed or endangered within the Federation, the President... may take all necessary steps for their restoration, intervening, if need be, with the aid of the armed forces. For the said purpose he may suspend for the time being, either wholly or in part, the fundamental rights described [elsewhere].[26]

The President also had the right to dissolve the Reichstag, and rule by decree for short periods of time in case of emergency. The individual states, through their representation in the Reichsrat, could delay but not stop the passage of laws. Proportional representation was guaranteed, with the result that minority parties continued to exist, but also that coalition governments would almost certainly always be necessary. The consitution came into effect on 11 August 1919, but carried with it an article (61) which would cause some concern for the Allied powers:

After its union with the German Reich, German-Austria will have the right to the number of votes in the Reichsrat to which its population entitles it. Until then the representatives of German-Austria will act in an advisory capacity.

Predictably, but still causing resentment in Germany for the interference in their domestic affairs despite the "self-determination" ideals of Wilson's Fourteen Points, the Allies forced Germany, on 22 September 1919, to strike this clause from its constitution.

But just as bitterness combined with some legal normalcy appeared to be returning to Germany, days after the constitution came into force, a Polish uprising in Upper Silesia began. Apparently in response to the killing of Polish miners in a work dispute by German authorities, wide-spread protests spread. The Polish government actively supported (if not instigated) the wider mass protests, in the hopes of influencing the outcome of the promised plebiscite for the mineral-rich region. Thousands of German soldiers and policemen were used to suppress the uprising, with the killing of apparently more than 2000 to follow in subsequent security operations. Many Poles fled the region as a result, to neighbouring territory under Polish governmental control, and the Allies were eventually forced to send in a military mission to restore order. As a result of the disturbances and popular reaction against the German actions, in local elections held that September in the region of Rybnik, more than twice as many Poles than Germans were elected to council.

For Russia, as well, the situation in the late summer of 1919 continued to be in flux. A regrouping of forces by the White General Denikin resulted in major gains against the Bolsheviks in the Ukraine, starting in August and lasting until the end of the year. Bela Kun's communist experiment in Hungary had by this time also unravelled. An inability to finally get Soviet help to arrive, along with controversial nationalizations plans for land which alienated the peasantry, led to domestic turmoil, and eventual refusal of the army to follow his orders; Kun was forced to flee the country at the start of August.

And as this was going on, more direct pressure on both Germany and Soviet Russia was being applied by the Allies. Although the blockade of Germany had by this time been ended, the Allies continued to maintain a blockade against Soviet Russia. On 21 August 1919, the Entente Powers demanded that Germany respect their blockade of Soviet Russia, something of no small concern to either government. Despite apparent, and luke-warm, compliance from Germany, the resentment at the dominance of the Allies served to focus the attention of both the Soviet leadership and the German military on developing a relationship with each other, as a counterweight to the Allies. The pressure of the blockade was compounded by successes of White Russian forces in September and October, in the Baltic regions. Under general Yudenitch, a White army march on Petrograd came close to actually capturing the city, by late October 1919. A vigorous defence mounted by the Red Army, however, prevented its fall, and in the subsequent counter attacks the White forces were compelled to retreat.

The German idea of coming to agreement with a state which was a fellow outsider in the international system was not limited to relations with European powers.[27] The government of China had not signed the Treaty of Versailles, in protest over the Allied decision to allow Japan control over Shantung instead of handing back to Chinese control. Given the civil strife in progress at the time, German armaments producers sensed an opportunity to establish commercial and military links. The Sino-German peace treaty ending the state of hostilities between the two countries was signed on 15 September 1919. It was the first step towards normalizing relations, and allowed for negotiations to begin, which resulted in a May 1921 treaty on compensation claims: Germany renounced all claims for compensation for the Boxer Rebellion and paid China, further, for the cost of maintaining German prisoners-of-war during the First World War. In return, formal diplomatic relations were opened, military missions were exchanged, and German firms were allowed greater access to the Chinese market; by and large, the German companies enjoyed a great deal of success during the 1920s. The possibility of working outside the Versailles system, settling old claims, and including the possibility of military-industrial cooperation and development based on the expertise of German companies was thus something which Germany had established as a precedent, while searching towards the development of its policy towards Soviet Russia.

In late September 1919, Enver Pasha was again active in attempting to act as a conduit between Germany and Russia. This time, in another note written by Humann to Seeckt, the matter consisted of the sending to Russia of another Turkish intermediary acting on Enver's behalf, Said Emin Effendi. The main significance of this attempt lay in the indication that General Goltz, far from acting on his own during this time, was so closely linked to Seeckt that Humann felt he could rely upon him to help in the plan—all the while that Goltz was apparently committed to fighting the Bolsheviks. Humann begged forgiveness for disturbing Seeckt in his letter, but had received news that a mutual friend, who demanded to remain incognito, had recently arrived at his offices. His concern was less his personal security, than the consideration that the British thought he was currently in Anatolia, and he wished to continue to keep them occupied with looking for him there. For this reason, Humann felt obliged to respect his wish. Apparently, Said Emin Effendi wished to go to Moscow, via Ukraine. He had approached Humann with the hopes of obtaining from him free passage to at least get through the German lines of local military positions. After discussing the matter with other officers, Humann decided to take Effeni to General Goltz, and to obtain his help (or, in the worst case, on his own) to make his way through the lines; Humann felt that Golz was likely to be the one in the best position to offer assistance and information on how to effect the journey. For this reason, Humann requested Seeckt to write directly to Goltz with a request for assistance for Said Emin Effendi "to travel to Moscow as an emissary of Enver Pasha". As Effendi was greatly concerned that his incognito status was jeopardized and wished to depart shortly, Humann requested the letter come as soon as possible. The number of attempts, and numbers of German officers assisting them, was increasing as the year 1919 wore on.[28]

From the Soviet perspective, it was already clear, based on the visits received by Radek, that dealing with the German military would likely provide more immediate and concrete results and benefits, than in dealing with civilian leadership of Germany. Radek's reflections upon his meeting with Walther Rathenau, at the end of the summer of 1920, speak to the impression which civilian leaders tended to make:

> [W]ithout any preliminaries, came Rathenau. I knew him only from his books, from his activity as president of the board of [AEG], and as the organizer of Germany's raw materials supply during the war. I had occasion later on to meet him many times in his capacity as German Minister for Foreign Affairs, and I was able to form a clear idea of this very complicated man. Already at the first meeting, his basic qualities became evident to me: a great abstract intellect, the absence of any intuition and a morbid vanity. Crossing his legs, he asked permission to give his views on the world situation. He spoke for more than an hour, listening attentively to the sound of his own voice. [...] "Marx merely gave the theory of destruction. From my works you will derive the theory of constructive socialism. This is the first advance in science since the time of Marx", he announced modestly.
>
> Noticing that I was smiling, he continued to hold forth: "The victory of the revolution in Germany is impossible for a long time to come. The German worker is a philistine. Probably in a few years time I shall come to you in the capacity of a technician, and you, the Soviet notables, will receive me as an old acquaintance in the Kremlin, wearing silken garments." "Why silk?" I asked him.
>
> "Because after many years of the asceticism of illegal revolutionaries, you will wish to enjoy life after victory. There will be

nothing wrong in that, as long as you do your job of creating the new society." With these words Rathenau, assuming the role of a gracious and indulgent control commission, concluded our first talk. Rathenau [later] brought the Director General of the AEG, the clever old Felix Deutsch, who had old connections with Russia and a very good knowledge of the Russian technical world. Felix Deutsch was very sceptical about the possibility of the existence of any system other than capitalism. [. . .] But let the regime be what it pleases, as long as we trade with the AEG. He inquired delicately whether we did not intend to return to them their confiscated factories. But when I laughingly inquired why we should make presents to them, he started to moan about my perverted views. But he too wanted to go to Russia.[29]

Radek remained sensitive to the importance of economic links between the two countries. To this, he emphasized the need for better industrial and commercial relations between Germany and Soviet Russia in a meeting held with the German Foreign Minister Walther Simons, Deutsch, and Kopp, on the eve of his departure.[30]

The unofficial German representative in Moscow at the time was Gustav Hilger—a German who had been born and raised in Russia, and who served as an intermediary to effect the exchange of prisoners-of-war between the two countries. He as well had learned of Enver's attempts to reach Russia and subsequent escapes. But despite having seen the latter several times after his successful later arrival in Moscow in 1920, Hilger claimed to have no knowledge about "the nature of his mission on behalf of General von Seeckt or his accomplishments [. . .] There are no indications, however, that the German feelers had any appreciable results",[31] beyond the fact of having occurred and indicating the seriousness of interest.

In the Soviet camp, more extremist believers in global revolution, such as Yoffe, who in 1918 served as Soviet ambassador in Berlin while Brest-Litovsk was still in force, had been complicit along with Radek in trying to infiltrate communist agitators into Germany to assist with the second communist revolution at the start of 1919. In mid-September 1919, he complained to Moscow of the inadequacy of the current Soviet policy—he felt that they were not aggressive enough, and offered by way of example that had there been even one illegal emissary in Bavaria to better coordinate the uprisings of the previous year, at the very least the local communists would have had a useful person with whom they could have consulted.[32] The strength of the Yoffe's position, and the momentum of international communism in general, received a boost with the decision, at the start of October 1919, of the Italian Socialist Congress to join the Comintern. The issue of dual-diplomacy, from the Soviet side, was one which was still actively debated and by no means settled, all the while that the Germans were attempting to make overtures to Moscow.

This prospect of turning Soviet attention outwards appeared more possible at the start of October 1919, given the fact that the Allies had begun to withdraw their direct support in the Russian Civil War. Despite France's desire to stay involved, only the British saw direct action against Bolshevik forces, and once the Treaty of Versailles had been accepted by Germany, both the British and the American governments no longer had the desire to offer anything more than fincancial assistance for the White Russians. The Allies retreated from Archangel at the end of September, and the remaining forces left Murmansk by the second week of October. Both cities fell immediately to Bolshevik control, once the Allied military forces had left.

In addition to withdrawing their own forces from the theatre of operations, the Allies as well pressed Germany to pull back its presence in the Baltic region. Although some sections of Goltz's army in Latvia had indicated a refusal to return to Germany as early as late-August, it was not until 8 October that the Allies formally demanded of the German government that it recall Goltz himself from the region. The Allies did not accept the German explanation that, since 21 September 1919, the official command of the forces had been transferred to Prince Avalov-Bermondt, and that the Freiwillige Russische Westarmee was not Germany's responsibility. Goltz was recalled, and the Freikorps unit began a long and slow withdrawal, finally reaching German territory in mid-December. The German evacuation of Lituania was effected by mid-December, in the same process.

The Red Army, then, gained control of eastern Russia by November, and was able to focus its attention on Siberia; after capturing Omsk on 14 November, they forced admiral Kolchak's army further east to Irkutsk. As a result of these retreats, Kolchak was forced to resign his command, in favour of General Nikolai Semenov; Kolchak was later captured by the Bolsheviks and executed, in February 1920. At the same time as Kolchak was resigning, General Yudenitch's failure to capture Petrograd led to a retreat by his army from the Baltic region as a whole, and in his decision to then disband the army and withdraw from the Civil War. The Soviets were then free as well to launch a major counter-attack in the Ukraine, against General Denikin's army, in December 1919; by the end of that month, most of the remainder of the Ukraine had been occupied by Bolshevik forces. The situation in the East, then, was proving more favourable for the Soviets, although instability with regard to Poland was evident. After the presentation of the findings of Lord Curzon, who had been charged by the Allies to fix Poland's eastern border along lines of local ethnicity, and who thus determined that Vilna should become part of Lithuania, the Polish government formally rejected the proposed "Curzon Line" as being their final eastern border.[33]

With the internal military situation improving drastically for Soviet Russia, and in response to the overtures attempted by Enver Pasha earlier, the Soviet leadership decided to press contacts with Germany from their end, as well. In November 1919, Victor Kopp, a long-time personal acquaintance and colleague of Trotsky, arrived in Berlin to be a semi-official diplomatic representative. He was, from his arrival onwards, actively engaged in dealing with military, foreign office, and civilian financial interests in Germany, with an aim to produce closer links in any and all fields. His initial contacts with the German foreign minister officials were aimed at improving the prospects of closer collaboration.

Specifically, Kopp wished to know what the German reaction was to the continued (as of the end of August 1919) Entente blockade of Russia. German Foreign Minister Mueller said that there was no change in their position regarding trade relations between the two countries. Kopp then informed the minister that there were in fact other countries interested in trade with Russia as well, and offered the example of an American firm, Manhatten Trade Corp, which was interested in creating a German–Lithuanian–American company for trade relations. With respect to the escape of Enver Pasha from Lithuanian custody (referring to an 18 October telegram in which one of the two Turks in the aeroplane was correctly identified as Enver), Kopp noted that the Lithuanians suspected that the purpose of the flight was for the negotiation of a trade agreement. The minister also noted that Radek's position in prison, thanks to the Foreign Ministry's representations with German judicial authorities, was improved from its earlier conditions.[34]

Radek's year in a Berlin prison covered some of the most tumultuous times of the Weimar Republic. His role in the events at the end of 1918 included, after entering the country illegally and in disguise, participation in the foundation of the German Communist Party and the uprisings of January 1919, a difficult relationship with Rosa Luxemburg (who viewed him, in short, with utter disdain for his condescending attitude of purveyor of communist wisdom from the one place in the world where Revolution had succeeded) which ended only with her assassination, and his subsequent arrest on 12 February 1919. The significance of Radek's prison term lies less in his ability at the time to provide a direct line of communication (for he was not in contact with Moscow until Victor Kopp arrived in November 1919) but rather in his ability to provide encouragement and information to his German visitors, and his influence after his return to Moscow, on forming Soviet attitudes towards the German outreaches which had developed as a result of this encouragement.

In the debates which would follow the evolution of a dual-policy from the Soviet side—encouraging Revolution in Germany, while simultaneously trying to trade and gain from it—Radek recognized the futility of the former, and the harmful effect it was having on the latter. As E. H. Carr pointed out, it was Radek who first saw the "the possibility of using the Versailles treaty as an instrument, not as Comintern first wished to use it for hastening the proletarian revolution in Germany, but for forging a military and diplomatic alliance between Soviet Russia and Germany".[35] By way of example of the openness of his relationship with the military circles by the end of his stay, was the fact that, in December,

> [. . .] I was permitted to move into the private apartment of Baron Reignitz, from which I was to start my journey. When I got up next morning, Baron Reignitz inquired whether I would object if Colonel Bauer, a German artillery commander during the war and chief advisor of Ludendorff, had lunch with us. [. . .] He implied that [. . .] it might he possible for the officer class to make a deal with the Communist Party and Soviet Russia. They realized that we were invincible and that we were Germany's allies in the struggle

against the Entente. I told him that only the German Central Committee could speak for the German Communist Party, and that with the Soviet Government it was necessary to negotiate in Moscow.

The civilian sectors of government, still with connections to the current establishment, included personalities of significant stature:

> [...] I had to move into the apartment of Police Commissar Gustav Schmidt, where I spent a few more days. He was very shaken when my first visitor in the new flat [...] proved to be the former Minister of Foreign Affairs, Rear-Admiral Hintze. Hintze, of small stature, elegant, with a motionless Chinese face, made a strong impression on me. He was a man deeply shaken by Germany's fate. [...] He was for a deal with Soviet Russia, and said that he would very much have liked to see our present conditions with his own eyes. In 1905 he had been naval attaché at the Imperial Court. He had watched the events in Petersburg, had hunted a great deal in Russia's forests, had had opportunities to observe the attitude of the landlords to the peasantry, and had convinced himself, on the basis of his observations, of the final downfall of the old Russia. He questioned me on the probability of revolution in the West, and whether it would come there before the Entente had swallowed up Germany.[36]

The British government was interested to learn, in late November 1919, that Ludendorff viewed the news of the Allied withdrawal from their participation in the Russian Civil War as amounting to a victory for Germany. The way was clear for Germany to increase its influence in Russia, so went the report, now that America was not in a position to do so. Ludendorff apparently continued on, during a meeting with his personal supporters, that a new Triple Alliance could be formed with Germany, Russia, and Japan, and that before long Germany would be in a stronger position than it had ever been.[37] Despite his ascent into political irrelevance, Ludendorff was nonetheless a German general and war hero, and thus his comments were taken in London with interest as a reflection of at least some currents among the commanding generals and German leadership.

The British were clearly further concerned by the potential that this new relationship could be realized, upon receiving reports in December 1919 that the Finnish government believed beyond a doubt that there were in fact German staff officers "directing Soviet forces". This was apparently reflected in a significant change in both tactics (and, correspondingly, success) by Soviet forces during the last month. A defector, further, was reported to have left Russian forces because "he could no longer endure German-Jewish intrigues at Petrograd". Reports of German officers directing operations among Soviet forces had filtered in from an arrested Bolshevik agent, as well.[38]

The German military's mistrust of the civilian branches of government was a Prussian tradition rather than a new development. This was accentuated during the war years given the increasing role played by the army in formulating government policy, and carried into the post-war years. With regard to the relationship with Russia, this translated mostly into a desire to pursue a separate, independent, and secret policy. The practical result of this was that the German Foreign Office (and indeed any German civilian agency) often had no idea what the army was doing, with whom it was meeting, and why. It resulted in the Foreign Office becoming dependent on accidental sources of information, to determine what policy was being pursued by their colleagues in the Reichswehr. It was clear at the end of December 1919 that the German foreign ministry was not informed of the contacts between one of the most important foreign prisoners in Germany—Radek—and other members of the German government; they learned second hand (via the Polish consul-general in Berlin) in the middle of that month of visits to him by defense ministry officials, to discuss the impacts of the Polish situation and Pilsudski's overall policies.[39]

In Moscow, the combination of Radek's contacts and Kopp's early reports gave enough impetus to exploring the possibility of developing closer and more concrete secret ties with Germany that a briefing paper was drafted, on 18 December 1919, for use within the Soviet administration on the ground-rules and goals of such collaboration. It emphasized the following points: (1) secrecy; (2) trade (especially exports to Russia); (3) trade imports from Russia. Echoing Kopp's comments made earlier, an American consortium via Lithuania was to act as the middleman for handling the details.[40] The desire for closer collaboration did not mean that either side particularly trusted the other; that Germany was informed of the Russian government's communications, and that the Soviets later were aware of it, was clear from Soviet possession of a series of German decrypts of Russian telegrams, including some from Chicherin to Lenin, on the situation in Germany in 1919, and on the potential for greater "exchanges".[41]

Certain facts become evident from the piecing together of the secret contacts between Germany and Russia in 1919. The German military showed the initiative, and had the presence of mind to take advantage of Radek's arrest almost immediately upon his capture. Their interest was not merely theoretical, but actual, pressing, and secretive—they began the process of trying to use a non-German—Enver Pasha—as their intermediary,[42] as a precaution against a harsh result from the Paris Peace Conference. The raised hopes at the start of 1919 for the potential for a Wilsonian peace to come from Paris did not influence Seeckt's overall opinion of where the best option lay for German future foreign relations. The impact of the Allied naval blockade, and the terms of Versailles, merely confirmed the German army's initial thoughts. The Russian Civil War had, understandably, occupied the Soviets' attention enough that no real attempt could be considered to begin to respond to the German overtures before the situation with the Whites was brought under control. That German troops actively involved in assisting the Balts in combat against the Red Army was not enough of a deterrent to prevent the Soviets from keeping open the option of collaboration, when the situation calmed somewhat towards the end of the year. Radek's imprisonment serves as an indicator of the overall tenor; his transfer to comfortable quarters from August 1919 onwards, the freedom he was given in receiving a wide range of visitors, and his eventual relocation to the private apartments of a German staff officer, before being sent back to Russia, all speak to the fact that the German army took care to keep a channel to Moscow open regardless of the surrounding political chaos.

4
Opening the Door Wider, Amid Rumours and Chaos

If the first year or so after the Armistice saw the German military, and then the Soviet government, come to the realization that perhaps their best interests lay in developing a closer relationship with each other vis-à-vis the western Allied powers, then the following year saw ever-more concrete steps taken towards turning the mutual interest into a working relationship. The process was by no means assured, and there were many false steps and hesitations. But the overall political climate of Europe, and the continued isolation of both states from the rest of the international community, ensured that the initial inclinations of the post-war year would be acted upon.

That a Russian section of the German Foreign Office was in existence was, given the practice in most foreign ministries, nothing unusual.[1] However, in order to specifically focus upon expanding and developing the relationship with Russia, the Reichswehr itself took a step in this direction, and created a specialized bureau to handle the contacts and negotiations. As a direct result of General Seeckt's desire for closer cooperation with the Soviets, a special working group for Russia (Sondergruppe R) was created within the army early in 1920, and was greatly expanded by 1921.[2] The most prominent personality within it was Captain von Niedermayer, who was sent as its main representative and liaison to Moscow; he was assisted in this task by another officer, named Schubert. There was still no official German representation in Moscow, and in order to camouflage the work of Sondergruppe R and to finance future joint ventures with the Soviets, a cover-company was created (Gewerblicher Unternehmangen [Gefu]), jointly based in Moscow and Berlin. The German Foreign Office was uninformed of the activities of unofficial diplomacy conducted by the army, and only later (towards the end of 1920) became aware of the existence of Sondergruppe R. Wirth, who after May 1921 was both Chancellor and Finance Minister of Germany, was informed in somewhat more detail, as the scale of the proposed eventual investment was too large to be hidden in the army's budget; it was through the finance ministry that considerable amounts of capital were placed into Gefu.

The objectives of the German army with regard to Soviet Russia were, broadly speaking: a concession contract for the construction of airplanes in factories in Russia, by the Junkers aircraft firm; the foundation of Bersol, a pharmaceutical (poison-gas) company jointly owned by Russia and Germany; and the manufacture for Germany of artillery munitions in Russian factories, with the technical expertise of German managers and workers. Many obstacles lay in the way of the successful or complete realization of the objectives. However, in addition to these immediate tasks, the objectives of Sondergruppe R went further still: to lay the foundation of a relationship which would allow for the establishment of pilot- and tank-training facilities in Russia, with German involvement. These initiatives were successful, and were eventually realized in practice.[3]

Major political events of international significance at the start of 1920 threw into relief the growing relationship. The League of Nations Council met for its first session in mid-January, with Soviet Russia and Germany noticeable by their absence. The same day, the United States Senate voted against American participation in the League of Nations, heralding the return of the isolationist tradition, and the final death of the Wilsonian interventionism and idealism for European politics. In France, Clemenceau was defeated in presidential elections by Paul Deschanel; both the political elite and the public in France turned against Clemenceau, in no small part, for not having fought hard enough to make Versailles harsher for Germany, thus giving Germany a clear indication of the opinions of the most important western Continental power. That the perceived Allied vindictiveness had not worn down with time was also apparent, in German eyes, from continued attempts by the Entente powers to have the Dutch turn over the former German emperor, Wilhelm II, to Allied authorities so that he could be tried for war crimes. Though the Dutch refused once again on 23 January, they did nonetheless agree to have him interned; he remained in Holland until his death in 1941.

General Seeckt was determined to keep his personal sponsorship and encouragement of German military overtures to Russia as secret as possible for as long as possible—especially from the German Foreign Office. Despite the fact that Enver Pasha had been sent to Moscow at Seeckt's behest, the general nonetheless naturally attempted to distance himself from any possible connection with even the events. Seeckt's involvement had been inadvertently acknowledged to the German Foreign Office by a member of his staff—Lieutenant Lange. When the potential implications of the admission was realized, the ministry of defence scrambled—to an almost paranoid extend—to correct the "confusion" for the Foreign Office. To this end, other officials within the ministry of defence accepted full responsibility for the conveyance of Enver to Russia. The military's disclaimer against Seeckt's involvement went so far as to deny that he had any personal knowledge of the voyage, that he did not authorize or sanction it, and further that he was on vacation at the time the events had transpired. Lieutenant Lange's statements otherwise were the result of a "confused mix-up" on his part. It was also claimed that the minister of defence and the minister of foreign affairs had both been personally informed of Enver's trip in advance, and that (for good measure) the minister of foreign affairs was claimed to have entrusted certain tasks to Enver as well. Given the political climate, the strictest of secrecy was deemed necessary. The support of private businessmen for this adventure was also justified and explained. If absolutely necessary, the ministry of defence was prepared to elaborate upon the details, but only if—given the political sensitivity of the matter—the ministry's involvement could be concealed.[4]

Although Enver had been successful in opening a dialogue of sorts with the Soviets, it was hampered somewhat by the continuing Russian practice of trying to stir up revolutionary agitation within Germany at the same time. Radek had used his time in prison not only to receive distinguished German personalities, but also to advise local communists. Though he had personally come to view with scepticism the prospect of a successful communist uprising in Germany in the near future, it would be a while before many colleagues in Soviet Russia felt the same way. The Comintern, especially, remained true to its goal, continued to press for agitation in the Reich, and thus kept open a source of friction with Germany. This Soviet agitation had understandably irritated German officials to the extent that steps were taken to control the situation, before any further progress on dealings—whether financial or military—between the two countries was made: to this end, on 18 January 1920, there was a draft treaty (in German) under circulation in the Russian Foreign Ministry, whereby each of the states promised to refrain from meddling in the internal affairs of the other.[5]

From the German perspective, the private enterprise component of the relationship effectively meant that in many instances the Germans visiting Russia could best be described as part of a military-industrial complex which maintained ties with, and operated under the protection of, the Reichswehr. To that end, a series of visits were made by industrialists touring the new Soviet state (especially the Crimea) in the first half of 1920, to simply ascertain the nature of local conditions before proceeding further with more concrete obligations and contracts. Their reports home about what they found described the decay of the Soviet industrial base, and that they were often pessimistic about the prospects of resurrection. Among other concerns, they discussed the difficulties involved with gold transportation, contracts, lists of locations of gold, steel production reports, coal reports, and other industrial metals. Overall, what resulted was a series of financial reports which painted a gloomy picture.[6] The reports continued into the year and, by the middle of 1920, also highlighted the concerns that the Russo-Polish conflict could conceivably spread to the 1914 borders of Germany.[7]

In an after-action report written on 23 January 1920, on the return of Radek to Russia, the German Foreign Office noted as well that Enver Pasha's continuing anti-English campaign was being conducted with the assistance of the Bolsheviks. There had been a significant amount of anti-English propaganda regarding Central Asia, and some degree of relief (in the German Foreign Office) that in the end the prospect of establishing a Soviet government in the region appeared unlikely. The British had also been letting it be known that the unofficial German position was that, despite the willingness to conclude trade negotiations with Russia, ultimately Germany stood ready to proceed with the Entente powers against Russia. Germany felt that it was urgently desired that Russia's Trade and Industry Commissar Krasin come soon to Berlin, to discuss improved economic ties.[8]

By the end of January 1920, Ago von Maltzan, state secretary in the German Foreign Office, was pleading for greater care in German approaches to the Soviets. His arguments were expressed in terms of economic as well as political terms: one had to admit and concede to German industry the possibility of defending itself against British competition in the indispensable Russian market; but on the other hand, one also had to consider that Germany's position vis-à-vis the Entente could be strengthened, with the careful handling of the relationship with Russia. From the perspective of the Foreign Office, improved relations with Russia meant economic matters, and the opportunity to use ties of this nature for political gains.[9]

In Russia, the end of January and start of February of the same year saw swings in the overall fortunes of the country. An initially successful seizure of control of the city of Vladivostok in the Far East by the Soviets was later repulsed by Japanese soldiers, demonstrating the Bolsheviks' inability to completely consolidate their authority. But on the other hand, the first days of February saw the signing of an armistice between Soviet Russia and Latvia to end hostilities between the two countries; a formal peace and treaty of friendship and cooperation would come on 5 March. The Soviets also offered formal recognition of the independence of Estonia, through the Treaty of Tartu; this ended Estonian participation in the Civil War.

The same month, however, saw a series of setbacks for Germany. The idea of holding a plebiscite for Schleswig was not, in itself, anathema to Germany.[10] The majority of the population was ethnically German, and it had been under German control since the Danish–Prussian war over the territory, in 1864. However, the Allies stipulated that the duchy, which historically had been a single entity, should be subject to two separate plebiscites, one for the northern third and one for the southern two-thirds. The boundary between the two plebiscite zones was chosen along ethnic lines, with the predictable result that the Northern Zone Plebiscite, held on 10 February 1920, saw three-quarters in favour of reunification with Denmark. Had a single vote been held, given the overall populations of the Danish and German nationalities, the result would have clearly allowed for the whole of the province to remain within Germany. The second vote, held on 14 March for the more populous and more ethnically German lower two-thirds of the province, resulted in an 80 per cent victory for the Germans. An international commission was established to administer the plebiscite, with three of the five members being provided by the Entente's Britain and France. To assist the commission, the two governments despatched four large warships, two battalions (one each from the British and the French armies), for a total of approximately 3000 Allied soldiers and sailors, and another 250 special policemen; the military force was under the command of a British admiral. The formal incorporation of northern Schleswig into Denmark occurred on 9 July 1920.

On the Polish frontier, Germany felt as if the situation was slipping further away from its control as well. In the days coming after the Northern Schleswig vote, the Allies, in response to continued clashes between Germans and Poles, occupied Upper Silesia on 12 February 1920. That the majority of the troops used were French, and that the Allies had just demonstrated themselves in Schleswig to be perfectly willing to simply divide disputed territories in order to obtain results which were not favourable to Germany, led to the Allied occupation being viewed with some trepidation in Germany. This was followed shortly thereafter with the Allied occupation of the port and city of Memel, on 15 February, and the beginning of the envisioned 15-year League of Nations administration of the Saar region, on 26 February. The combined impact of these moves was to drive home the reality of the dismemberment and occupation of the country, and to deepen the enmity felt towards the Allies.

The Allies were aware that one potential impact of their actions might be to push Germany and Soviet Russia closer together, and openly discussed this as a distinct possibility late in February 1919, at the London Conference. Lloyd George summarized the Allied position by stating that the Allies should not recognize the Soviet Government "until the Allies were satisfied that it conformed to principles guiding ordinary civilized Governments", and that the Allies "[...] should prosecute our endeavors to secure raw materials essential to the rehabilitation of European trade".[11] Nitti, the Italian prime minister, warned a few days later (23 February) that the Allies had to more constructively engage with Russia, and that this meant the resumption of political relations: "[...] If we did not, and if Russia then turned to Germany, and these two powers made common cause, a most gravely dangerous situation would be created." Italy was, however, isolated, as Japan backed France; England sided with them while pretending that there was in fact no difference of opinion between any of the powers. With regard to Poland, France wanted the Allies to urge the Poles not to sign a peace deal with the Soviets; the British and Italian position was that unless the Allies were prepared to back the Poles militarily, it was an issue best left for the Poles themselves to decide.[12]

In a report sent on 24 February 1920 from the French government in Paris to their embassy in London, concerning German–Russian relations, the Germans were described as being well informed of ongoing trade talks between the Soviets and the British. Kopp, apparently, even informed the French that an accord would soon be signed between Germany and Russia, allowing for the return of prisoners-of-war, the establishment of economic relations, and the establishment of rail and postal communications. Kopp denied that anything more than this was being planned, in contrast to other French reports that Germany was in fact attempting to lay the groundwork for a long-term political accord with Russia. The French wondered at the British willingness to withdraw and allow Germany too much free room for manoeuvre; if this continued, when in fact the Allies should be doing the opposite and placing themselves in a better position in Germany from which to observe all developments within that country, then it would surely be only a matter of time before the entire structure of the peace crumbled.[13]

Starting in February 1920, and continuing in the months which followed, a flurry of reports between the British Foreign Office and its various representatives on the Continent dealt with rumours and possibilities of varying forms of German–Soviet propaganda. While ranging widely in accuracy, they are nonetheless worth examining if just to appreciate the impact which the echoes of the real contacts were having; the more so, as the reports came closer in accuracy as the months wore on, and as they give an increasingly apt description of how the private industrial aspects provided an effective shield for the military negotiations underway up at the same time.

A Polish intelligence report which was forwarded to the British, and whose reliability was admittedly judged to be "doubtful", stated that the German and Soviet governments signed an agreement in March 1920 whereby Germany undertook "1. To equip the Russian army and industry so that the same could resist the English in Asia and

Poland. 2. In every possible way to support Russia in her peace negotiations with the Western States." The Soviets apparently undertook to "1. place mines, railways, canals, and big enterprises for exploitation by the Germans". The text was supposedly signed by Lenin, Trotsky, and Chicherin, and by Noske, Erzberger, and Bauer. The number of German instructors in Russia would amount to 20,000. The original report was apparently bought by an English agent for 18,000 pounds, sent to Warsaw, and then sent to the British Foreign Office.[14]

On 3 February 1920, the British Foreign Office wrote to their embassy in Berlin that reports had been received from British military sources to the effect that a delegation of the German General Staff had arrived in Moscow. This was supposedly in connection with an agreement reached between the German and Soviet governments, which stated that the German government would send military specialists to the Red Army, if the Soviet government would abstain from propaganda in Germany. Information was also received that a training camp had been established in the interior of Germany, and also at Heidekrug, where officers and men of Bermondt's army underwent training with a view to service in Bolshevik Russia. The Foreign Office asked their Ambassador to discuss the matter with the British military representatives there, as the "reports on the subject of German relations with the Soviet Government are so conflicting [...]".[15]

Shortly thereafter, the British Foreign Office sent further word to the embassy in Berlin that a report which "should be reliable" had reached London. Ludendorff was apparently the head of a secret organization to bring an armistice between Reds and Whites in South Russia, with the aim of launching a combined Bolshevik/Spartacist attack on Poland. Ludendorff would, at a propitious moment, lead a coup in Germany. Lord Curzon advised Lord Kilmarnock, the British chargé d'affaires in Berlin, to inform the German government that a planned coup was afoot, and promised to check out the information, which included a list of approximately 200 names of German officers serving with the Red Army.[16] Kilmarnock's reply, on 9 February 1920, was that it appeared that some people connected with Ludendorff spoke of such an alliance to attack Poland, but no evidence existed of a planned coup. Major-General Neill Malcolm, of the British Military Mission in Berlin, further stated that London's information "in several respects" did not agree with his own. Kilmarnock then wrote that talk of a coup and alliance and attack on Poland appeared to be part of a move designed to scare Britain away from demanding the handing over of war criminals.[17] The bogey of German–Russian conspiratorial relations occasionally, thus, took on what in retrospect appeared to be fantastic proportions, but which in the context of the times commanded the serious attention of usually sober statesmen.

In a report closer to reality, Kilmarnock wrote to London on 17 February 1920 that he had learned from a good journalistic source that coming representatives from Soviet Russia [i.e. Kopp], would ostensibly discuss issues concerning the repatriation of prisoners-of-war, but in actuality would also discuss a possible economic agreement between the two countries.[18] One day later, on 18 February, Curzon wrote to Lt. Col. Ward (the British military representative in Kovno) that General Malcolm in Berlin had received a report (which he believed) that the Germans were sending a Dr Shoeneberg to Kovno to open negotiations with the Soviets, but that his orders were in fact to procrastinate as much as possible. Kilmarnock then wrote to London (with reference to a 11 February report of General Malcolm), making it clear that Britain was well informed of the German–Soviet mutual interest, and that it involved in some sort of military cooperation, economic ties, prisoners-of-war, and other matters. Kopp was viewed as being the Soviet lead. According to Malcolm, "[. . .] I would point out that Herr Schlesinger (not to be confused with Dr Erich Schlesinger), who with colonel Bauer is responsible for the department of the Kriegsministerium that deals with prisoners-of-war, is a man who is much in sympathy with Bolshevism."[19]

On 24 February, Kilmarnock wrote again to Curzon that the German Ministry of Foreign Affairs had declined and downplayed Radek's attempts to expand conversations between the two countries on prisoners-of-war, to include other matters, such as commercial agreements; Germany apparently said it would limit and restrict the Soviets to prisoner-of-war issues, not least because there was little that they thought the Soviets had to offer for export in any event. A series of notes and reports written in the following week, however, gave the impression among the British diplomats that something more than simply prisoner-of-war affairs was being discussed in the negotiations. According to the British Military Mission representative Major Hedley, "Any agreement arrived at will I feel confident, be far-reaching in its nature and will include arrangements for re-opening of frontiers and general economic relations. Whether it will or will not comprise some sort of military convention is at present uncertain." Hedley also wrote that Baron von Maltzan, head of the Russia section of the German Foreign Office, informed him that Herr Schlesinger would be the German "O'Grady", but the firms like AEG would conduct their own negotiations separately. However, in the opinion of another British officer, Captain Breen, in a 20 February note, Schlesinger was himself pessimistic of the value of German–Russian trade, and "Germany urgently needs the financial help of America and England".[20] By 11 March 1920, Curzon received from Kilmarnock a report from an informant, dated 9 March, stating that Schlesinger and Kopp had agreed to include chemical and medical firms in their discussions, including "[...] the dispatch to Russia of German chemists and medical stores in return for certain concessions granted to German enterprises in Russia".[21]

On 2 March 1920, Kilmarnock wrote to Curzon that, in conversation with Mueller of the German Ministry of Foreign Affairs, the latter "professed complete ignorance" of Enver Pasha's presence in Germany, and thought it unlikely that he would be in the process of flying to Russia on Germany's behalf. British sources, on the other hand, indicated that Enver Pasha was heading over that week.[22] On 11 March, the Earl of Derby, the British ambassador in Paris, wrote to Curzon that the Conference of Ambassadors decided it could not really ask Germany to arrest Enver and Talaat Pasha as "war criminals" when (a) the Allies had temporarily suspended the prosecution of war criminals and (b) the two were not on the list of 46 for Leipzig anyway. It was better, they thought, to simply ask the Germans to expel them for abusing German hospitality.[23] Later, on 30 April 1920, Kilmarnock wrote to Curzon that he had been informed by the German secret police (via Baron Eckhardstein) that Djemal Pasha and two other Turks were heading to Russia in disguise, and that the trip was being planned in conjunction with Kopp. Kilmarnock urged that Finnish and Estonian police have them arrested for travelling on false documents.[24] By 7 May 1920, the British asked for their arrests; their object was (according to a report dated 28 May) to meet up with Enver Pasha in Moscow, pick up forged 50 pound banknotes, go to Tashkent, buy gold from sheiks, and then foment anti-British hostility; there was no mention of other activities being conducted on behalf of the German military.[25]

The failure of the German government to prevent any effective resistance to the perceived Allied injustices concerning the occupation and handing over of German territory was something which would prove too much for extreme nationalist forces in Germany to bear. The Kapp Putsch, which began in mid-March but whose impact was felt for months to come, demonstrated the army's indifference, disloyalty, and independence from the civilian leadership.[26]

Dr Wolfgang Kapp, a former president of East Prussia, associate of Admiral Tirpitz, and founder of the monarchist Fatherland Party, had levelled a series of complaints against the federal government, starting in January 1920. Designed mainly as a pretext for later action, they questioned the legitimacy of Ebert's rule, arguing that the constitution demanded the election of the President by the nation and not only the National Assembly; Kapp also argued that the government itself was illegitimate, as it had been formed for the purpose of negotiating a final settlement to the war, and nothing further. He complained as well of the government's inability to effectively maintain order and improve the economy. The only solution to his grievances were for immediate national elections. Ebert and Chancellor Bauer ignored Kapp's demands, whereupon the latter began to plot for a coup against the government; the timing of the coup was likely earlier than Kapp had initially envisioned, as he was afraid that the government had learned of the plot.

Be that as it may, General von Luettwitz, the Commander of the First Division of the army, was Kapp's main military ally, and with the support of his troops as well as many of the returned Baltic Freikorps, a seizure of power was launched on 13 March. Ebert and Bauer's appeal to General von Seeckt for the assistance of the Reichswehr was met with the observation that soldiers did not fire upon fellow soldiers, and Seeckt further compounded the military's inactivity and paralysis by taking an indefinite leave of absence. With no support from the military, Ebert and the government fled the capital to Dresden; they subsequently were forced to continue to Stuttgart, to avoid arrest by Freikorps soldiers in Dresden. Kapp made a public declaration that the Ebert–Bauer government was no longer in existence, that he had assumed command as Chancellor, and that General Luettwitz was the new Minister of Defence; the assumption of powers were stated to be temporary, with new elections to follow shortly in order to "restore constitutional conditions". No mention was made of the ulterior intention of re-establishing the monarchy, at this time, despite the fact that the older imperial black-white-red flag was flown.

Ebert's response was to call on the only force left in the country which could conceivably stop the coup, the working classes in a general strike. In an appeal issued by Ebert, Noske, and Bauer, the public was exhorted to commit to a general strike:

> The military revolt has come. Ehrhardt's naval brigade is advancing on Berlin to overthrow the government. These servants of the state, who fear the dissolution of the army, desire to put reactionaries in the seat of the government. We refuse to bend before military compulsion. We did not make the revolution in order to have again to recognize militarism. We will not cooperate with the criminals of the Baltic states. We should be ashamed of ourselves, did we act otherwise.
>
> A thousand times, No! Cease work! Stifle the opportunity of this military dictatorship! Fight with all the means at your command to retain the republic. Put all differences of opinion aside.
>
> Only one means exists against the return of Wilhelm II. That is the cessation of all means of communication. No hand may be moved. No proletarian may assist the dictator. Strike along the whole line.[27]

The impact of the appeal was immediate, and decisive. With the exception of a few pockets of support (East Prussia, Pomerania, and Silesia), there was little enthusiasm for Kapp's attempt. The governments of Baden, Wuerttemburg, Bavaria, and Saxony actively and openly supported Ebert, and the general strike was especially effective in the capital itself, where a refusal by Berlin workers to work led to the complete paralysis of the city. With no way of governing, and most of the army now watching with concerned "neutrality", Kapp had no choice but to resign, on 17 March.

Given the declarations by Ebert that new elections would be forthcoming, Kapp claimed a Pyrrhic victory; a Reichstag would replace the "illegitimate" National Assembly on 6 June. A different, and unforseen, sort of victory came against the workers, as Kapp's forces withdrew from the capital on 18 March.

With the government of Ebert en route to Berlin once again to attempt to retake control of the city and the country, the Freikorps troops loyal to Kapp were making their final way past the Brandenburg Gate. In response to jeers from the gathered crowds of civilians, the last unit in the column fired a volley, killing many of the onlookers. When the proper government returned to Berlin, they found a city enraged, and out of control. In parts of Berlin, soviets were already being set up, and the radical leader Ernest Daunig proclaimed himself the president of the "German Communist Republic".

The radicalism spread outwards from the centre, and a new Spartacist uprising was underway—this was viewed by the German army as something which had to have been conducted with the assistance of Soviet agitation, thus complicating the relationship with Russia. In many parts of Germany, workers refused to heed the government's call for an end to the strike, and the government almost found itself without control over portions of Bavaria, Wuerttemburg, West Prussia, and especially the city of Leipzig. Given the success of the general strike against Kapp, the KPD then attempted to use the same weapon against Ebert. The level of support from the public was not the same this time, however; but the major difference proved to be the support of the army, which rediscovered its loyalty to a government threatened from non-soldiers from the Left. As bad as the situation was, it had the merit at least of remaining something of a domestic crisis. But with the success of the communists in the Rhineland, the government's attempt to regain control brought it in direct conflict with the French.

France was no supporter of Bolshevism, but it was even less interested in seeing a return of German soldiers to the demilitarized zone; with the exception of a police force, Germany was not allowed, under the terms of the Treaty of Versailles, to station any soldiers there. The local German police were entirely not in a position of strength from which they could combat the KPD, who took control of Essen, Wesel, and other points, before declaring an alliance with Soviet Russia. Utterly unable to deal with the situation any further, Bauer resigned as Chancellor on 26 March, to be replaced by the former Foreign Minister Mueller. The resulting moderate coalition cabinet tried to find a way to allow for German soldiers to enter the Ruhr to restore order, without coming into open breach of Versailles; to this end, it formally requested the Allies for permission to send the

German army into the Rhineland for the sole purpose of fighting the insurrection.

Attempts by the British and the Italians to find some compromise method in order to allow this included: the threat of a potential direct occupation and demilitarization of an even wider zone should the German army not promptly withdraw once it was no longer needed to fight the communists; having Allied officers accompany the German army; or simply demanding whatever guarantees Marshal Foch desired of the Germans as a precondition. France countered the British and Italian proposals by demanding the right to occupy Frankfurt and other cities as "hostage", to be evacuated only once the German army left the Rhineland. This was something the German government could not bring itself to do, and with the situation in the Ruhr becoming more desperate, Mueller decided to risk whatever consequences would come, and sent the German army in anyway. Although some fighting occurred, the military, which entered on 3 April, was able to take the KPD strongholds within two days. France responded by ordering its own soldiers to occupy Frankfurt and Homberg, which they did on 6 and 7 April.

The bitterness roused by the French willingness to thus manipulate the desperate domestic situation in Germany was intense. Matters were not helped by the fact that Senegalese troops were among the French occupiers, which the Germans in Frankfurt viewed as an additional insult. Protests developed, resulting in deaths and injuries from the use of machine-guns against a civilian crowd. Although the British were not pleased with the unilateral manner in which the French acted, nor were they pleased that Germany had, in the end, taken the right to violate Versailles into their own hands.

Despite a lengthy speech in which the German Chancellor blamed Kapp, the communists, French militarism, and the decision to employ black soldiers in the occupation as causes for the current tensions, Mueller recognized that the letter of Versailles had been violated, but argued that the spirit of the treaty had not: if the maintenance of public order was not foreseen by the Allies, then they would not have made allowance for the continued presence of German police in the demilitarized territory. The only issue at hand was that the size of the police was inadequate to maintain order, and that they needed extremely temporary reinforcement by the military to put down an open insurrection. That the German army accomplished its task quickly, and was mostly withdrawn in the following weeks, did not assuage the Allies very much.

At a meeting of the Supreme Allied Council at San Remo on 19 April, a British and Italian proposal to invite Germany to participate in a resolution of the conflict was refused by the French. The German government was, in the end, simply told that so long as they did not carry out the disarmament clauses of Versailles (i.e. completely withdraw), the Allies would continue to occupy Frankfurt, and that the German request to increase the size of its army to above 1,00,000 men could not even be considered. Other pre-existing complaints about delays in reparations and coal payments were also included in the note sent by the Entente powers to Germany, but along with them was a statement that the Allies had in fact no intention of acutally annexing any German territory. After more notes were exchanged between the two sides, the German government agreed to the limits demanded by the Allies, and the extended French occupation ended on 17 May. The event, however, proved to be a precursor to the later occupations of the Ruhr, in 1923.

Perhaps while on his "indefinite leave" during the Kapp Putsch in March, Seeckt found time to write out his thoughts and offer general advice on foreign policy to any official of significance. In a report written during this time for the higher echelons of authority (the President, Chancellor, Foreign Minister, and Defence Minister), Seeckt deliberated upon "Germany's next political tasks".[28] He noted possibility that soon the Red Army might be victorious over the Poles; this would mean that one of the fundamentals of the Treaty of Versailles (an independent Poland separating Russia and Germany) would be eliminated, and that Germany would have Soviet Russia on its borders. This would herald a dangerous time, as then Germany might also become a competitor for Russia. Whoever allowed the initiative to be taken away, Seeckt intoned, allowed for his fate to also be taken away, which could signify the utter downfall for Germany. The "Russian question" had to be assessed with regard to its repercussions on the German people, for the political and military position of Germany vis-à-vis the Entente on the one hand and Russia on the other.

Seeckt was worried that the ideas of the Russian revolution might prove strongly attractive for the German people (which would have been music to the ears of Yoffe and the Comintern). With use of arms alone such developments, amid the global crises of the day, could not be simply kept down. Rather, one had to meet the developments and direct them, along with the future of the people, in the appropriate direction. A struggle against Russia would deepen the divisions within the German people, the general believed, as a fight against their new ideals; it would as well lead to new uprisings internally, which, if dealt with by the state's proper power, would paralyze the country. A struggle against Russia would not be one with the unified nation behind it; it would therefore be hopeless. It would be met with sharp resistance from the working-class masses and in the end would bring about Bolshevism in its worst form, as experienced in Russia—something which Seeckt wished to spare the German people. And lastly, the Bolshevik leaders in Germany would side with Russia, and follow the path which a far-sighted German policy with regard to their own people should from the start demand. As well, from the point of view of the Entente, a Russian victory against Poland had to be prevented; the Entente powers had a great interest in setting Germany against Russia. A complete and direct Entente victory against Russia directly could be ruled out, Seeckt felt, because the huge land and population of Russia made it simply invincible. If Germany fought against Russia, it would therefore fight a hopeless cause, become a vassal of England, and thus simply a victim whom Russia could vanquish when no longer it was needed by the Allies.

Seeckt further believed that "Russia had the future to itself". It could not sink, because it bore new powers on its huge territory. It could, once its disorganized economy again began to produce, create a profusion of raw materials and food. It needed Germany (as Lloyd George feared) as an industrial partner, as a supplier of intelligence and organization. Germany and Russia needed to be reminded of how their relations were before the war. If Germany joined sides with Russia, it would become invincible as well; other powers would always have to keep Germany in regard, as Russia could not be ignored. If Germany placed itself against Russia, it would lose all future hope, and find itself promptly in war. There was no future to be had alongside the Entente, Seeckt wrote for his readers; with it, Germany would forever remain an exploited nation which allowed itself to work for others. And with such a future, Germany would become internally divided and would suffer the heavy fate of becoming a nation of slaves ("Helotenvolkes").

An entirely different situation would arrive if Germany opened itself up and placed itself immediately on Russia's side. This opportunity could also be missed, because Germany had to first wait to see the outcomes of the power-struggles within Russia and without, and to see if Russia would be strong enough to support Germany in a breach with the Entente. Correspondingly, Germany had to demonstrate to Russia with the fullest openness of its peaceful intentions and declare that it wished to live in friendship with Russia, with reciprocal extensive economic exchanges, on the basis of full reciprocity. But this had to be dependent upon Russian respect for the 1914 Imperial German borders, as Germany felt an obligation to protect the territories which, up until the war, were part of Germany. Russia would look for friendship from Germany and respect its borders, because Germany would proceed cautiously and wisely, because Germany has always respected the right of self-determination of states, and also because Russia needed Germany's labour and industry. If Russia halted at the 1914 borders, and if the Entente undertook no hostile actions against Germany, then Germany would stand as a potential broker between the two sides, and thus would have its hands free in terms of its bargaining position for the political and military scene outside Germany.

In short, according to Seeckt, Poland remained a common "mortal enemy" for both Germany and Russia, and it was only with an alliance with Russia that Germany's position as a world power could be regained. This was not only the direction for Germany's next political tasks, but served as an explanation and later justification for his entire programme of military collaboration with the Soviets. Seeckt could not have offered a clearer statement of his, and hence the German military's, vision.

A futher sign of the inter-governmental rivalry within Germany, however, was demonstrated by the fact that contacts between the Reichswehr and Red Army were often the subject of German secret police reports, which made their way to the Foreign Office. The State Secretary for the Protection of Public Order reported to the Auswaertige Amt in early May that several Red Army generals had been noted in Berlin, in the company of a Russian general, Werchoski; apparently, they were attempting through intermediaries to contact

German military circles.²⁹ These reports represented a cause for concern, given the context of the failed attempted coup led by Kapp.

The stability of Soviet Russia's internal and external position at this time continued to undergo significant changes, and spoke directly to the concerns and goals raised by Seeckt. By the end of March, the Red Army had effectively eliminated General Denikin's forces in the Ukraine, forcing him to turn over formal command of all White Russian forces in Southern Russia to General Wrangel. After initial successes which saw the Red Army capture Baku, Wrangel was able to effectively reorganize the White forces, and take advantage of the troubles between the Soviets and Poland. These flared up on 27 March, with the Polish demand that Soviet Russia formally recognize the 1772 borders, thus placing territorial demands upon Belarussia, and setting the stage for the war. After the third week of April, Poland's main offensive operation was launched, with the aim of capturing Kiev. An independent Ukraine was an integral part of Pilsukski's hopes for an anti-Bolshevik alliance of states along Russia's periphery. The Polish army did not have great difficulties in its early encounters with the Red Army, and managed to take the Ukrainian capital of Kiev on 7 May. This was in some part, at least thanks to the diversion provided by a major offensive launched by general Wrangel's White army, beginning at the same time, and which overran much of southern Russia, from the Sea of Azov northwards.

Although the contest between the Poles and the Russians would continue onwards through the summer and into the autumn, the mere fact of war between the two did much to ensure that Germany and Russia would see the common objectives of their national interests, as Seeckt both predicted and desired. The primary enemy was the same for both countries, but more important was the determination of France (and by extension, the Allies) to support Poland. Poland was the offspring of Versailles, and the countries left out of the peace of the First World War found much to agree upon with regard to the newly resurrected state.

Soviet forces launched counter-attacks at several places in the south, during the early summer months. After defeating the White fleet on the Caspian Sea, the Red Army established a foothold in northern Persia, and established a Soviet Republic of Gilan. At the same time, in Central Asia, the Red Army forced Armenians out of

Karabakh, and had occupied much of Armenia by the middle of the month. Further northern gains made by the Soviet Cossack cavalry led to major breaches in the Polish–Ukranian lines in early June, thus allowing for the main Soviet forces to begin to push through. The Red Army recaptured Kiev and its surrounding areas by the middle of June, and continued their advance westwards. Prominent in action against the Poles was the young General Tukhachevsky, whose force exceeded 100,000 infantry and more than 10,000 cavalry, and was supported by both artillery and machine guns.

With regard to the recent Russian advances against Poland, the French received indications, on 31 May 1920, that Ludendorff and the German extreme nationalist circles in general were torn between two contradictory impulses, with regard to Russia: to support traditional Prussian expansionist aims, with the support of a Red Army led by Prussian officers, or to play upon the fears of a Bolshevik advance into Europe in order to win from the Allies the right to re-establish a Great Prussian state as a bulwark against the coming revolutionary tide. The French opinion was that in no circumstances should the Allies allow themselves to be manipulated into a position in which they became dependent upon the whims of Germany.[30]

The Soviet administration took an active interest in possible developments between Germany and Poland, and demonstrated this in a series of correspondence exchanged between Chicherin and Kopp, from June 1920 onwards. Included in a note from Chicherin on 22 August 1920 was that he had dispatched a further representative (named Bratman) to Berlin with instructions for Kopp regarding continuing negotiations with Germans. On 23 August 1920, in a letter to Kopp on German neutrality (in the Polish war), Chicherin pointed out that any deal with the Germans on any military matters had to have the approval of Seeckt—that he was the real power behind these issues.[31]

The British, by this time, were getting ever more suspicious of Kopp's activities in Berlin, and noted the clear links with German industry. On 20 June 1920, Kilmarnock wrote to London that the

> German government have given extra-territorial rights to Kopp and his mission. Result is that every Bolshevik agitator in Germany can escape police control by sheltering himself under the aegis of Kopp's mission. *Although Chancellor and Minister of Foreign Affairs*

are probably ignorant of what is going on [emphasis added] close relations are maintained with Kopp by Head of Russian Department of the Minister of Foreign Affairs Herr Behrens and by Geheimrat Schuler who controls personnel. These officials are under influence and protection of Disconto Gesellschaft, Mendelsohns Bank and Herr Deutsch of A. E. G. all of whom have large economic interests in Russia. Herr Deutsch especially is in favour of an alliance with Russia and works hard for its realization.[32]

By the end of June 1920, even the German Ministry of Defence found itself on the defensive in reply to inquiries from the German Foreign Minister as to the activities of Kopp in Berlin. Apparently, compromising letters between Kopp and a German officer-association had been intercepted, which gave the impression of activities and negotiations of a political nature, which would normally fall within the prerogative of the Foreign Office. The Foreign Office viewed the Offizierbund as, effectively, a front for the German army, and thus held the Ministry of Defence accountable for what had been discovered. The army downplayed the accusations, stating that with reference to a previous inquiry from the start of June the assumption the Kopp had dealings with the Deutsche Offizierbund (having Russian counter-revolutionary (i.e. White) tendencies and meddling in inner-Russian affairs) was simply incorrect. The signatory of the intercepted letter to Kopp was unknown to the Offizierbund, and nor did the Offizierbund apparently have any knowledge of other officers named in the letter. The Offizierbund was, explained the Reichswehr, independent of the Ministry of Defence. It was simply an organization which dealt with the financial interests of its officer members; political endeavours would run contrary to its own statutes. The Reichswehrministerium further claimed that, through its oversight of Russian organizations and individuals in Germany, it was mostly aware of their activities, but that it had nonetheless already exchanged its information with both the Foreign Ministry and Ministry of Public Order, in monthly reports to those bodies, since May 1920; and thus could not be accused of acting with subterfuge.[33]

More reports were filtering in to the German Foreign Ministry from its own sources, however, hinting of closer collaboration than was being admitted to by the German army. In mid-July 1920, informants in Warsaw indicated that Prince Sapieha was also strongly advocating the disarmament of Germany, to prevent the linking of Germany with Bolshevik Russia. The prospect of such a union was nurtured by the Polish intelligence services, and was gaining more and more credence in the press—in some measure, at least, due to "occasionally careless and irresponsible German missteps".[34] An example of the Polish attempts of the time to play up the dangers of German–Soviet collaboration was a report sent the very next day to London: "Polish Military Attaché informs British Military Representative that ship containing 400,000 rifles and 200,000,000 cartridges bought by Bolsheviks in Germany will sail from either Hamburg or Luebeck for Reval. Name of ship and date of sailing unknown."[35]

The continuing problems of reparations payments made matters more dire for Germany. At the Spa Conference in early July, the heads of states of France, Britain, Germany, and Belgium were present, along with their foreign ministers and, often, defence ministers.[36] The main issues of concern were reparations, but also the disarmament of Germany. Germany attempted to mitigate the demands of the French by offering their own counterproposals. Before meeting with the Germans, however, the Allies first settled upon a formula for receiving the future German payments: 52 per cent for France, 22 per cent for Britain, 10 per cent for Italy, 8 per cent for Belgium, 5 per cent for Serbia, and the remainder to be divided upon the smaller countries who fought during the war. In return for having had its guaranteed neutrality violated, Belgium was further given the right to transfer all of its war debt to Germany, and was to receive the first major payment of the German reparations. Germany agreed to coal deliveries to help maintain their payments, and further agreed to establish a system for the better monitoring of its disarmament. The formal request of Germany to be allowed to surpass the 100,000 men limit on its military imposed by Versailles was met with continued reluctance on the part of the Allies, as Germany still had at that point in time 200,000 men in uniform. General Seeckt, in direct negotiations with the Allies, managed to gain until 1 January 1921 for the reduction of the German army to the size envisioned by Versailles, to allow for it to occur in an orderly fashion. In the meanwhile, other paramilitary organizations under the army's direct control, such as military units of the secret police and the approximately 500,000 strong citizen's defence reserve (Einwohnherwehr), were to be disarmed completely.

In the second week of July, Germany experienced the next set of plebiscites concerning territory contested with Poland, in Allenstein and Marienwerder. The International Commission of four appointed to oversee the two plebiscites was staffed with representatives from Britain, France, Italy, and Japan. As per Article 97 of the Treaty of Versailles, two battalions of British soldiers, two battalions of Italians, and a small French contingent, all under the command of the British, were assigned to maintain order. The overwhelming majority (more than 95 per cent in both regions) voted to remain part of Germany. In a 23 July 1920 note, with the the Marienwerder and Allenstein plebiscite zones decided in favour of Germany, France replied to a British request that the Allies withdraw their troops from these areas and further allow Germany to advance troops to their eastern borders (in East Prussia) by way of Poland, with a refusal. France thought the British request was premature: the precise borders of the plebiscite zones still had to be set, and France feared that by withdrawing their troops too soon, they would be abandoning the Poles to German pressure. Further, France did not understand the logic of the British reasoning that Germany needed to further fortify its frontier against a danger of possible invasion by Bolshevik forces; Germany had, after all, declared its neutrality in the Russo-Polish conflict, and thus was hardly at odds with Soviet Russia.[37]

By early July, Soviet advances against the Polish army were gaining momentum. Tukhachevsky's attacks, which had begun on 4 July, had progressed to the point where Polish forces were generally retreating by 7 July. Polish attempts to use old German fortifications from the First World War did not slow the Red Army advance, and by 14 July the Poles were again in retreat. In the midst of these advances, Soviet Russia finally settled relations with Lithuania, thus securing that border against potential distractions from the main war with Poland. The Lithuanians and Soviets had been at war since the withdrawal of German troops from the country at the end of 1918, and the Soviet seizure of Vilnus in January 1919 ensured that the conflict would continue. It was partly due to the Polish intervention on the side of the Lithuanians in driving the Soviets from the capital, that the Russo-Polish conflict escalated into war in the first place. The Allied decision to award Vilnius to Lithuania rather than Poland led to a falling out of the two former allies, and facilitated the negotiations between Lithuania and Russia for an end to their conflict.

In signing the Treaty of Moscow of 12 July, which recognized the independence of Lithuania with Vilna as its capital, the Soviets also removed one more source of disaccord with Germany, as it had been Germany's policy to support an independent Lithuania—Germany indeed had driven out the Soviets in the first place, in 1918. The Soviets followed this Baltic success with the 11 August Treaty of Riga, which recognized Latvia's independence, renounced Soviet claims to any Latvian territory, and thus ensured that Latvia as well would no longer be a cause for military concern in the region.

By the end of July 1920, Soviet advances against Poland were so far along that the issue became one of the very survival of the Polish state. The Red Army was pushing forwards as much as 40 kilometres along some sections of the front, and captured Brest-Litovsk on 1 August. In a letter from Maltzan to Chicherin, dated 20 July 1920, in consequence of the German declaration of neutrality in the Russo-Polish war, the German Foreign Minister proposed the attachment of a German military representative to the right (i.e. northern) flank of the Red Army. This officer would have direct contact with both the German and Soviet armies, and thus would be in a position to coordinate the prevention of unwanted misunderstandings at the German border between the two armed forces.[38] This delighted Seeckt, as it would provide official cover and sanction for a direct link with the Red Army; in early August 1920, the Reichswehr wrote to the Foreign Office to tell them that, in the event that they required a German officer to be sent to the Russian General Staff, they were pleased to recommend Major Schubert,[39] who was, conveniently enough, a colleague of Niedermayer and prominent member of Sondergruppe R.

At the same time, it was noted within the Soviet administration that the German Foreign Ministry (in addition to the German army) was interested in pursuing closer links with Soviet Russia for geopolitical in addition to economic reasons. Kopp, who since August 1919 unofficially represented all Soviet interests in Berlin, and whose position since 19 April 1920 was made more official due to his role in overseeing a prisoner-of-war exchange treaty signed by the two states, firmly believed that what motivated the Germans was the possibility that through cooperation with the Soviet Union, the Polish corridor separating East Prussia from the rest of Germany could be rendered frail.[40]

Chicherin was supportive of the German position, and commented upon the creation of friendly relations with Germany as being "especially desirable"; on the other hand, he did not wish German interests to entrap Russia into further conflicts, especially given that Moscow shortly expected a communist uprising in Poland. Ultimately, his opinion was to simply remain as flexible as possible, "in order to be better placed to transform the map of Europe".[41]

British concerns, by late summer 1920, were that in the process of disarmament, German arms might somehow make their way to Russia. They reported to London that Seeckt "apparently has issued stringent orders" to all officers of the German army not to hinder disarmament: "if any officer put slightest obstruction in the way of disarmament he would take strongest measures against him even to explusion from the Army." Further, they were of the opinion that the German government was in fact doing its best to carry out compliance with the disarmament terms, but that "[...] bribery and corruption are rampant in German offices and there is no question that missing rifles (number perhaps two million) [...]" were being re-routed to both Russia and Poland by a "secret organization".[42]

For his part, Seeckt's pragmatism regarding the Russian relationship never infringed upon his perception of Bolshevism as a serious domestic threat to Germany. In a general order issued to all commanders and general staff officers of the army on 31 July 1920,[43] Seeckt warned of the "dangers of contact with communism and the Soviet Union". The recent Russian gains over Poland, Seeckt wrote, awakened many moods and hopes which the Reichswehr had to eliminate, through clear directions on how to deal with them. The advances had especially once again evoked the thoughts that Germany could only hope to escape the Treaty of Versailles by launching a new war, with Communism [the Soviet Union] at its side. Seeckt warned directly against the pursuit of such trains of thought and overestimations of the help which Soviet Russia could afford Germany. Citing Radek, Seeckt maintained that the Red Army owed its success against Poland to its ability to tap into an old current of nationalist strength, against which Poland was not able to offer opposition. But neither in terms of numbers of soldiers nor in terms of the conduct of the war could this fight be compared with one against the West. At Germany's border in the East there could be no more than 5,00,000 Red troops; in the West they stood opposite to one million. The Russian railroads were taxed to their fullest to provide only this little army with enough supplies; how could they be expected to relieve Germany against a new blockade? The Putilow-factories, the largest military factories in Russia, which once employed 42,000 workers, and which now employed only 7,000, were wholly insufficient to supply the arms, ammunition, and technical material needed by the Red Army for a western war; even the whole of Russia's civilian industries could not produce them. The further allegation, that Entente troops, having already failed in Russia once, would not thus wish another fight against Bolshevism, was illusory and irrelevant: there was no reason to believe that these troops would not be used on the Rhine. The insufficient immediate help which could be offered by Russia would not be nearly as costly as Germany's transition to Bolshevism. In the simplest analysis, the Russia's three-year-old people's government had driven economic activity into the ground.

Seeckt referred to the published reports of socialist study-commissions on the failure of the Communist system, and Russia's desolate situation. The cities were starving, and were becoming desolate; in St Petersburg alone 280,000 workers had migrated out of town. Corruption, tax evasion, and embezzlement had bloomed, and the currency had been completely devalued. The civilian leadership, which could have worked in providing a suitable structure, had been decimated. The Communist Bukharin allowed the decline of industry. Only the predominance of the peasantry prevented Russia from starving. Such a situation would be brought to Germany by communism, Seeckt warned, if Germany were to reach a hand out to it. For the industrial state they signify total ruin, which would engulf even its best strengths and which no structure will resist.

The only way to steer Germany through the dangers of the present lay in its self-assertion against both the Entente and Bolshevism, and thus in remaining strictly neutral against both. While it was conceivable that Germany could enter into a friendly economic exchange with Russia, and assist with its internal rebuilding, thus potentially contributing to the perception that a communist government was healthy and feasible, it was nonetheless imperative that the door be closed to International Communism. The absolute priority had to be domestic order, and the sharpest fight against any disturbance to it. Only through the full exertion of all of the state's authority and forces, as well as the commitment of each individual towards the existing state and economic system, and the unselfish work of each person within his abilities towards the service of the inner strength of the state, could Germany drive such politics away. The people had to see, Seeckt intoned for his generals, that Germany's salvation did not lie in foreign help or inner turmoil, but only through hard, sober, healthy work. It was in this sense that the Reichswehr had to act: "I must expect that each leader will spread this understanding to his subordinates and shield them from anything else".[44]

With no small measure of irony given his inactivity during the Kapp Putsch, Seeckt followed this commentary with another general order for the army on the need for "political reliability" of the Reichsheer:

Germany faces difficult decisions. We don't know [...] what the events in the East will signify for us. One thing is certain, however: Germany can only overcome the serious dangers which lie ahead if the government can rely on the unanimous help of the nation and all the resources of the state. Whoever would even consider otherwise, in the belief that he knows best for the Fatherland and attempts to impose his will upon the government and departs from the rule of law, will only ruin Germany completely. Only a minority would follow him, and general-strikes and civil strife would result, rather than the hoped for national unification. I emphatically warn the leadership of such a movement to be sure of what part of their plan is driven by patriotism, and what part may be driven by personal ambition and selfish motives. I especially warn the groups which, under the guise of national goals, only wish to bring Bolshevism to power in Germany. [...] As such a forcible revolt could play into the plans for a union of the Germans with the Bolshevism in the East, what remains of Germany, defenceless, would then fall easy prey to foreign countries. I already [...] commented on how wholly unsuitable Bolshevism is, as an effective ally for us against foreign countries, and and pointed out the economic and cultural annihilation it brings. This warning is reinforced, today. [...] No threatening foreign dangers, regardless of how large they may appear, must seduce us, and destroy the work of the previous year, and the successful future unification of our people, for playing games with federal unity.[45]

These public warnings against Bolshevism and in favour of loyalty and unity were accompanied, at the same time, with private advice to the Foreign Minister, commenting on the military situation in the East in general, and on the need for a more pro-active Russia policy. In his memorandum, Seeckt elaborated that whatever the results of Russian–Polish cease-fire negotiations, Germany had to work on the assumption that either they would fail or that if they did not, war might nonetheless flare up again. The Red Army's right-wing had as of 30 July reached Kolno with its cavalry, and was therefore not much more than 100 kilometres away from Soldau. Thus, the war had moved into the immediate proximity of the Polish-occupied German provinces ["der an Polen abgetretenen deutschen Provinzen"]. It was not inconceivable that the Danzig to Warsaw rail-links could be interrupted.[46]

It was, Seeckt wrote, urgent that the German people of the occupied areas, who hoped for German assistance, were not disappointed. While this could not be accomplished by force of arms, at the least a public request could be made to the Russian government to spare the populations of the former-German territories from the ravages of war. It was not yet known if the Entente troops would be sent via Danzig to support Poland. In this eventuality the further duration of the war in the provinces was likely with West Prussia becoming the battleground for fighting between the Entente and Poland on the one hand and Russia on the other hand. However, even if the Entente did not send troops, or if they were sent to help via a different route, the remnants of the Polish army could still spill back into the German provinces. The probability that the provinces would not be spared from war by the quick and total conclusion of fighting should induce Germany to direct the proposed request to the Russians. Such a step would reflect the hopes of the German people and would not fail to make a deep impression upon the German and Polish populations of the occupied areas. It would demonstrate in a loyal manner to the whole world, to both Russia and Germany's enemies, that Germany—despite its new borders—had an obligation and debt to these territories, which had been culturally part of Germany for more than 100 years. This would be the basis for the eventual procurement of the lost lands.[47]

Political considerations, Seeckt went on, precluded support of the affected areas by armed force, to roughly the 1914 borders. If Germany were to enter West Prussia with troops, it would be a "significant infraction" of the Treaty of Versailles. Germany would therefore be able to expect an armed intervention by the Entente in the West. As well, an advance into now-Polish lands would also likely lead to a collision with Russia in these areas: "We then would have to face the Russians as enemies in the East. A policy which makes us enemies of the Entente and Russia can not be justified." Germany had to demand, both to the Entente and to the Russians, to be directly involved in any conferences proposed for the resolution of the conflict, if simply to ensure that England and Russia did not somehow settle their wider overall differences, to Germany's disadvantage. Article 117 of the [hated] Treaty of Versailles was to be cited, to prevent Germany from being excluded from any treaty consultations and negotiations.[48]

Seeckt argued that admission to such a conference would qualify as an "extraordinary success", as it would indicate progress for Germany towards dealing with and being equally entitled to participate in world politics. The first step had to be taken in order to lead Germany out of the "miserly small fights" and to take the major lead in global- (and especially Eastern-) politics. At the very least, if Germany were not admitted to a conference, it would have demonstrated—both abroad and at home—that it was willing to negotiate again, and that it was not willing to allow itself to be simply pushed around; this too would be a success, in Seeckt's view, which could be used in the future, as it would allow for the possibility of organizing a plebiscite for the lost provinces.

Ultimately, Seeckt proposed that the overall question of the "Polish-occupied areas of Germany" be raised at the same time as discussions for an end to the Russo-Polish conflict. The German point was to argue that it was not trying to change the Treaty of Versailles, but rather wished to fulfill it, in that it proposed to examine thoughtfully the rights of self-determination of peoples, for Danzig, West Prussia, and Posen on the basis of what was done for Allenstein and Marienwerden. As for Wilson's principle that Poland should have a free and unobstructed access to the seas, this simply could be argued to mean guaranteed access, as opposed to territorial sovereignty.

Seeckt believed that Russia, for whom the principle of self-determination of the peoples had always received special emphasis, could take up this thought and make it part of its programme—if only out of its enmity for Poland. If this occured, Germany was already half way to its goal. It was impossible to predict when next the overall picture would be so favourable at the level of international politics, to demonstrate Germany's resolve to be re-integrated into the system, as well as to simultaneously raise the issue of West Prussia and the Polish question, or if in the foreseeable future Russian and German interests would ever again run so largely parallel they did then. But, these steps should only be taken "in full public light"—it was in the public realm that the possibility lay for the guarantee of success in the world, with Russia, and domestically.[49]

Seeckt's concerns about the Soviet advance were seemingly justified in the short while following his reports. On 2 August some units of the Red Army were only 100 kilometres from Warsaw.[50] The Poles had managed to slow down the Russians on their Russian front, but the perilous situaiton at the capital forced a rapid withdrawal, as all available forces were required for Warsaw's defence. A Soviet-backed Provisional Polish Revolutionary Committee had been set up to hopefully inspire the workers in the newly "liberated" lands—the impact was the opposite, as Poles rallied in waves of nationalism rather than class consciousness. Tukhachevsky had, by this time, begun to overstretch his resources, and the British–French Allied military mission, under General Weygand, had already arrived and was offering advice to the Polish defenders of the captial. Lack of cooperation among Soviet commanders, in part the result of political bickering between Stalin and Tukhachevsky, would also play a significant role in the coming Battle of Warsaw.

By 11 August 20, the relationship between Seeckt and Moscow was advanced enough that Enver Pasha was able to arrive there to enter into direct negotiations on a wide range of military matters; this was noted in a letter reporting the event from Feliks Dzerzhinskii, founder of the Soviet secret police, to Lenin.[51] This was followed later that month with direct attempts (again, noted in reports written by Dzerzhinskii) by the Soviets to purchase arms from Germany, and on making the practical arrangements for their receipt by railroad—something which was decided upon and approved at the Politburo level. Trotsky approved of the deal, and wished to hasten its completion.[52]

Chicherin as well wrote to Lenin, in mid-August 1920, of the meetings he had had with Enver Pasha, concerning proposals carried by the latter from the Germans. Enver wanted the Soviets for their part to attempt whatever they could to assist for the restoration of Germany to its 1914 frontiers. In return, Germany promised to offer "unofficial" help, through sharing its expertise with munitions and through the possible organization of revolts in Poland. Chicherin further wrote that, with regard to the plans for using German help with the development of munitions factories, the negotiations had already begun. Enver was aware that the Soviets might attempt to negotiate with other circles in Germany than just the military, and in an attempt to restrict contact to the army, he warned Chicherin not to rely on any word from Germany unless it came with Seeckt's approval. In an attempt to add weight to his offer, Enver stated that the Entente had already made territorial offers to Germany in return for its support against Russia.[53] What Chicherin finally believed could be conceded to Germany was a call for the people of the Polish corridor as expressed through a plebiscite, to expel the Polish troops. However, he added, it should not appear too obviously to be a pro-German act, and any attempt to force back the return Polish regions to German control was impossible.[54]

In response to the inquiry of Enver regarding potential Soviet armed help against France, should it be necessary as a result of Germany's maintenance of its earlier declaration of neutrality (of 20 July) in the Polish–Russian war, Chicherin noted, perhaps with irony, that would likely involve allowing the Red Army to move troops up to the Rhine.[55] While waiting in Moscow for a full reply from Chicherin, Enver had the chance to meet Lenin, as well.[56]

Enver Pasha's version of his visit to Moscow in August was, in part, captured in a letter written to General Seeckt from Moscow on 25 August 1920. "Dear friend, today an officer of General Staff paid me a visit. In response to your message, opinion in their General staff is divided. One part wants to fight the Entente-imperialist powers with the help of socialist Western states, while another is in favour of an invasion of India."[57] Enver wished to coordinate action at the Turkish, Persian, and Afghan borders, but the situation was on hold until the spring; he wished to learn Seeckt's thoughts on the matter, and had apparently spoken with senior aides of Trotsky on the matter.

In response to Seeckt's suggestion that Enver seek Russian help in obtaining arms for an Anatolian Army, the Soviets replied that they were unable to be of assistance; however, should such arms be procured in Germany, the Soviets were willing to let them be transported through Russian territory—an option Enver hoped Seeckt would give positive consideration towards.[58]

One day later, on 26 August 1920, Enver wrote again to Seeckt that he had spoken with the "crucial factor of Trotsky". There was in Russia a group, to which Trotsky belonged and which possessed real power, which was in favour of an understanding with Germany, and this party was prepared to recognize the German borders of 1914. "And they see that the only way out of the current global chaos is through common cooperation with Germany and Turkey." In order to assist the party in shoring up its strength enough to win over the entire Soviet leadership, at the very least it would require unofficial help from Germany, and if possible the selling of arms. Enver felt that it was very important for Seeckt to meet directly with the Soviets' representative, so that Germany's situation could become clarified and stabilized. The Russians could help in the Polish Corridor or an otherwise suitable locale, with the raising of a volunteer army or instigating a revolt.[59]

In another version of Enver's letter to Seeckt, the Soviets were more explicit in their willingness to help Germany:

> Yesterday I had a conversation with Sklanski, [sic: E. M. Sklyansky, deputy-People's Commissar for War and] right-hand man of Trotsky.... A party here, which possesses real power and to which Trotsky also belongs, favours an understanding with Germany. Sklanski said his party would be willing to recognize the old German frontier of 1914. And they see only one way out of the world's chaos: co-operation with Germany and Turkey. And in order to strengthen this party's position and to win the whole Soviet government for the cause, [he asked] whether it would not be possible to render some unofficial help: for example, [to provide] reports about the Polish army and, if possible, to seel arms and have them smuggled...[60]

F. L. Carsten points to Brockdorff-Rantzau's September 1922 letter to Chancellor Wirth, in which he claims that Seeckt was in league with Trotsky as early as the summer of 1920—something which was not denied by Wirth. "It thus seems likely that Enver Pasha's emissary [bearing the letter] was received by Seeckt or by one of his subordinates."[61]

The British continued to fear that something was afoot at the time. A member of their commission for the Baltic states, Colonel Tallents, wrote to London in mid-August 1920 that Yoffe (the chief Soviet representative at Russo–Lithuanian negotiations at Riga) had left for Moscow, and that he had remarked independently that a Russo-German treaty was likely to be signed soon. "Having regard to Kapp's [*sic*: Kopp's] presence in Moscow I infer that he may be destined for negotiations in Berlin."[62]

The British suspicions of German collaboration with the Soviets grew stronger as August 1920 wore on; the Poles were complaining to London about being effectively boycotted in the war, while the Soviets apparently were not: the Polish Minister of Foreign Affairs had stated to the British representatives that many recently manufactured Mauser rifles had been captured from the Bolsheviks, and claimed further that proof existed that more German war materials was destined for the Red Army.[63]

General Seeckt was not the only one who expected a Soviet victory over the Poles at Warsaw. Public opinion in Britain was not favourable towards Poland, and Lloyd George urged Pilsudski to make peace under whatever terms he could obtain. The British Labour party, sympathetic to the Soviets, urged British workers to not assist Poland in any way, and to block supplies heading to Europe which could be used to assist the Polish armies. French socialist newspapers followed suit, and industrial actions in parts of central Europe mirrored the activities of the British workers, in refusing to handle goods destined for Poland. The French government remained committed to France, however, and included among the officers sent with Weygand, Charles de Gaulle. Although their symbolic presence was appreciated, the Inter-Allied mission to Poland did not play a significant role in the outcome of the fight.

The battle for the capital, of crucial importance not only for Poland, but for the future of German–Soviet relations as well, began on 14 August. The "miracle of the Vistula" was less than miraculous given the infighting and disobedience within Soviet ranks by the time they reached the river. Many of Tukhachevsky's senior officers simply disobeyed his orders—occasionally under the influence of political commissars such as Stalin. The military attacks were not always well coordinated, and the Poles fought with greater elan in defending their capital than the Soviets, exhausted by such a quick advance thus far, could muster. Matters were not helped by the fact that Tukhachevsky was attempting to coordinate the battle from Minsk; by the time he realised the magnitude of some of the local defeats, the main Soviet army was already routed. Lack of effective communications sealed their fate, as many orders were simply not arriving on the front. From this point on, the Polish army began to chase the retreating Soviet forces, back into parts of Belarus.

Chicherin, all the while, continued a dual-track diplomacy in correspondence with his German counterpart, in late August 1920. Here, however, he would find a more tentative reception. The German Foreign Minister Simons was apparently disappointed with the outcome of his contacts with Chicherin, of August 1920. Simons was unable to make a further impression on the nature of proposals from Moscow, and was under the impression that the Soviet side wished to engage in talks with Germany only with regard to the issues of transit through the Corridor.[64] An additional consideration, not forgotten, was that the establishment of normal relations with Soviet Russia could be provisional to a hostile British reaction, as well as complications arising from the war-zone as well; the German Foreign Minister added that he might not yet be ready to attempt to lead a grand political move towards Russia, as Germany could too easily get its fingers "caught in the gear-works".[65]

The fear of getting publicly caught in an embarrassing transaction was not enough to prevent the German military from conducting individual deals for weapons with the Soviets. A note from Trotsky to Lejava (Deputy Chairman of the Commissariat for Foreign Trade) instructed him to immediately conclude the final arrangements for a "previously agreed to" deal for arms, under terms negotiated by Unshlikht (member of the Revolutionary Military Council on the Western Front). The same day, a telegram from Trotsky to Unshlikht informed him that the transaction had been approved, and that the gold (worth 27 million marks) would be delivered partly in German marks, partly in English pounds; later again that day, another telegram stated that the initial route for sending gold was considered "difficult", and exploring alternate options of getting the money to Kopp in Berlin was being considered.[66]

The British had finally had enough of the rumours of that month, and directly approached the German Foreign Minister with their misgivings. The German response, sent to London on 31 August

1920, was that the German Minister of Foreign Affairs Simons "[...] volunteered emphatic denials" of secret Russo-German deals under preparation. What had happened was that as Kopp did not have authority to carry on full negotiations, Simons gave him a letter for Chicherin, in which he said the time might be approaching when economic relations might be officially resumed, but before this a satisfactory account was needed for the murder of Germany's ambassador to Moscow, Mirbach [in July 1918].[67]

Chicherin noted, at the end of August, in a lengthy commentary on the wars and Europe in general, the importance of Germany's reactions to the events, that "[our] relations on all questions, concerning Germany, have not changed". However, the Soviet government refused to consider any form of apology for the murder of Mirbach.[68]

Rumours of a developing Russo-German relationship were not limited to the diplomatic arena. Many short press clippings from August 1920 (*Times of London*, *New York Herald*, and *Le Petit Parisien*, among others) of a supposedly secret agreement between Germany and Russia were noted with dismay by the German Foreign Ministry. The official German reply prepared for them was that this was misinformation spread out by Poland (probably at the behest of the French) in response to the German declaration of neutrality in the Russian–Polish war, and the subsequent Russian pledge to respect the German frontier. With regard to specific allegations of the sale of arms to Russia, the Foreign Office explained that:

> It is a well-known fact that the Russians formerly took some tens of thousands of German prisoners, who were naturally disarmed. It is also well known that, in the autumn of 1918, large quantitites of German arms fell into the hands of the Bolsheviki in South Russia and Lithuania when the German troops withdrew. Lastly, very large quantities of arms and ammunition were, by order of the International Baltic Commission, handed over to Lithuania by the Russo-German Bermondt troops when they withdrew from the Baltic provinces, and a large proportion of the same may well have got into Russia. It is, therefore, not at all surprising that the Poles should possess [fn: In the original German the words are "erbeutet haben sollen" [should have pillaged].] German rifles, but this fact can in no event justify the conclusions drawn by the Polish Press Bureau.[69]

A German foreign ministry report from the end of the month noted an accidental confirmation of the Soviet pledge to respect the German frontier: a Russian soldier who had been caught with a small patrol on German territory by the border guards (as noted in a report without date, but stamped 25 August) pleaded that it was a personal (i.e. navigational) error, and confirmed that the Red Army was under strict orders to not cross into German territory.[70]

A German border police interrogation report of another incident that month (of 27 August) called into doubt the veracity of the Soviet officer's claim. Another group was caught on German soil, consisting of two Soviet officers (Gawrilow and Wuttge [who was a German national]), and one political commissar (Tomaschow). Upon interrogation by the border police, it appeared that one of the officers had served during the First World War in Morocco as member of the Turkish cavalry in the German–Turkish armed service, while the other had personal ties with the Russian representative in Berlin, Kopp, who was "apparently to attempt to conclude a trade-agreement with Germany to the end of manufacturing in Russia airplanes, automobiles, bicycles, boots, ammunition and guns". The large German financial concerns were apparently hesitating, because factory machinery in Russia had been worn out, and specialized workers were lacking. An agreement with the German government for the dispatch of 16,000 German specialists did not bear fruit. One of the captured three claimed to have met, on 8 August, with a supposed lieutenant of the German Foreign Office, in order to cultivate meetings and discussions for German support and supplies to the Red Army. And then, the political commissar made what the border police thought was "an interesting declaration" concerning none other than Enver Pasha—the reason for which the report was sent to the Foreign Office. Enver had been in Germany for approximately 14 days and then, in contact with the Bolshevik army, came across the German border illegally. The political commissar claimed to be an eye witness. Enver Pasha then made his way to Moscow. Copies of border police report were sent to the Foreign Office, the Ministry of Justice, the Defence Ministry, and the Federal Commissar for Public Order, thus widening the circle of those in Germany who might deduce something of the military's attempts.[71]

In an early-September note to Chicherin, Trotsky, and Lenin, Victor Kopp reported from Berlin that sympathetic circles existed among the German nationalists, who wished to find a modus vivendi with Russia, concerning Poland.[72] That same day, 7 September, news came of the Franco-Belgian military convention, which served to coordinate French and Belgian policy in most aspects of foreign policy; that is, against Germany.

Despite the earlier German denials to the British of any exceptional liaisons with Soviet Russia, events continued to crop up which demonstrated to the British that the denials were not entirely credible. A mid-September note from the President of the Inter Allied Aeronautical Committee of Control (IAACC) to the President of the German Air Service Peace Commission wanted several issues to be cleared up. Among them was that "It has besides been proved that aircraft travel between Germany and Russia and one has found on a pilot forced to land in Poland, an order, defining the duties of the pilots charged with the liaison with Soviet Russia, signed by General von Horn, and dated Breslau (20th July 1920)." The IAACC noted that the pilot was a military aviator, that he was using a military plane, and that he received orders from a general in the German army. It wished to know, specifically, "what steps have been taken against the organisers and performers of the liaison by aircraft between Germany and Soviet Russia [and demanded the giving of] the necessary orders for the dissolution of the secret formations which have been employed in this liaison work and which exist round about Breslau".[73]

The popular press in the Entente countries also continued to hound at the matter, as exemplified by the Paris newspaper *Le Petit Journal*. In an article on "The Role of Enver Pasha" of 18 September, their correspondent claimed that Enver had, in Berlin and Munich, conferred on occasion with the German Minister of Defence, as well as Generals Lucendorff and Hindenburg, ostensibly for the purpose of obtaining German military help for Turkey. Apparently, Enver then went to Moscow to claim success for his mission, claiming that soon a cadre of 50 German high-ranking officers (of whom the correspondent claimed he could offer some names) would be on their way there. These Germans wished only one thing: a military alliance with the Bolsheviks against Poland, and then against France.[74] Aside from the last comment on France, the reporting was remarkably accurate, all things considered. The only difficulty was in determining how one was to separate the wheat from the chaff of rumours of the time, and then what could or should have been done about it.

The end of the month saw another territorial revision of the German landscape, as a result of the League of Nations decision that Eupen and Malmedy be ceded by Germany, despite the fact that over 80 per cent of the inhabitants were German speakers. Although the outcome was ratified by plebiscite, Germany complained of intimidation and fear of reprisals within the conditions in which the vote was conducted (including the requirement for names and addresses of the voters on the ballots); the results were nonetheless recognized by the international community.

Partly as a result of this, matters within the German camp had solidified enough that Kopp was able to report to Chicherin, on 20 September 1920, that the idea of long-term military cooperation, with active support from both the German and Soviet sides, had gained ground in Berlin.[75] A few days later, on 25 September, Kopp wrote directly to Lenin to inform him that increased trade with Germany would definitely lead to closer overall cooperation between the two countries—that is that trade was simply to be considered as the first step. Specifically, a major impetus on the side of the Germans were the provisions of the Treaty of Versailles which gave the Entente first priority on German gold, for reparations. From the German point of view, transferring their gold to Russia (in payment of agreements) was preferable to simply losing it.[76] An inquiry from Kopp to the German Foreign Ministry, on 29 September 1920, attempted to determine the status and rights of the Russian government in German courts, with an eye to non-recognition but the possibility of trade agreements between the two. The German reply, of 13 October 1920, was reassuring. As a matter of formality, the Soviet Russian government, not being recognized by the German government, could not have official standing as a party before German courts, without the consent of the courts. However, such consent could easily be obtained by way of prior agreement, if it was outlined in the contracts signed with the German firms in question.[77]

On 9 October 1920, Lithuania paid for its earlier decision to abandon the Poles to the Soviets. Polish irregular units, led by General Zeligowski, captured the city of Vilna, and declared it to be part of Poland. Given the Polish successes elsewhere on the battlefield by then, this was to be expected. The unwillingness of the League of Nations to assist Lithuania regain the city condemned that organization to being viewed with increasing cynicism. The Polish advances against the Soviets by this time were so great that at the signing of the preliminary Treaty of Riga, on 12 October, saw Poland able to claim much more territory in the east than had been envisioned by the Allies. Freed from the worry of having to deal with Poland further, after the armistice of 12 October, the Red Army was able to concentrate its resources on dealing with the continuing fighting in southern Russia against the White forces. Their attacks against General Wrangel's army began in late October, and by 1 November had forced them down into the Crimea. By 14 November, the White forces had been evacuated to Constantinople, and the Soviet Russians had finally eliminated the White threat from the south and the Ukraine.

Seeking more breathing space and the ability to simply concentrate their forces, Soviet Russia next signed, on 14 October, the Treaty of Dorpat, recognizing Finnish independence and thus allowing for the end of Finnish involvement in the Civil War. Although Finland gained a small territorial outlet to the Arctic Ocean, the issue of Karelia remained unresolved between the two sides.

By mid-October 1920, the British were convinced that not only did a military arrangement of some sort between Germany and Russia exist, but that significant smuggling of arms was underway. A Russian steamer, the Subtonik, was apparently in Hamburg, having recently brought to Germany by some Russian trade-union delegates. The British government believed that arms and ammunition had been concealed on board the vessel for its return journey, and formally asked the German government to investigate the matter, with extreme haste, before the ship left port.[78] The reply sent back from the German Foreign Office demonstrated the difficulty in separating rumours based on the echoes of truth, from simple hubris. Dated 25 October 1920 and written by the local chief of police, it stated simply that "Found were 14 guns and 500 cartridges, which were for use by the ship's personnel and which had been stored in a locked crate formerly belonging to the Norwegian customs-authority. The existence of the case was communicated to the Hamburg Senate, and it is still on board the ship. I hereby view the issue as settled."[79]

Later that month, again without their prior knowledge but with the complicity of the army, Enver Pasha was noted by the German Foreign Office to be in Berlin once again, travelling with false papers. He was apparently in the company of Grigory Zinoviev, the chairman of the Executive Committee of the Comintern, and on a mission to buy arms and weapons for use by the "Transcaucasian Bolshevik Armee in Asia" for use against the British in India. Enver was described as having "threads" leading back to General Seeckt, who was an "old friend" from earlier times. It was therefore recommended that rather than take any action on the matter, General Seeckt be approached to ask for his advice on what to do.[80]

At the end of October 1920, it was reported to the German Foreign Office that Trotsky himself was to travel to France; a three-day stay in Berlin along the way was planned, because "baseless newspaper attacks" concerning his wife in Berlin caused him problems which needed to be dealt with. The visit was also somehow related to the business of the Geschaeftsunternehmen Baltiskbank in Copenhagen, and Berlin was requested to determine whether a return journey through Germany was authorized, and if it was, for how long.[81]

It remained an open question as to what should be the relationship between Soviet diplomacy and Revolutionary propaganda, and which was the more serious pursuit; this was a direct comment on the relationship between the Comintern and the Soviet foreign ministry. The first major conflict between the two institutions with regard to Germany came in October 1920, as Zinoviev went to the USPD Congress as the official representative of the Soviet government, after receiving permission to enter Germany through the Soviet representation in Berlin. Zinoviev's resulting speech to the Congress was considered subversive and explosive. The German government was not at all content to see their diplomatic hospitality thus abused, and Simons was so upset that he later stated in the Reichstag that a lawyer might well be needed to consider whether or not Zinoviev's comments were judicially actionable, despite the fact of his diplomatic protection.[82]

The first contacts within the relatively pragmatic and productive framework which Kopp had attempted to set up did not prove very successful. At the request of the Commissar for Foreign Trade Krasin, S. G. Brygkov was sent in November 1920 to Berlin to buy arms; the Reichswehrministerium could not, on account of the Treaty of Versailles, deal officially or directly with him. The idea of placing Brygkov into touch with an arms-dealer was considered wise by Kopp, but the individuals proposed by Niedermayer were considered by Kopp to be of dubious reliability, and made it impossible to conclude business; in Brygkov's own assessment, the who business seemed rather haphazard and vague, and thus cast doubt on Niedermayer's (and by extension, Sondergruppe R and the army's) commitment to a serious relationship.[83]

Given the direct contacts in Moscow between Enver Pasha and Sondergruppe R's Niedermayer, on the one hand, and the Soviet authorities there, it was not surprising that, on 1 November 1920, Chicherin told Kopp to keep his focus in Berlin on trade matters (leaving military matters to be dealt with in Moscow). On the whole, based on the notes sent by Chicherin to Kopp at this time, a completely firm or consistent policy by the Soviets towards Germany had not yet been developed by the end of 1920; beyond the desire to maintain and develop links, and to conclude individual agreements and deals, a longer-term policy was difficult, given the fluidity of the overall political situation in central and Eastern Europe.[84]

While the Soviet leadership was less internally divided (despite the Comintern's activities) than their German couterparts, they sometimes appeared to forget that the German Foreign Ministry was not entirely informed of the overall picture. Even relatively normal requests, such as for entry passes for specific purposes, continued to catch the German Foreign Ministry unawares: indicative of the situation of the time was a note dated 6 November 1920, in which one Vladimir Romm was requesting entry for 15 days in Berlin for the purposes of "consultation with the Reichswehrministerium for exchange of information regarding Poland". Clearly caught by surprise, advice was solicited by the Foreign Office on how to handle such requests from Moscow in the future—the note itself was signed off by Maltzan, among others, on 8 November 1920.[85]

Although it would be some time before negotiations between the Krupp firm and the Soviets would bear fruit in 1921, some tentative steps had already been pursued by Kopp, in accordance with the instructions of Chicherin. In early November 1920, the British Foreign Office received a report from Stockholm stating that Swedish banks had refused to be the gold middleman for a deal negotiated by Kopp and Krupp, for 1800 locomotives in return for Soviet gold. The British representatives in Berlin, as well, reported that Dutch banks were apparently considering the opportunity passed over by the Swedes, but that even so German firms and Hugo Stinnes' Industrial Group were skeptical that the deal would ever come to pass. The

British firm Vickers and the North British Locomotive Company were looking for possible British participation, but only for a longer-term deal; Vickers was willing, in any case, to sound out Krupp on the details of the deal, on behalf of the British government.[86]

By the end of the month, and through the start of December 1920, Kopp continued to press the German Foreign Ministry for closer and more formal trade relations between Russia and Germany. Trade was the only thing mentioned—it was clear that the Soviets were now respecting and supporting the Seeckt approach keeping the negotiating tracks for military and trade relations separate, and keeping military matters out of the hands of the German Foreign Ministry.[87]

The British government wanted, on 18 November 1920, clarification on a confidential report which stated that on 4 May of that year an agreement had been signed between Schlesinger (for Germany) and Kopp (for Russia) which had three principles: (a) if the neutrality of Germany were violated by the Entente sending support to Poland, the German government would not obstruct the open recruitment of German officers and men for the Soviet army; (b) if German neutrality were not broken, the German government bound itself to support the Lithuanian army, in return for timber concessions in Lithuania and the instructs were to have grants of land in Lithuania; and (c) the Soviet government in return bound itself to return the Danzig corridor to Germany.[88]

The response, which came from General Malcolm of the British Military Mission in Berlin, was that was "most improbable" that Schlesinger was involved with such a deal. Schlesinger was described as an important personage in 1919, "as he was put into the Reichswehr Ministry by the Soldiers' and Workmen's Council to superintend the Officers. Incidentally he was very useful to the British Military Mission at that time." His main charge now was prisoner of war affairs, for which he had much contact with Kopp. Although it was possible and probable that he discussed commercial matters, no proof of that existed, and Schlesinger was further considered not to have enough authority any more, to be able to negotiate or sign such an arrangement as the one reported.[89]

Although initial military personalities, who contacted Radek while he was in prison in 1919, had close links with Ludendorff, his influence on relations with Russia was never strong, and differences of opinion between him and Seeckt had become wide, before the end of 1920. In response to a request from the German Foreign Ministry, in November of 1920, for the Reichswehr's thoughts on recent public pronouncements by Ludendorff and Hoffmann for an anti-Bolshevik campaign in conjunction with the Entente powers, Major von Boetticher sent a note to Simons, bearing Seeckt's dismissive reply:

> The German people are not for an attack against Russia. The German people will not march on Moscow, not under the leadership of Ludendorff or Hoffmann, and certainly not under Foch. In earlier times a prince's desires were met with a mercenary army, but today the people must go with and lead the war. Fighting against Russia means fighting for Poland, shoulder to shoulder with the French under the supreme command of the Entente. This is a monstrosity which German officers and the German people will not accept. A foreign policy which leads to a campaign against Russia would bring in return the hatred of all of Russia. [. .] The plan of General Ludendorff is therefore politically a Utopia, militarily inoperable, and, even if it were feasible, malignant for Germany. The revolts [i.e. Kapp's] teach us, however, that even the oddest of thoughts can be considered seriously by wide currents of the German people, especially if they are spoken by men like General Ludendorff, and that the fear of Bolshevism clouds the brains and momentary pressures make the attainment of grand political objectives appear easy, without regard to the consequences.[90]

The British, in late November 1920, continued to be plagued with fears and doubts about the growing indications they were receiving of relations between Germany and Russia. The British Foreign Office, in a 24 November 1920 note highlighted as "Very Urgent", asked for the specific details of any actual trading transactions between the two countries in the last few months; a week earlier, on November 17, Lord D'Abernon, the British ambassador to Germany, had reported from Berlin a statement (attributed to the German Foreign Minister) which indicated that "Germany had already made deliveries to Russia to value of several millions."[91]

The French, as well, were concerned. General Niessel, Chief of the French military mission in Poland, sent a report at the end of December 1920 to Marshal Foch, on the dangers of increased contact and cooperation between Germany and Soviet Russia. The German–Bolshevik relationship was not something which could be denied. The German intention was not only to take advantage of the economic possibilities in Russia, but to help stabilize and strengthen the Red Army, which in turn would be able to lend support to Germany. The German government apparently thought that it could, with impunity, attempt to circumvent the requirements of Versailles while remaining immune domestically to the dangers of Bolshevism; this was, according to Niessel, sheer blindness on the Germans' part, as all indications received thus far were that the Bolsheviks were continuing with their efforts at propaganda and destabilization against Germany. But given the uncertainty of the future situation in Russia, Germany was clearly trying to place itself in the best position possible in terms of economic and military gains. The danger of this, for Poland, was clear.[92]

Although Kopp had been instructed by Chicherinto to keep his focus on trade matters, he nonetheless continued to occasionally come into contact with members of the German military in Berlin. A report from Kopp to Moscow, dated 2 December 1920, reported on a wide-ranging conversation between General Seeckt himself and Kopp. Kopp described the general as a "typical reactionary", but one who nonetheless led the "Eastern Orientation" [i.e. pro-Russia] among the generals in Germany, and who was also at odds with Ludendorff. Seeckt saw the advantages of some cooperation with Russia, especially with the situations in Poland and Upper Silesia so undecided. Further, if things got out of hand with Poland, Seeckt made it clear to Kopp that Germany would (in some, undefined way) offer assistance to Russia. However, Seeckt wished to restrict contacts between two armies via Niedermayer. It was, Kopp reported, a wide-ranging conversation dealing with most of the geopolitical issues of the day, and Seeckt's views were expressed in a generally open and forthright way.[93] Building upon this in a series of communications with Kopp, at the end of December 1920, Niedermayer directly proposed the exchange of military attaches between the two sides. Chicherin's eventual response was that this would first have to await the re-establishment of formal diplomatic relations.[94]

Reports from Entente papers of military collusion could be relatively easily ignored, but if a major German newspaper commented upon it, and mentioned the official Soviet representative by name as being part of it, then the government took the matter more seriously. The accusation had appeared in a *Deutsche Tageszeitung* article of 7 December 1920 on the apparent transport of arms from Stetting to Russia, and apparently (once more) caught the German Foreign Ministry by surprise. The German treasury ministry's response to the foreign office inquiry on the issue was that there had indeed been an arms purchase made by Kopp before, but that the German government was not officially involved. The transactions were generally concluded in a roundabout manner:

> German individuals and groups go to the Soviet delegation in Berlin, among other things with the intention of offering the sale of arms. Both Kopp and the government of the German Reich avoid the conclusion of anything connected with the sale or transfer of arms, in Berlin or elsewhere in Germany. The Soviet delegation under no circumstances contravenes German laws and regulations concerning the sales of arms. The arms dealers, therefore, go to Stockholm, to live in the "Grand Hotel" [. . .] and discuss the deals with Soviet representatives there. The ships must go to St Petersburg harbour, and receive first the payment in gold, for among other things guns (of "model 88 or 98 400").

In other words, according to the German treasury, even if the particulars of that particular newspaper report were true, the only thing that really mattered was that no laws on the purchase or transport of arms had been contravened.[95] This was not the first time in 1920 that the subject of German arms exports had been brought to the attention of Allied governments, however. On 22 April 1920, the French foreign minister informed his ambassador in London of a recent decision by the Conference of Ambassadors to issue a resolution making representations against Germany for the illegal export of arms. Apparently, German arms had already been noted en route in Holland, Sweden, and Finland.[96]

5
Confirming the Contacts, Building a Framework

The year 1920 saw the two countries move closer towards an arrangement, and the increasing number of exchanges between the Soviet government and the German army. It was the year in which Seeckt became more convinced of the validity of his Ostpolitik, and in which the Soviet administration was coming to realize that it would likely have to abandon the Comintern impulse for exporting revolution to Germany, if it wished to be able to accrue the greater benefits of military-economic arrangements. The following year, in the run-up to the Treaty of Rapallo, saw these opinions confirmed and solidified by the international events occurring around the two countries.

In mid-January 1921, Chicherin's main fear was that the current international political climate could potentially lead to the military isolation of Soviet Russia, should Germany somehow come to terms with the western powers—the victory of the "Churchill view", as he called it.[1] Chicherin expressed extreme interest, therefore, in the continuation and intensification of the contacts with the German military. Sondergruppe R's Niedermayer proposed to Kopp that he come once again to Moscow to confer directly on the potential framework for greater cooperation; Chicherin not only permitted this, but expressed himself to be strongly and personally in favour of accepting the request, as an important step towards reaching "longer-term objectives", as he wrote to Kopp on 19 January of 1921.[2] As for the fundamental suppositions behind his own commitment, Chicherin had professed, five days before this, that he considered the continuing contacts as one means of helping the German government weaken the anti-Soviet right-wing elements within it.[3]

Trade negotiations were easier to deal with, and events moved more quickly than military negotiations at this time, within the Soviet camp. By 21 January 1921, a protocol on Soviet–German trade relations had been drafted by Chicherin, Krasin, and Alexey Rykov, Orgburo member as well as the Chairman of the Supreme Council of National economy, and special representative of the Council of Labour and Defense for food supplies for the Red Army and Navy. As well. Chicherin took great personal interest in detailing the appropriate replies to foreign inquiries regarding concessions.[4] Trotsky was occasionally, but not directly, informed of the nature of all the contacts with Germany. In a letter to him from Kopp, dated 26 February 1921, the former outlined the results of a meeting he had recently conducted with Stinnes, who knew that Russia was in crisis and wanted to know if Russia was interested in greater cooperation with Stinnes, possibly using British capital.[5]

At the Paris Conference held at the end of January 1921, Germany's Foreign Minister formally stated that the country could pay 30 billion gold marks in reparations. This was considerably less than what the Allies had expected. At the Brussels Conference of mid-December 1920, the Allies had concluded Germany would pay, over a 42-year period, 230 billion gold marks. Even though the British had felt at the time that this sum was likely more than what Germany could afford to pay, they too were underwhelmed and angered at the German proposal. Despite the expressed willingness to continue talks one month later in London, France pushed ahead with military arrangements aimed at Germany.

The Franco-Polish Mutual Assistance Treaty of 19 February 1921 promised direct aid to one another in the event of an attack by a third party. It was a clear indication that France viewed German revisionism as a real threat to European stability, and that France was preparing to create an alliance system which would encircle Germany. The treaty ensured coordinated foreign policy in general terms, and was amended by secret appendix on 21 August to clarify its applicability specifically to Germany and Soviet Russia.

On 1 March 1921, in a letter to Chicherin, Kopp reported on a meeting with Simons, in which the latter expressed hopes for good and improved relations between Germany and Russia. Kopp told Simons that the Hoffmann–Ludendorff plan was categorically unacceptable. Simons replied (as per Seeckt's views) that this plan was a personal fantasy of those two men, not official German policy, and that the German people were opposed to any intervention against Soviet Russia. Simons proposed sending an emissary (a Second State-Secretary named Ausamt), quickly to Moscow for talks, saying that this could be quite independent of the London Conference proceedings. If things went well and he did not require too many consultations with Berlin, an agreement could be signed in Moscow by mid-March. The basis of the future agreement would be three points: Germany would renounce its claims for Russia, especially military matters (resulting from the war) and nationalizations; Russia would promise to renounce claims/rights given it by Versailles; and a Russian–Polish peace would not be signed before the Silesian plebiscite (1 April). Simons clarified that these were his own points, but said that he would take them to Cabinet for fuller discussion, and promised to inform the Soviets of the response by 7 March.[6]

In further letters, Kopp reminded Chicherin that some German representatives who had been sent to Moscow (i.e. "Schteller") were in fact only empowered formally to discuss trade matters. Kopp argued that if Russia was to be content with low-level trade contacts with Germany, then the current level of representation was sufficient. But if Russia wanted firmer and fuller relations, it would need a more formal level of representation.[7]

At this time, the Soviet administration came to realize that dealing with the German Foreign Office could be more frustrating than dealing directly with the German army. Simons was mistaken if he had hoped that the terms which he offered to Kopp for the framework of an "improved" relationship with Russia would be well met in Moscow. On the Soviet side, the German interest in pursuing matters was seen as degenerating into needless delay, by 7 March 1921. In reply to the German suggestion that the Soviets hold off on signing a peace treaty with Poland until after the Upper Silesian plebiscite,[8] Chicherin wrote angrily back to Kopp that all in all it seemed to him as if the German–Russian relationship was taking an inexplicable turn. The German government had to be reminded that it needed to have improved relations with Soviet Russia, should it find itself in a difficult international position and dependent on Soviet support: "They must change their behaviour toward us in an extremely radical manner, if they expect to receive anything from us." Specifically, the German government seemed to believe that Moscow was somehow indebted to it, and would immediately do everything which was of use to and in Germany's interests. To a strange degree, Chicherin went on, the German government neglected to realize that political cooperation was founded on reciprocity. In their general policies, the German government had not lifted a finger to help Soviet Russia, and looked upon the activities of the extreme elements of the White Guard and the Tsarists in Berlin with complete silence. Such a stand, Chicherin summarized, was absolutely unacceptable, and he could not understand how the German government could expect that the Soviets would, as a result, offer even minor political support to Germany.[9]

The month of March 1921 proved tumultuous for Germany in many instances, and should have impressed upon the German Foreign Office the need for new allies—a need which was not lost on Seeckt and the German army. From 8 March, France occupied the Ruhr cities of Duesseldorf, Duisberg, and Ruhrort for 6 months, in response to the German government's failure to meet their reparations payments. To throw the matter into further relief, and also to demonstrate to Germany that they were not the only country interested in coming to an arrangement of sorts with Russia, was the announcement on 16 March of an Anglo-Russian Trade Agreement, in which the two countries agreed to attempt to re-establish normal trade relations, without either side giving ground on the earlier points of disagreement over Tsarist debts. The Soviets made further advances in normalizing their border situation with the 18 March Treaty of Riga, which formally ended the Russo-Polish war. But as important as these events were, they were overshadowed by the question of Upper Silesia.

The long-awaited plebiscite in Upper Silesia was conducted on 20 March 1921. As per the Treaty of Versailles, an International Commission was appointed, comprised of one member each from France, Italy, and Britain—there was supposed to be a fourth from the United States, but that country declined to participate in the end—and was to be in accordance with Article 88 of the Treaty of Versailles. This stated in part:

> [...] the inhabitants will be called upon to indicate by a vote whether they wish to be attached to Germany or to Poland [...] The plebiscite area shall be immediately placed under the authority

of an International Commission of four members to be designated by the following Powers: the United States of America, France, the British Empire, and Italy. It shall be occupied by troops belonging to the Allied and Associated Powers [...] The Commission will maintain order with the help of the troops which will be at its disposal, and, to the extent which it may deem necessary, by means of gendarmerie recruited among the inhabitants of the country.

[...] The result of the vote will be determined by communes according to the majority of votes in each commune. On the conclusion of the voting, the number of votes cast in each commune will be communicated by the Commission to the Principal Allied and Associated Powers, with a full report as to the taking of the vote and a recommendation as to the line which ought to be adopted as the frontier of Germany in Upper Silesia. *In this recommendation regard will be paid to the wishes of the inhabitants as shown by the vote, and to the geographical and economic conditions of the locality.* [emphasis added]

There was no indication in the Article that the plebiscite area had to be treated as a single, indivisible geographical entity. In support of the International Commission, France sent ten battalions of soldiers, Great Britain sent four, and Italy sent two. While each contingent was commanded by officers of their respective countries, the overall command was given to France. The result of the plebiscite (approximately 60 per cent in favour of Germany, and 40 per cent for Poland) was interpreted in Germany as an absolute victory.

The sense of victory in Foreign Affairs was short lived, however, as by 24 March 1921, the Allied Reparations Commission, frustrated by the February proposals of the Germany, found it to be in default of its payments, and subject to sanctions.[10] The first step was the British Reparations Recovery Act, in which a 50 per cent import duty was placed on all German products as a means of capturing some of the missed payment. This served to confirm as well the French occupation of earlier March, and presented a unified Allied front to Germany. It also set the stage for the later presentation, in May, of the final bill for reparations.

The KPD attempted to take advantage of the growing discontent and anger in Germany, over these events. After internal splits within the party, the main elements, spurred onwards by the Comintern, decided in March 1921 to attempt to light a revolutionary spark in the country. The "March Action" did not take root beyond the core area of Saxony in which some factories had been occupied, and some of the docks in Hamburg. The revolutionary activity was easily suppressed by the authorities, who this time did not need to resort to the support of the Freikorps to re-assert control. The communists later claimed that several hundred were killed in the pacification operations, and thousands arrested. The only certain result was that over 20,000 members of the KPD left the party in disgust.

Kopp made a personal, if not necessarily intended, contribution to the evolution of the relationship between the two states in his assessment to Chicherin of the March 1921 KPD actions. Up to that point, there still was hope—especially within the Comintern—that a revolution might yet be possible in Germany, and so the agitation which so irritated the German Foreign Office and the Reichswehr had to continue. Kopp's report went some way towards disabusing Moscow of notions promoted by the Comintern representatives. As early as 2 March 1921, well before the formal uprising had begun, he wrote that despite the impressively threatening outward appearance, the events in Germany had no serious revolutionary nature. He went on to roundly critique the KPD leadership and organization as being very weak, and possessing little control over radical elements. What little militant momentum had been gathered in the previous months was being needlessly squandered, Kopp wrote, and the overall position of the KPD was in actuality "extremely tenuous".[11] That Kopp was proven correct by the later ease with which the action was suppressed would provide support to those in the Soviet leadership who, in June, sought to curb the influence of the Comintern's activities in Germany.

A few days later, in a 7 March 1921 letter to Chicherin on the growing crisis in Silesia, Kopp made it clear that the Germans saw war as a possible outcome: the Poles were moving divisions from the Russian border over to the German border, so as to be able to be in Berlin in 5–6 days after receiving permission from the Entente. The note made clear the magnitude of the crisis in Germany, and the important potential role of Russia. There was also a growing crisis along the Bavarian border with Czechoslovakia—for this, Kopp blamed Balfour and the British as being provocateurs. He went on to say that he had not yet received Ausamt's full reply to earlier proposals.[12] On 21 March 1921, Kopp was informed of the official mandate of Feliks Galle as "specialist" voice to discuss issues relating to collaborative work, until 1 June.[13]

Shock at the audacity of the prospective collaborative partner was not exclusively the preserve of the Soviets. Simons, in reacting at the end of March 1921 to the Comintern support of the KPD revolt, while the Soviet government concurrently pursued negotiations with Germany, noted that a "considerable" amount of self-control was required in trying to deal with the Russians while they were setting "fire to the roof over one's head". But nevertheless, he was in favour of leading negotiations with them to a conclusion.[14]

From the end of 1920 through to March of 1921, when the Anglo-Soviet trade agreements were signed, Radek, in a circular written for the Soviet leadership, noted that British diplomats had actively discouraged peace between France and Russia. Moscow perceived the existence of a not inconsiderable wedge between the Entente powers, which could be effectively exploited in other areas.[15]

With the March uprisings suppressed, and Kopp issuing assurances to the Germans of greater future control of Soviet agitation, more detailed correspondence between Soviet and German authorities was finally exchanged from 3 April 1921 onwards, on the establishment of air-links between the two states.[16] The correspondence was supplemented by later letters, on the direct negotiations for a Berlin–Moscow air route, led by a German firm "Sabbatnig".[17] These would, however, drag on for more than a year.

A memorandum dated 5 April 1921 from the Politburo, on Kopp's reports on Germany, included as well a note from Chicherin to Molotov dated 7 June 1921. Letters and notes during this time referred, in general, to Kopp's work in Berlin, including clarifications and elaborations for what policy Kopp should be pursuing. Included in this was a somewhat detailed assessment of Germany's military interests and capabilities, and approval for Kopp (on 12 July 1921) to continue pursuing closer links. As well, the Politburo approved the sending of more representatives to Berlin to assist Kopp (Y. Kh. Lutovinov). Lutovinov would prove, however, to be less assistance than trouble for Kopp, as he came to fulfill the aims of the Comintern rather than the foreign commissar.[18]

Meanwhile, Enver Pasha continued to send information back to Seeckt, from Moscow. On 19 April 1921, he informed him that a colleague was on his way to Berlin on Enver's behalf, who bore information on the situation in Russia which the general would be very interested to hear.[19] This was the second time in which Enver personally sent information to the general this way, during this period—the first had come in February 1921.[20]

Although Lenin did not take an active part in directing the negotiations, and rarely responded directly to news of the evolution of the relationship, he remained informed by Chicherin in general terms. In a note from the latter to the former dated 20 April 1921, Chicherin offered an update on the state of negotiations in Berlin between Kopp and Scheidemann: the Germans believed that an agreement with Russia can be had in "months".[21] Kopp's charge to focus on purely trade matters had slid into disuse by this time: on 21 April 1921, he met with General Staff officers and the directors of Krupp, to discuss direct technical military collaboration.[22]

Brockdorff-Rantzau, though without office, was not without influence, and wrote at the end of April 1921 a lengthy memorandum on the general political situation facing Germany at the time. After outlining what few friends Germany had and how the Entente cared only for the destruction of German power in all spheres, he observed that the Soviet government was itself split, the Red Army was poorly equipped and without discipline, and the country (and peasantry) were in revolt. In every way, there was little to be gained in the immediate present from an alliance with Soviet Russia, especially given the dangers of Bolshevism to the health of the German people. However, Brockdorff-Rantzau was also of the opinion that when faced with an enemy which was ideologically ultimately bent on destroying Germany, it was better to engage it at an international level and thus at least in some ways attempt to keep control of the initiative, rather than simply sit back and allow fate to take its course. He was therefore of the opinion that Germany should, given the current situation, with extreme caution be prepared to have contacts with Russia. To this purpose, Brockdorff-Rantzau was prepared to go to Moscow, while being under no illusions as to the difficulties of the tasks involved. It was also especially important for Germany to bear in mind, he wrote, that the Soviets could well try to simply play Germany off against the Entente powers, and that the Soviets would place greater value on the Allied Forces than on an alliance with Germany. Nevertheless, even with this possibility, given the dangers of the current international climate, one still had to make the effort. If Germany did not, then it could come back to harm it; if it did and succeeded, it could bring the greatest of benefits.[23] Brockdorff-Rantzau wrote a shorter note directly to the President of Germany on a 25 April 1921, in which he reiterated these points, and urged great caution in negotiating with the Soviets.[24]

That Kopp's early-March scathing assessment of the KPD, and by extension of the Comintern position as a whole with regard to Germany, had an impact was evident just a few short months later. On 2 May 1921, Chicherin complained directly to Lenin of a recent Comintern radio-broadcast about Germany, which had preached the need to continue the Revolutionary struggle, and so on. In Chicherin's view, it was completely counterproductive to Soviet Russia's interests, and worked to give assistance to those in Germany who were against a Russo-German rapprochement. The broadcast itself had drawn a formal protest from Berlin, as it had been aired by a government radio station in Moscow, and could hence said to have official sanction. "Such propaganda is a weapon in the hands of enemies of an agreement between Germany and Russia." Kopp as well was reportedly upset, as this directly undermined his negotiations with the Germans. He asked for a disclaimer from the Soviet Foreign Commissariat, and that future Comintern broadcasts and propaganda be subject to scrutiny before being aired.[25]

One of the central players of Sondergruppe R, and concerning whom little documentary record of his direct activities in Russia exists, was Niedermayer. His flair for self-promotion included the preference for being referred to as the "German Lawrence" [i.e. of Arabia], as a result of his wartime activities: he had been sent to Afghanistan to stir up anti-British activities, and had managed to avoid capture by both Imperial Russian and British forces. Upon his arrival in Moscow in the summer of 1921, he went, along with Gustav Hilger (who was apparently only empowered to discuss issues relating to prisoners-of-war), on an inspection tour of armaments factories and shipyards in St Petersburg, with the intention of determining their suitability for collaborative projects with German firms. Germany was to offer technical and financial support for the restoration of the factories, in return for a proportion of the output. Both the Soviet Vice-Commissar for Foreign Affairs Karakhan and Kopp accompanied them on the tour. Hilger later wrote:

> The impression von Niedermayer and I received from the inspections was devastating. Most of the factories and shipyards were not in operation because raw materials were non-existent and because a large part of the workers had taken refuge in the villages in order to escape starvation in the city. Roofs everywhere were damaged, so that the machinery was exposed to the destructive effects of rain and snow; and for the most part the machines were in an unspeakable condition. It was clear to us that any German participation in the reconstruction of Petrograd's industry was, under these circumstances, out of the question, since it would have demanded more than Germany at that time could afford. All the more remarkable is the fact that the Soviet government did succeed in subsequent years in restoring Petrograd's industries to running condition without foreign assistance. Obviously, it had underestimated its own strength in the summer of 1921; otherwise it would hardly have thought of asking German capital to participate in the reconstruction of Petrograd's armament industry and of thus offering Germany a good look into a branch of the economy which constituted such a vital part of Russia's military capacity. Or was the attitude of the Soviet government based on the conviction that the days of capitalism in Germany were numbered and that, therefore, her economic possibilities and technical capacities could be used for the benefit of the Soviet Republic without any danger?[26]

Niedermayer remained in charge of Zentrale Moskau, as Sondergruppe R's Moscow bureau was called, throughout the Weimar years, and had greater contact with the Red Army than any other German official in Russia. According to Hilger, "For security reasons, the official military attaché was not allowed to have any contacts with von Niedermayer and his group, so that he had no opportunity to talk to the constant stream of German Army personnel passing through Zentrale Moskau on their way to or from different places within the Soviet Union."[27]

The British government, as well as other states in central Europe, were also beginning to get informed of the possible directions of Soviet policy at this time. One representative wrote an assessment for the British Foreign Office, based on a report "founded on the investigations of Czecho-Slovak Secret Agents in Russia and which I believe to represent the truth, the Czechs being really the only non-Russians who understand the Russian mentality." Both wings of the Communist Party in Russia were apparently viewing the coming international conferences as opportunities to advance their cause of world revolution:

> [...] the Bolsheviks hope to score an easy victory at Genoa by gaining de jure recognition (which is all they care about) without having to give effective guarantees, and they think that they will be able to postpose all discussions on the economic reconstruction of Russia with its consequences and conditions to a later date when with their new recognized status they will be in a better position to deal with the Powers and pursue their object of dividing them in order to triumph over the capitalist world.[28]

Further reports to London discussed apparently more direct agreements. A dispatch from 21 March 1921 indicated that there was a firm plan in place for restoring the Bolshevik fleet with the aid of Germany. The ships were to be sold to Germany, which would repair and crew them, and thus have them ready for "joint action in the event of complications between France and Germany leading to the outbreak of hostilities". The negotiations were apparently still underway, as the only outstanding question concerned how many ships Germany would take. As well, the British had been informed (by again, Czechoslovakian sources) that "[...] arrangements have been made for the shipment of artillery via Sweden. As well, a small arms contract between Germany and Russia was rumoured to have been signed. In payment for the ships, Germany was supposed to supply aeroplanes and other military requirements."[29]

This information reached the British via Czechoslovakian sources as their government was taking more public steps to guarantee themselves against Germany: the Romania–Czechoslovakia alliance signed on 23 April was the first step towards the Little Entente,

France's attempt to encircle Germany with military agreement among its neighbours to keep it in check.[30] That there was some grounds for questioning the German and Austrian commitment to the territorial status quo became clear the next day, as citizens in Tyrol voted overwhelmingly in favour of union with Germany. The terms of Versailles clearly prohibited the act from being carried into reality, and so the exercise was a lost cause from the beginning.

Germany received further setbacks at this time concerning the issue of reparations. The United States, whom Germany had formally asked to serve as a mediator in the crisis over repayments, refused the German request on 24 April 1921. Shortly thereafter, the Allied Reparations Commission announced that Germany's full and total reparations under the Treaty of Versailles would be 132 billion gold marks.[31] The sum, while less than 230 billion proposed by France, still left Germany shocked, as did the decision, at the London Conference between 29 April and 5 May, to have Germany pay one billion gold marks by the end of May or face an occupation of the Ruhr. Germany borrowed the funds from London to be able to meet the deadline. The final reparations were divided into three series of bonds: "A" bonds worth 12 billion marks, "B" bonds worth 38 billion, and "C" bonds worth 82 billion; the "C" bonds would not be issued until after the "A" and "B" bonds had been paid in full, and were considered by some to be a form of insurance by the Europeans against their own debts to the United States. But the instability of the moment was compounded by the fact that while the conference was in progress (and with no coincidence of timing), a Polish uprising began in Upper Silesia, after 2 May.

Upper Silesia, with an industrially vital sector as well as agricultural zones, was according to Versailles to have its future decided by plebiscite, as described earlier. But with the fear that the Allies might award the entire plebiscite area to Germany as a result of the total vote of the area (approximately 60 per cent to Germany, and 40 per cent to Poland), the Polish nationalist leader Albert Korfanty organized mass demonstrations from March of that year, and led an armed uprising from May, with support from the Greater Polish Army, against any sign of German authority.[32] This was seen in Germany, and elsewhere, as an attempt to influence the final decision of the

International Commission, and in apparent violation of Article 88 of the Treaty of Versailles:

> [...] The Polish and German Governments hereby respectively bind themselves to conduct no prosecutions on any part of their territory and to take no exceptional proceedings for any political action performed in Upper Silesia during the period of the regime laid down in the Annex hereto *and up to the settlement of the final status of the country.* [emphasis added]

There were numerous accusations of atrocities made by either side, and both Germany and Poland began to attempt to recruit volunteers for defence forces against the other's armed units. The Inter-Allied Commission, under the influence of French General Henri Le Rond, did not initially intervene, but rather prohibited Germany from recruiting volunteers from outside Upper Silesia proper. While France clearly favoured the Poles, the British and the Italians tended towards support of the Germans; Lloyd George made a speech in Parliament actively denouncing the insurrection. The initial military results were successes for the Poles, with the Germans complaining of being tied by the restriction against sending support from outside the province. Eventually, on 1 July, Allied troops were sent in to pacify the region, taking advantage of an offer made earlier by Korfanty to relinquish control of the majority of territory he had captured to Allied—but not German—control. The Allies declared a general amnesty for any actions committed during the rebellion except cruelty and revenge.

Unable to reach agreement among themselves, the Allies turned the matter over to the League of Nations for resolution. With more Allied troops sent to the territory in the meanwhile, the situation was calmed significantly. The League promptly turned the matter to a commission comprised of four members—from Belgium, Brazil, Spain, and China. The commission, after deliberations which included input from both Germany and Poland, as well as its own experts, decided upon the partition of the province, as much as possible upon ethnic lines.

Despite the precise text of Article 88, noted earlier, this was perceived by the German public as giving in to armed revision of the plebiscite results—and an indication that the Treaty of Versailles would only ever be interpreted against Germans, and never in their favour; it also discredited the fledgeling League of Nations in German eyes. As a result of the division, Germany received the majority of territory (comprising primarily of agricultural lands), but lost the important industrial zones. Poland gained almost one half of the population of Upper Silesia, and just under a third of the total land. In terms of industrial output, Poland gained possession of resources accounting for roughly three quarters or more of the province's total coal, pig-iron, lead, and zinc output. In additon, Poland also gained the major towns of Königshütte (Chorzow), Kattowitz (Katowice), and Tarnowitz (Tarnowice); not insignificant minorities of Germans also lived in the newly Polish territory. The League of Nations asked Poland and Germany to enter into negotiations to deal with economic matters resulting from the division, as well as for the protection of minorities.

Faced with the outcome of both the recent reparations conferences and the results of the Upper Silesian question, the government of Chancellor Fehrenbach resigned on 10 May, rather than accept responsibility for what was widely perceived as another Versailles Diktat. His replacement, Wirth, under the threat of occupation of the Ruhr, introduced a policy of fulfillment. Wirth, as mentioned earlier, continued to hold the position of Finance Minister, and proved willing to consider the investments in both legal and illegal enterprises in Soviet Russia.

The continued instability in Germany seemed to offer at least some hope to Comintern officials in Moscow, that the dream of a German revolution could still be realized. Not all of Moscow felt the same way as Kopp and Chicherin, however, concerning the greater value placed on cooperation with Germany rather than in trying to foment revolution. The prospect of using a relationship with Germany was considered by Lutovinov as simply a tool for the eventual (Comintern) goal of social revolution on a larger scale. On 20 May 1921, he wrote to Chicherin from Berlin that Soviet Russia had to help Germany regain its fighting potential so that Germany would be placed in a definite position vis-à-vis the Entente—a situation which Soviet Russia could exploit. To be perfectly clear of the utilitarian nature of the collaboration, he wrote that no peaceful relations between Russia and a capitalist state could save Russia; only, rather, non-stop war, which would lead to social revolution.[33] Chicherin, with Lenin, Trotsky, and Bukharin in support, informed Lutovinov on 30 May 1921 that if peaceful talks were to be sought with the capitalist states, excessively aggressive Comintern demonstrations had to be avoided.[34]

For the German Foreign Office, at least, the issue of Germany's relations with Russia were not perceived as they were by the army. Politically, the need to take some account of Britain became relevant, as noted by Maltzan in late May 1921. A "tacit" agreement was in existence with Britain that Germany's relationship with Russia should not infringe upon the British–Russian relationship.[35]

This informal arrangement came as the British lowered their tariff on German imports to 26 per cent for reparations, on 20 May 1921, with the Reduction of Reparations Recovery Act; in response to the economic troubles facing Germany at the time, the timing of the move was an attempt to provide a softer face to Germany than what was being presented, in general, by the French. This leniency did not extend, however, to matters of more traditional geopolitics: when Salzburg voted in violation of the treaties of Versailles and St Germain, on 29 May 1921, to join Germany, the Allied governments were quick to provide a unified front and threatened to intervene directly, thus ending any hopes of the separatists. The principle of self-determination, even when supported by over 98 per cent of the votes cast, was simply not open to negotiation with regard to Austria's relationship with Germany.

As early as June 1921, while Niedermayer and Hilger were making their way around St Petersburg factories, drafts were being prepared by the staff of the Red Army (with the approval of the Foreign Commissar) for German–Soviet agreements to jointly renounce all claims relating to the war. In essence, these were drafts of the substance which was later formalized at Rapallo—nothing exceptional, in other words, except perhaps the early date.[36] On 27 July 1921, another report was circulated within the Russian war and foreign ministries outlining the possibility and desirability of German renunciation of war claims against Russia, in return for other—that is, military—agreements.[37]

At the start of June 1921, Lenin recommended to the Politburo the adoption of Kopp's recommendations concerning secret military collaboration alongside trade negotiations, accepting the need as well for complete secrecy. Lenin was not clear about what form the structure for collaboration should take, but did raise the benefits of economic concession investments, as this way Russia would avoid responsibility for whatever the licensees ended up producing—thus Lenin demonstrated an appreciation for the principle of deniability.[38]

Lutovinov, in his reply to accusations of political irresponsibility, rose to the occasion on June 1921. He described the German collaborators of Kopp as being a group of military adventurers, who were politically isolated and who, accordingly, could lead Russia into difficulties and trouble not only with Britain and Poland, but also within Germany itself. He recommended instead that Russia should deal with the extreme right-wing group "Orgesch", as they were in any event the moving force behind the entire affair.[39] As a result of this initiative, the Central Committee met and, as Maxim Litvinov, chief assistant to Chicherin and roaming ambassador for the Soviet government, reported back to Lutovinov on 7 June 1921, came to a series of decisions, including the possible separation of activities of the Soviet Government from the Comintern. Litvinov further stated that there were some limits as to what would be done for the economic concessions given to German firms; and there thus appeared to be some backtracking from Lenin's position, in the name of the Comintern.[40]

Despite a later attempt by the Central Committee (in mid-August) to more strictly separate the actions of the Comintern (revolutionary activity abroad) from those of the Soviet government (the successful nurturing of the interests of the Soviet state), the peace within the Soviet camp was not lasting.[41] The ability of the Comintern to keep a steady stream of revolutionary invective alive during this time was demonstrated by the Varga Bureau (officially, the "Statistical-Information Institute" of the Comintern in Berlin), which oversaw the production of newspaper articles and pamphlets in Germany throughout this period. Their activity proved to be one long series of attacks against the German state, and exhortations to keep the revolutionary spirit alive.[42] With regard to the intensification of contact and negotiations with Niedermayer, it was agreed to by the Politburo that they proceed, in Moscow, but that they be treated with extreme care.[43]

In a report concerning his 1 June 1921 meeting in Essen with the directors of the Krupp firm, Kopp wrote that the encounter was friendly, but also that "spies" of Britain were already informed of the meeting, and were further interested in the military dimensions which could possibly arise from Krupp's dealings with Russia. Kopp then wrote of the details of the proposed Krupp ventures, including how to have factories which could be easily converted to military from civilian uses.[44] On 2 June 1921, the Soviets received a note outlining (in German) the conditions which were to be met by Russia before concession talks with German firms began, for iron development in St Petersburg for 50 years: agreement as to the size of the areas of the concession, and German bank financing. The German firms were quite clear about dual civil–military nature of the venture; in the abbreviations page of the report were entries for such weapons as artillery, shells, gun-barrels, gun mounts, munitions wagons, and even submarines.[45]

These meetings with Krupp came as the Little Entente in south-central Europe was finally completed; the Yugoslavians signing an alliance with Romania on 7 June 1921, thus linking these two countries with Czechoslovakia under French tutelage. This gave a greater sense of impetus to the German–Russian talks, as seen with the continuation of the Krupp talks the following month.

In early July 1921, the Krupp firm further analysed the situation in Russia to see how the company could regain and develop their position which was lost because of the war and revolution. The leadership of Krupp showed particular interest in St Petersburg, as it was "the most important port at present in Russia" and "the only large entrance way to Russia and the water-ways which connect it with middle-Asia", recognising thus the perspective of further economic expansion from the periphery into the interior of the country. "It has to be seized [...]" and "more hostile, especially English" influence had to be eliminated. The chief representative of Krupp in Moscow, Petersen, stated grandly in a memorandum that he thought not only the city, but the whole "economic region of St Petersburg" should be directly or indirectly involved and developed. For this, he reiterated the earlier points that a concession to be created for iron-works factories to be controlled for a period of 50 years. Moreover, the Russian government should offer guarantees to the remaining industries of the economic area.[46]

Kopp then reported to Chicherin, on 21 June 1921, that Krupp specified its interests as being: "the production of agricultural machines and appliances, production of machined instruments, household-merchandise and mass-produced articles for rural economies, the repair of locomotives, construction of locomotives and rail-wagons, construction of merchant-ships (especially for river-use)". While cognizant of the Russian interests in the military application of its expertise, Krupp apparently was not particularly interested in the arms-industry except insofar as it had to engage in it to further its main—and presumably more profitable in the longer term—civilian industrial interests. From the German side it was imperative that everything was done to distract Britain away from the military-political aspect of the relationship, so as not to give them a pretext to place direct pressure on Germany to drop economic cooperation with Russia. Krupp went further to propose, specifically with regard to St Petersburg, "firstly to strongly declare the intentional subordination of military to civilian industries as the long-term goals of a public German-Russian programme, including the immediate dismantlement and re-building of the arms industry, in order to undermine one of our enemies' most important arguments". Kopp, however, maintained that there was "great and serious interest" within German industry for military cooperation, though after his interviews with Krupp he had to concede that the immediate fate of the arms-industry "becomes blurred somehow into the fog".[47] At the end of June 1921, he commented that one had to be careful to the possibility that "military group" might fall entirely under the influence of the Krupp firm; at the same time, he urged the Soviet government to strongly impress upon the Moscow representative of Krupp, Petersen, that economic collaboration was not of value in and of itself, but only "in a particular political context".[48]

Krupp was of course not the only firm which was being encouraged by Seeckt, through Sondergruppe R, to open facilities in Russia. Junkers continued with discussions with both the German military and Foreign Office on the possibilities of conducting business in Russia, by sending a director to Berlin for meetings in the fall of 1921; principally, the firm wished to know what support the government could offer the company in return for establishing factories in Russia. In doing so, they were following up on a July 1921 visit to their offices by Niedermayer, who had inquired if the firm was willing to cooperate with the defence ministry in Russia: these military plans, he claimed, were supported by a political undercurrent and would be financed by the government.[49] The war ministry, through Sondergruppe R's Tschunke and Fischer, allowed for the discussed projects to take on more concrete form, by providing the necessary working funds to get the ventures off the ground.[50]

The British were proving to be well informed of the Comintern's activities in Germany, and of the German Foreign Office's frustrations which resulted from them. As D'Abernon reported to Curzon on 11 June 1921, in a recent with Maltzan, the latter stated,

> The Soviet Government is still spending a large amount of money on propaganda in Germany. There is no good in attempting to stop this. If I [Maltzan] stop them in one direction it will be spent in another. [...] the danger from communism in Germany is certainly less than it was, but it must not be neglected. Compared with last August there is improvement—great improvement. Last year the whole of Germany would have become Bolshevistic if Warsaw had fallen. That is quite certain. I can prove it by documents—chapter and verse. At that time the Bolsheviks had succeeded in capturing or hoodwinking the Nationalist organisers here, telling them Russia and Germany must work together to throw off the Western yoke. All our extremists on the Right took the bait. At the same time Moscow told their communist friends in Germany: "We will only employ the Nationals until we have won the position—then we will cut their throats and enjoy pure communism."

Maltzan claimed to have a list of the proposed communist committees which were to rule Germany, with Radek at the head. "[...] As regards the attribution or partition of Upper Silesia, Maltzan's view is that Moscow favours the Polish solution, merely because it is the worst available. The Poles are certain to mismanage the industry—its collapse would be another capitalist failure, which would rebound to the advantage of communism."[51]

If the Comintern was actively involved in Germany, the same could not be said of Trotsky's Red Army staff itself. In a rather bland note to Chicherin of 29 June 1921, indicative of the peripheral role played by the Red Army in the early negotiations, Trotsky simply wrote that he agreed with Chicherin on the need for foreign trade contacts (including military-economic matters), and encouraged "someone" to look into the matter further.[52]

On 23 July 1921, Kopp wrote to Chicherin on meetings with, among others, Rathenau, in which he learned of German fears of France concerning Silesia, and British "economic repression".[53] As well, Kopp could confirm for Moscow the willingness of universities in Berlin, Munich, Leipzig, Heidelberg, and Goettingen to receive Soviet professors on "academic exchange".[54] Thus, Kopp was able to slowly expand the fields in which a collaborative relationship between the two countries would encompass.

Chicherin spelled out, on 6 July 1921, the motivation behind the current talks with Germany in clear terms to Molotov. The greatest danger which Russia faced lay in the unification of the capitalist states into a single front with the goal of economically exploiting Russia. It was for this reason that Moscow had to support all the efforts of individual states to develop separate relations with Russia. "We even value the German plan [for military and economic collaboration], as it leads Germany toward a policy which allows for the independent actions of Russia."[55]

An obvious counter-argument against military cooperation with Germany was related to the question or possibility that arms manufactured in Soviet factories could conceivably be used by the German authorities in repressing revolutionary workers and fighters for socialism inside Germany. Chicherin replied to this Comintern concern in a 10 July report to the Politburo, in which he stated that arms would be stored with the approval of the Germans in Soviet arsenals, "up to the moment of a new war".[56] Financing for such activities were to come via Deutsch Orentbank (Disconto-Gesellschaft), and would require a minimum guarantee of 6 per cent return on investment.[57]

Chicherin, who already at the 10 July 1921 Politburo meeting reported some indications that the military component of the relationship was possibly being diluted, admitted in a private letter to Kopp on 18 July 1921 that he was "not just a little irritated" by the developments, and restated his stand on the "political meaning" of the collaboration. The inclusion of the military-industrial component, he stressed, was the only guarantee that the entire business, as desired, did not remain only a business-trade venture with Germany.[58] Later, on 18 July, Chicherin reiterated the opinion expressed earlier that month to Molotov that the military contacts with Germany were a precaution against the development of a political-economic unified front of the western states against Soviet-Russia.[59] To ensure that they had a good grasp of their prospective partner, a relatively detailed 50-page booklet on the military, political, and economic situation in Germany, dated 1 August 1921, was prepared by the Red Army staff. It provided a good basic introduction to German military affairs, with a detailed breakdown of the size, strength, and Order of Battle (down to the level of trucks, in some units) of the German army.[60]

Not infrequently, Niedermayer on his own initiative promised more to the Soviet leadership than he could deliver. The reactions against his extravagances would prove, later, to be of help to Brockdorff-Rantzau in the bureaucratic infighting which would develop between him and Seeckt over the summer of 1922. In a series of notes between Chicherin and Lenin from July to August 1921, it was apparent that Niedermayer had also been involved in a gaffe concerning personalities within the Russian camp (Kopp versus Lutovinov); the reaction from the Soviet side (Lenin and Chicherin) was one of outrage and clearly demonstrated that Niedermayer had more or less worn out his welcome.[61] However, his presence was tolerated in Moscow to the extent that he was expected to be able to deliver concrete plans for future cooperation to Trotsky, as of 6 August.[62] Lenin remained, however, angry with Niedermayer. At one point, Lenin suspected the German to be playing a double-game with Russia, and demanded an immediate test: either agree to an "alliance against England", or send Niedermayer back to Berlin in disgrace. But Chicherin won the day, wanting no such undiplomatic gesture; he suggested that Niedermayer catch a serious case of "diplomatic flu", arguing that "he will still be useful to us".[63]

It was at this point in time that the United States finally, on 25 August 1921, signed a separate peace treaty with Germany, to formally end hostilities from the First World War. The United States Senate ratified the treaties with the Central Powers, in late October, thus paving the way for improved contact with Germany.

In a letter to Molotov for the Politburo, Chicherin again stressed, on 27 August 1921, the extraordinarily high value that he placed on the military contacts he had, and that he characterized the relationship with Seeckt's group as being of "the highest importance" and forming "one of the most important and largest perspectives of our policies".[64] By September 1921, with tensions high in Germany due to the ongoing problem of Poland and Upper Silesia, discussions took on a firmer character.

A consortium of German industrialists and banks had materialized, but the German army, which had initially also been involved with a significant financial stake, had to withdraw, in part due to the demands by the industrialists for a clear separation of civilian and military industrial aims. The industrialists could rely upon Chancellor Wirth to resist the military group, whom Seeckt had put pressure upon with descriptions of internal and external political upheaval. Wirth had fundamentally no objections against military contacts; he simply wanted to commit to dealing with actual rather than potential dangers, and realized that the military and civilian economic projects, both of which could be useful in promoting an independent German policy towards Russia, were often at odds with one another. Moreover, he believed that a disentanglement of the military from civilian economic cooperation with Russia could improve the manoeuvrability of German foreign policy.[65]

A total debacle of the military cooperation, which Kopp had warned Niedermayer was possible (if he continued irritating Chicherin and Lenin), had been avoided, in that the new negotiations between the two sides succeeded in establishing a framework and guidelines for future German–Russian military partnership. The direct negotiations at this time were conducted between Seeckt's aide Hasse of the German army and Krasin and Kopp on the Soviet side. Krasin stated that Russia did not wish to develop closer economic ties with the Entente powers, that the construction of airplanes by Junkers should begin shortly, and that contact with Krupp should take on a stronger form. Although Seeckt, who was informed of the meetings by Hasse in early October, did not take part in the discussions, he delegated others to continue with the talks over the coming weeks. Seeckt, knowing that financing of a not inconsiderable size would be needed, informed Wirth (who was both Chancellor and Minister of Finance) of the specifics of the plans under consideration, which now included the possible participation of both Junkers and Stinnes.[66] The Soviets also wanted clear Germany military support in case of a renewed attack on Poland.[67] Seeckt's recommendation to the Chancellor was that given the risk that France and Czechoslovakia would immediately intervene against Germany in the case of support for

Russia against Poland, the best course of action for Germany was "benevolent neutrality".[68]

The Soviet version of these meetings came in the form of a report by Kopp to Chicherin, of 20 September. In it, the German side was labelled the Voeyenni Gruppoi (military group, i.e. Sondergruppe R: Hasse, as well as Niedermayer, Schubert, and Tschunke), and on the Russian side were Kopp and Krasin. The two sides agreed to the establishment of a Russo-German Trust for arms manufacture, which would produce, in order of priority, heavy artillery, airplanes, as well as gunpowders and shells. With regard to funding for the venture, from the Soviet side it would come via the government, while from the German side it would have to be determined in due course.[69] On 24 September 1921, Kopp clarified to Moscow (in a letter to Bogdanov, with copies to Chicherin and Trotsky) that he was speaking of 1000 aeroplanes, 200 armoured vehicles, 200 battlefield artillery pieces, 200 machine-guns, and 3000 pieces of ammunition for each weapon. Further, with reference to the military side, he had already agreed upon preparatory specifications for the first order.[70] Kopp then wrote directly to Chicherin that the collaboration was, as a result of the September meetings, becoming more concrete. A full and detailed plan would arrive with direct contact between the two general staffs, but the German group had agreed on the need for a fuller representation in Moscow than had been the case thus far, in the form of a military commission. The first major initiative was to be with regard to the production of aeroplanes.[71]

Demonstrating that it was clearly uninformed of what was going on, the German embassy in Moscow wrote to Berlin a few days later, on 14 September 1921, that "Captain Niedermayer, aide to the minister of defence, [is] here with special orders, about which we are not informed. Please check/verify."[72] The foreign ministry back in Berlin was equally in the dark. In their message back to the embassy of the same date, they noted that to the best of their knowledge, Niedermayer, until that time officially an adjutant of the Federal Defense Secretary, had been in Moscow for a long time, and that he was involved in special Russian military issues.[73] A further reply from the embassy in Moscow on 29 September was that they now believed Niedermayer had returned to Berlin three weeks previously, and had still not returned to Moscow; a few days after that, the embassy was able to further report that Niedermayer was up to something suspicious, but that it was probably with the Chancellor's knowledge.[74]

Niedermayer's presence was apparently disconcerting enough for the German Foreign Office to prompt yet another update, on 1 October 1921: Niedermayer's visit to Russia was described as being strictly confidential, but the Chancellor and Foreign Minister had apparently been informed of his task. As well, Hilger (in apparent contradiction with later claims in his memoirs) was also informed of Niedermayer's local mission. They could learn no more than that he was apparently on a mission of "economic observation". But as they noted,

> The wording of the job "economic" observation is naturally somewhat conspicuous. I have taken the precaution of ensuring that I am informed of his reappearance here. I reckon, however, that his presence here was without my official knowledge because I [Wiedefeld] was the official representative of the Reich. The ground is here is so hot, that such a parallel pursuit of German aims can only be described as extremely dangerous. Only an absolute consistency in the leadership of this business can slowly move us forward.[75]

By 16 October 1921, Wiedenfeld, the senior German representative in Moscow, was able to report back to Berlin that he had been informed that Hauptmann Niedermayer alias Dr Neumann was expected to return on around 20 October, but that his mission there was still unknown.[76]

At the start of October 1921, Kopp echoed Chicherin's desires for the need for a relationship with "political" meaning; it would be difficult and undesirable to separate the military contacts from the greater political context, he wrote, especially with regard to the German military's ability to raise or access the funds needed for the joint projects. He dismissed as wishful thinking the nationalist circles in Germany, who hoped to provoke serious conflicts between Soviet Russia on the one hand, and Poland, Romania and the Baltic states, on the other.[77]

In 1921, Ludendorff wrote a public attack against Brockdorff-Rantzau. Although not directly related to the poor relations Brockdorff-Rantzau had with Seeckt, and despite the growing personal contempt which Seeckt felt for Ludendorff, the fact that it was a general with links to the nationalist circles of the right in Germany gave a foreshadowing of the situation which would evolve in the summer and autumn of 1922. The main complaint of Ludendorff was that Brockdorff-Rantzau had apparently helped the "Ostjude" come to power in Russia. This would mirror the accusation of immoral character, as Seeckt would also accuse Brockdorff-Rantzau of more or less treason, for his apparently "unpatriotic" role at Versailles.[78]

By mid-October, a settlement of the Upper Silesian problem was reached by the League of Nations decision to divide the territory. As noted, although territorially the smaller portion, the section awarded to Poland contained the industrial zones of the province, while the section given to Germany was mostly agricultural in nature. The decision to partition the lands led to such widespread dissatisfaction in Germany that Chancellor Wirth felt obliged to resign. The new government had no choice, in the end, but to accept the League's decision, but did not do so enthusiastically. Troubles between the German and the Polish communities continued, and the threat of renewed conflict led to a late November German–Polish conference. The negotiations eventually resumed in February 1922, and the German Polish Treaty of May 1922 finally confirmed the reality of the League decision. Although this in turn diffused a major possible source of open conflict, the overall problems between the two (the Corridor, Danzig, and the lost provinces and citizens) ensured that a general hostility in Germany towards Poland would continue to form a fundamental common point with Soviet Russia.

However, even among German diplomats there were differences of opinions on how best to proceed. On 21 October 1921, the French ambassador to Germany, Charles Laurent, reported to the French Minister of Foreign Affairs, Aristide Briande, on a supposed split within the German Foreign Ministry on Germany's relations with Soviet Russia. Maltzan was in favour of developing an immediate economic relationship with the Soviets, in order to gain thus for Germany more room for manoeuvre vis-à-vis the Allies. Others, on the other hand, were in favour of a return of the Russian monarchy, and for this reason wished to use Berlin as a base from which exile-Russians could gather and prepare for an eventual return. Maltzan was apparently supported by Rathenau and Deutsch (of AEG), while another member of the foreign ministry, Behrendt, was supported by more right-wing industrialists, such as Stinnes. Maltzan was optimistic about the longevity of the Soviet regime, believed that reports of the famine in Russia and the Ukraine were exaggerated, and further believed that the recent reign of terror within Russia was the result of Trotsky and the Cheka's initiative, and that with Lenin's return to dominance of the decision-making scene the matters were calmer again. Although the Russians were unable to pay in advance for foreign industrial orders, the prospect of offering long-term economic concessions was a way around the problem of financing. Although Maltzan himself wished to retain for German factories and workers all the orders which would come from the relationship, Rathenau and Deutsch were more pragmatic about the need to come to some more flexible understanding within Russia.[79]

Miscommunications within the Soviet camp could occasionally lead to potentially embarrassing public situations as well. At the end of October 1921, the Politburo found itself unexpectedly in a difficult position as security forces in Russia had arrested a foreigner who proved to be, in the end, a "cinematographer" for the German military group Sondergruppe R; they released him, and indicated a hope for greater "coordination" with the Germans in the future, to avoid such occurrences which might otherwise spill into the public eye.[80]

Despite the sense of progress which had come earlier that summer, the Soviets, by 1 November 1921, were beginning to feel frustrated with what they perceived to be the drifting nature of the negotiations with Germany, and the institutional incoherence it represented. They referred the relations as being at a "freezing point".[81] On 3 November 1921, Litvinov wrote to Nikolai Krestinsky, future Soviet ambassador to Germany, that Soviet Russia's diplomatic interests would be furthered if they happened to be coincident with those of Germany—and that relations with Germany should not be unduly tampered with for the sake of diplomatic etiquette.[82]

At the start of November 1921, Krestinsky's main task was to find out what possible ways could the German government develop even more directly political links and relations between Soviet Russia and Germany. This sounding out had to be conducted "in an extremely careful manner", in Litvinov's words in early November 1921. Moscow was in favour of extreme discretion for several reasons: for one, they suspected that the German government, within the context of the policy of fulfillment, might simply try to manipulate Soviet advances to try to reinforce their position in the West and to gain further concessions from the French. Secondly, Litvinov argued, "[although] our own stand for such a political connection has generally still not been clarified, it would not be of harm in any event to [first] have an idea of the position of Germany". On the actual occasion of the inquiry, he argued that one had to wait and react to the outcome of the Washington Conference and the Allied declaration on Soviet debts. "Joining with Germany", he wrote, in making clear the current evaluation of the Weimar republic in Soviet calculations, "must be considered seriously, in the event that the Allies in Washington take toward us an irreconcilable position or put upon us unrealizable demands."[83]

In November 1921, Reichswehr officers (General Wurtzbacher and Colonel Hasse) again visited the Junkers firm at Seeckt's behest, at their Dessau works, to reach an oral agreement with them: Junkers should build an aeroplane and engine factory in Russia for which the defence ministry would provide the means.[84]

The German Foreign Office was aware that there were differences of opinion as well as frustration within the Russian camp regarding their general policy towards Germany, and received a report which shed light on these differences on 21 November 1921 from a Swedish Communist official named Berklund. It spoke of a lack of unity within the Russian Communist Party on account of changed tactics towards foreign powers, financiers, and large industrialists. Although true Communists did not have the intention, Berklund claimed, of making ideological compromises, the Party had before it great difficulties. Apparently, a "well-known party-worker and member of the All Russian Headquarters Executive Committee" named Newski had been successful in moderating somewhat the long-standing sharp exchanges between Lenin, Trotzky, Radek, and Chicherin and thus kept open the possibility that they could continue their common tasks. It was the decision made to allow for economic concessions—and how much foreign and thus anti-bolshevik influence should be allowed—which most greatly divided Soviet thinking. For traditional communists, the members of the Soviet government in favour of closer collaboration at such a cost were considered more interested in gaining and maintaining Soviet power in Russia, "regardless of whether or not the land gets run to ruin or not".⁸⁵

On 22 November 1921, Laurent in Berlin wrote again to Paris, on Russo-German relations. Krestinsky, recently arrived in Berlin as a representative of the Soviet state, was accompanied by an ever-growing number of assistants, giving proof to the growing importance of relations between the two countries. Rumours had even been heard that soon Radek would be arriving in Germany again, and that Karakhan, recently in Berlin as well, was trying to develop not only an economic partnership, but a military alliance as well. These growing contacts between the two sides, however, were causing worry among elements of the extreme-right in Germany, as had been demonstrated with a series of articles in the right-wing press in Berlin.⁸⁶

A few days later, on 24 November 1921, a note received in Paris from their embassy in Poland indicated that German industrialists, led by Hugo Stinnes, were more active than ever in pursuing closer links with Russia. Apparently, the deciding factor in the rise of Maltzan's general policy were Upper Silesia, and the recent defeat of the Soviets in Poland. The Germans desperately needed a Red Army success in Poland, in order to better make their case that only Germany could serve as a buffer against Bolshevism in Europe; in the process, they hoped to favourably influence the League of Nation's deliberations regarding Upper Silesia. But the "Bolshevik scarecrow", so profitably used in the past, had disappeared, leaving the Germans with little choice but to simply get on with developing their relations with Russia as best they could. No mention was made, however, of a military dimension to the relationship.⁸⁷

Nikolai Petrovich Gorbynov, within Chicherin's Commissariat, wrote to Lenin on 28 November 1921 with a non-official list of contacts and negotiations between the two sides. First on the list was Schlesinger, who had dealt with prisoner-of-war issues for the Germans earlier before continuing on to become an "unofficial representative of the German government and of German capitalist consortia". Agreements dated 28 December 1921 were apparently concluded with Deutsche Bank to develop oil, with financing via the National Bank, and a German firm "Soblatnik" to rent two Russian factories for the production of aircraft and motors (which would be signed by 6 February 1922).⁸⁸ At the end of November 1921, Kopp wrote directly to Trotsky, informing him of the trip to Moscow via

Riga of a director of Junkers named Saxenberg, and an engineer von Bentheim; they were on a sales trip.[89] Marking the more direct involvement of military men from the Soviet side, in December a mixed German committee which included representatives of Junkers and several officers of Sondergruppe R, among them Hasse, had meetings in Moscow with Trotsky and the Russian Chief of Staff Lebedev, during which the question of common action in case of a new Russo-Polish war was also discussed. Niedermayer apparently felt confident enough to state that the Reichswehr was now in a position to offer German capital to Trotsky.[90] While in Moscow, the group also met with Radek, who later reported his impressions to Chicherin; this marked the re-entry of Radek into direct contact and negotiations with the Germans, since his release from prison in Berlin at the start of 1920.[91]

Seeckt, at the start of December, was eventually persuaded to meet directly with the Soviet negotiators in Berlin, but could not offer the financial backing they desired;[92] this was in contrast with what Niedermayer had told Trotsky just a short while earlier, further undermining Niedermayer's credibility with the Soviets. Seeckt informed Krestinsky that Sondergruppe R's activities in Russia would have to come under the firm umbrella of the German commercial enterprises working there, that the legal cover of private citizens working abroad was an absolute necessity.[93] He was in favour of a "not so direct approach" between the two sides, but did not doubt the potential of the relationship: "One is told, that Count Schlieffen said upon his death-bed: make the right-wing strong. So, too, we can say to German politicians: keep my back clear."[94] With the meeting with Seeckt already concluded, and the way apparently open for closer and more concrete relations, Litvinov sent a letter to Kopp on 22 December 1921, a telegram from Litvinov to Berlin, formally authorizing closer cooperation.[95]

Chicherin informed Lenin on 27 December 1921 that Krestinsky would meet Loran when next in Berlin, and that Russia's policy towards Article 116 of the Treaty of Versailles,[96] which the Germans would be reminded of, was that Russia had never given up its right to it.[97]

Radek made a further entry into the negotiating forum with a visit to Wiedenfeld, on 30 December 1921. In the latter's report of the encounter to the German Foreign Office, one day later, he noted:

Radek spoke yesterday, in the course of a long interview with me, of his gratification over the dissolution of the Staatskommissariats for Public Order, and the dismissal of Mr Weissmann. The impact of the latter will, in his opinion, have a portentous effect on the establishment of German–Russian relations. That the German government needs Secret Police is obvious, however the whole organization of Weissmann's business was blundering, and in no manner useful to the interests of the German government. The agents were very poorly paid, and become, based on this, tempted either to exaggerate news, or to sell German intelligence/information to foreign powers. Radek opened at these words his notebook and handed over to me a large package of photos of documents, of which the majority carried the marks of the State Commissioner for Public Order, the Ministry of the Interior, the Editor of "Ost-Information", etc. He pointed out especially a letter of Baron Uxkuell of which Mr Weismann, firstly, allowed to get away, which had been altered, and which at the same time touched upon the question of an honorariam. A more detailed study of the documents, whose genuineness I could not confirm, was naturally not possible, because Radek only gave me a quick overview of the many he was holding while standing! He furthermore informed me, that he has documentary evidence that Regierungsrat Schwartz sold certain anti-bolshevik and anti-Irish documents to the English government. Furthermore, he showed a letter of the Staatskommissariat, which indicated that two officials within the German representation to Moscow conducted "special jobs", of which Mr Wiedenfeld knew nothing about.[98]

Overall, 1921 brought several significant advances to the Russian–German secret military relationship. It was in the course of this year that major German firms were brought more concretely into the process; Sondergruppe R served as the bridge, and was able to ensure that the military component of the relationship was not submerged by the businessmen's desire for safer—and larger—profits from a more traditional economic relationship relating to civilian industrial exchange. On the Soviet side, the schism between the Comintern and the Soviet government became open and obviously contradictory, forcing the Politburo to come down on the side of Kopp. Though some frustration had been expressed by the Soviets for the occasionally slow pace of negotiations by the German side, preliminary deals with concrete numbers of military objects (planes, artillery, etc.) had been outlined in the end. The international events of the year served as catalysts towards reconfirming the necessity of the relationship. And although the German military had been the initiator in opening the contacts, by the end of 1921 the Soviet side seemed at least, if not more, intent on preventing the purely civilian side of the relationship from overwhelming the military component. The other main change, from the Soviet end, was the increased participation of Trotsky and the Red Army in the contacts; they had been scarcely involved at all in the earlier years, but were finally brought into the negotiations once Chicherin and Kopp had managed, with the German military, to make concrete enough steps as to bring the Krupp and Junkers representatives to the table. Lenin's role throughout remained surprisingly distant—he intervened or commented upon the negotiations rarely, and then almost always to simply agree with the direction in which Chicherin was taking matters.

6
Under the Umbrella of Rapallo

The year 1922 is of significance to European diplomacy primarily because of the Treaty of Rapallo. This exploded upon the scene in mid-April, just as the Allies were trying to develop a common front against Soviet Russia over the issue of past debt and the ending of its economic isolation. At the time, the news of the normalization of diplomatic and economic relations between the two outsider states of the European (and indeed international) system was not widely believed to be the full picture—stories were rife with secret military clauses which would allow for more nefarious plots to develop between the two. The rumours were only partly incorrect, in that a secret military relationship which would allow for nefarious plots to develop was indeed in existence, but it had begun long before the Conference at Genoa (from where the German and Soviet delegations shuttled away to the resort town of Rapallo). In allowing for direct and open contact between the two states, the treaty in fact provided a cover for the continuation of the contacts into more substantive arrangements. Rapallo, in allowing for formal diplomatic representation, also had a decisive impact within the German leadership, as the civilians of the Foreign Office would become more assertive over their rights to control all aspects of relations with Soviet Russia; the appointment of Brockdorff-Rantzau as the first German ambassador to the newly recognized Soviet state ensured that a show-down with General Seeckt would prove inevitable, over how future contacts with Russia would be conducted.

Initially, the new year brought temporary financial respite to Germany, as the Allied governments, at Cannes Conference at the start of January, agreed to temporarily postpone German reparations payments due to the ongoing economic crisis in the country.

The start of January 1922 saw the Soviet side of the relationship with Germany prepared to build upon the momentum of the last few months and push matters forwards, with an emphasis on the need to use the military contacts and the direct benefits they could bring as part of a larger economic advantage to be gained by the Soviet state. In the foreground, the armaments industry stood out as a natural starting point; it was this sector of Soviet industry which most required, in a report of Radek at the time, "swift and definite help" from the Germans.[1] Radek was under no illusions as to the vehemence of anti-communism in the German army, but he viewed this as being secondary (in the same way that pursuing the communist struggle in Germany was) to the fact that both countries needed a relationship with each other; nonetheless, he would find the agreements to be of such advantage to Soviet Russia that he would later exclaim, "We have the Reichswehr in the bag!"[2]

In a 9 January 1922 letter, Maltzan informed Brockdorff-Rantzau that the German cabinet was in endless discussion about the Russian problem, trying to come up with a united front, but that the Prussian state-ministry and its subordinate inner authorities were making obstructions, and that it was feeling like a Sisyphusian task. The threat of the previous few months of danger from France had diminished recently, with much effort. The "egocentric" actions of France, who wished to use Article 116 of Versailles to force Germany to pay Russia's pre-war debts, had allowed for Germany to come closer to Russia, while finding little favour with either Britain or America. The French negotiations with Russia had by no means stopped, but they had been toned down of late, in the run-up to the coming conference in Genoa. Maltzan expected representatives from Moscow to arrive in the next few days, "with whom we can hopefully have a positive exchange of views on further German—Russian developments, so that we have a common defensive front before Genoa". He then went on to say that Wiedenfeld was on his way back to Moscow on an economic mission, and that Schlesinger had already concluded very good economic projects, which had to be implemented.[3]

On 25 January 1922, Gorbynov, on Chicherin's behalf, again reported to Lenin that negotiations had been conducted between Krupp's representatives in Berlin, and Rykov, Krestinsky, and Boris

Stomonyakov, the later Soviet trade representative to Germany. The German firm Schering would soon sign an agreement (on 6 February) for chemical-pharmaceutical development in Russia, while the credit financing from two German sources would amount to five hundred million gold marks.[4] A separate report of these meetings sent to Trotsky by a Soviet official named Vemach described the Kruppled consortium's proposals for concessions and the establishment of manufacturing bases in Russia as being a little on the "theoretical" side (i.e. premature, or early), and not particularly advantageous for the Soviets. The problem, as Vemach saw it was the number of foreign workers that would be needed in Russia, the lack of control over the plans, the current political situation (i.e. Versailles), and, most importantly, the amount of capital which would be needed for the ventures. He believed the investment capital could only come from outside Russia (i.e. England), but that the situation was unlikely to come to pass.[5] By early February 1922, the concrete negotiations between Germans and Russians on the construction of aeroplanes by Junkers in Russia were also proving to be admittedly difficult and time-consuming, for which each side blamed the other.[6]

Radek made, for the first time since the ending of his arrest, a return visit to Berlin; only this time he was accompanied by a German officer—Niedermayer. Upon his arrival, Radek expressed the wish to see General Seeckt as soon as possible. This meeting was put off, however, until after one of the Sondergruppe R officers, Fischer, conducted initial negotiations with Radek. On 10 February 1922, however, a meeting with Seeckt finally occurred. It was perhaps the meeting of the highest placed personalities to date, and the range of conversation reflected it.

Radek wished to establish direct links between the general staffs of the two armies in order to better discuss the overall military situation, the use of German technical military literature and expertise in the training of Soviet officers, and also thought that Germany "was siding too much with Britain". Seeckt replied that "at the moment and in the immediate future Germany was forced to side with Britain who alone could curb France". Radek intimated that Russia was considering a spring offensive against Poland, and for this reason needed aeroplanes above all else.[7] Radek aspired to conclude with Seeckt direct military grounds for cooperation between Germany and Russia against Poland. Seeckt refused, for fear of starting an immediate war with France and Czechoslovakia. Seeckt recalled that he had earlier recommended to the Chancellor German neutrality in the Russo-Polish war—a friendly act for Russia. Radek, in response, wanted comparatively more binding military agreements. He laid great stress on the reorganization of the army in Moscow, and hoped not only for help with rebuilding the arms-industry, but also for help for the training the officer-corps. Seeckt frankly agreed that this lay among the common future goals of Germany and Russia. Given that Seeckt was speaking directly with Radek, he feared that the meeting would not remain secret for long; he further suspected that Radek was also conferring with representatives of the Entente.[8]

The Soviets' visit lasted from 25 January to 17 February, and the Russian side was initially represented by Radek and Krestinsky; they were joined later in February by Christian Rakovsky, Chairman of the Ukrainian Soviet government and its Commissar for Foreign Affairs, and Krasin. The discussions were on economic, political, and military issues, demonstrating how interrelated they had become, even for the German army. Seeckt, in Radek's report to Moscow, was described as being extremely closed and non-animated.[9] As much as possible during Radek's visit to Berlin, Seeckt attempted to deflect him onto intermediaries from Sondergruppe R, such as Hasse, Niedermayer, Thomsen, and Fischer.[10]

As Genoa was fast approaching, the German Foreign Office wrote up an internal memorandum for eventual use by the Minister, dated 11 February 1922; in it, they listed the advantages and disadvantages of collusion between Russia and Germany. Among the advantages were,

> That Germany would, in general terms, gain more than Russia from the relationship. Russian feared winding up dependent, and therefore in an inferior position.
> Germany's level of required foreign-currency reserves would become less expensive.
> The geographical situation of both states, with regard to each other.
> German industrial expertise in production for Russian business was expressly acknowledged.
> The German workforce and experience was especially suitable for the rebuilding of the Russian economy in the country itself (in situ).
> The wish to resume diplomatic relations.

Factors against the relationship included:

The Russian desire for a political understanding with the Entente powers.
The financial power of the Entente.
French advances.
The hoped alleviation by satisfaction of pre-war and wartime debts.
The Russian desire to conclude agreements before Genoa, namely concerning credits. The hope of American-backed financial reserves.
That German labour was not involved in most of the decisions in the early, preparatory stages (expertise, representatives of interested groups with particular skills concerning Russia, etc.).[11]

With longer-term perspective in mind, one desirable outcome of cooperation between the representatives of Reichswehrministerium and the Red Army General Staff was for the possibility of a "high degree of uniformity" in the military equipment produced by both countries.[12] In more direct geopolitical terms, only informal agreement on common military actions could be made at this time. But the option was in existence, and the common enemy was clear: Poland, Seeckt told Radek, would be divided as soon as Russia or Germany were strong enough.[13] Seeckt's words were significant, especially given the fact that they came on the eve of the start of a League of Nations–sponsored German–Polish conference on Upper Silesia.

On 20 February 1922, in a letter to Krestinsky, Chicherin discussed the general situation in Europe at the time of the approaching conference in Genoa. In his opinion, it was very important to be careful of how their actions played out with Britain—more so than with France.[14] In a later note, of 7 March 1922, he wrote that the French delegation on the eve of Genoa could be expected to try to unify a front against possible German–Russian agreements, that the use by the Soviet delegation of agitation would deepen French mistrust for relations with Moscow, that the French would aim to prevent behind-the-scenes negotiations, and that the Soviet delegation should keep the French delegation at a distance, if it wished to try to cause a falling out between France with Britain and Italy.[15]

On 6 March 1922, Litvinov wrote to Krestinsky that the most recent offer of financial credit from Germany was "miserly", but that it was likely not the last word from them on it. Further, damages from the Communist Revolution were to be included as being exempt from future claims, as well. A few days later, on 9 March, Litvinov made mention of the difficulties being complained about by the Germans (Wiedenfeld) about visa problems and the opening of a German consul in St Petersburg. He had the impression that the Germans were upset that the situation seemed contrary to earlier agreements and understandings.[16] But despite these frustrations, on 15 March a preliminary contract was signed between Sondergruppe R and Junkers, according to which Junker was to start immediately with the construction of aeroplanes in Russia, and Sondergruppe R was to pay 40 million marks and put at its disposal another 100 million as a capital sum.[17]

By 22 March 1922, indicating that the military agreements were certainly not hastily concluded in the heady atmosphere of Genoa, a letter was sent to Sklyansky from a German "businessman" Herr Petschersky (who, nonetheless, ended his letter by writing that he had come to Moscow "as a soldier and not as a businessman", and referred to the need to provide clear and unequivocal answers to his "Chef" [likely Seeckt] in Berlin). Written in German, it requested direct clarification in Trotsky's name for precise details of the military cooperation between Germany and Russia which could be expected, on the position of the Russian military leadership regarding the continual "partitioning" of German territory [i.e. losses via plebiscites]; a common position between the two countries' military leaderships on the issue of officer exchanges; exchange of information on questions of weapons calibres, for infantry, and light/heavy artillery; discussions on reciprocal mobilizations in time of war; and permission on both sides for the attendance at individual lectures at the military academies.[18]

On 8 April 1922, Radek reported to Karakhan of a 1 April meeting with Germans—an important meeting in which the final details of what was later signed at Rapallo were negotiated. Formal agreement would have to wait for final approval from Wirth and Foreign Minister Rathenau after meeting with Chicherin and Litvinov. On 3 April, this meeting took place, and the Soviet record of it referred mainly to compromises on issues of trade and nationality.[19] Chicherin spoke to the Chancellor quite openly of "the work of German officers in Russia". The Chancellor left it to Seeckt's judgement to decide "whether this activity should be denied by Germany". Negotiations between the two sides continued in the train-ride south to the conference at Genoa, with the possibility of restoring Germany's 1914 frontiers being discussed, as well as the curtailment of communist agitation in Germany. Rathenau, however, expressed surprise when Seeckt, immediately upon the signing of Rapallo, informed him that the German officers had been active in Russia earlier. The Reichswehr, in contrast, was fully informed of the course of the political discussions at Genoa which were leading to the Treaty of Rapallo; Hasse, of Sondergruppe R, was an accredited member of the German diplomatic delegation, and was updated by Wirth. Seeckt was glad for the Treaty, because it represented the "first attempt to conduct an active foreign policy [. . .]". He informed the Chancellor that it should be considered the first step towards closer "military rapprochement" with Russia.[20]

The Genoa conference, which lasted from 10 April to 19 May, was meant to be an attempt by the western states which had a financial interest in Russia, to try to come to some arrangement with the Soviet government over past debts. It marked the first time that both Soviet Russia and Germany were invited to participate as equals at an international gathering. Without altering its previous stand against honouring Tsarist debt, the Soviet willingness to have the matter discussed at an international level seemed to indicate that some form of progress or compromise might be possible. From the Soviet perspective, it was also an attempt to simply begin the process of reintegration into the international system. With the exception of the United States, the remaining nations demanded that the Soviets recognize the Tsarist debts, compensate firms and individuals for property which was confiscated, and offer legal guarantees for future contracts. The furthest that Chicherin was willing to go was to accept the Tsarist debt in return for compensation for damage caused by the Allies in the Civil War, new financial credits for the Soviet government, and cancellation of the Russian war debts.

In a five-page memorandum dated 12 April 1922, while the negotiations were underway in Genoa, Brockdorff-Rantzau outlined his position on the Russian question once again: basically, while Russia was interested in maintaining good relations with the Entente powers with an aim to its external security, its internal problems, especially with famine and continuing food shortages, implied that a trade-relationship with Germany was equally important for the authority of the regime, and hence for its survival. Brockdorff-Rantzau offered recommendations and guidelines regarding what had to be achieved through the Russian relationship vis-à-vis German rights, as well as what could be expected in terms of reactions and repercussions with England, France, and other countries. Significantly, there was no mention at all of any military matters; the German army's monopoly of the topic was still intact, and that German foreign affairs establishment did not have serious military collusion in mind when considering the ongoing negotiations.[21]

In the end, the treaty signed at Rapallo on 16 April represented the logical conclusion of the difficulties each power had in the preceding year, in their dealings with the Allies. Signed by Chicherin on behalf of the Soviets, and by Rathenau, on behalf of Germany, it was relatively short by the standards of international diplomacy:

> Article 1 The two Governments are agreed that the arrangements arrived at between the German Reich and the Russian Socialist Federal Soviet Republic, with regard to questions dating from the period of war between Germany and Russia, shall be definitely settled upon the following basis:
>
> [a] The German Reich and the Russian Socialist Federal Soviet Republic mutually agree to waive their claims for compensation for expenditure incurred on account of the war, and also for war damages, that is to say, any damages which may have been suffered by them and by their nationals in war zones on account of military measures, including all requisitions in enemy country. Both Parties likewise agree to forego compensation for any civilian damages, which may have been suffered by the nationals of the one Party on account of so-called exceptional war measures or on account of emergency measures carried out by the other Party.
>
> [b] Legal relations in public and private matters arising out of the state of war, including the question of the treatment of trading vessels which have fallen into the hands of either Party, shall be settled on a basis of reciprocity.
>
> [c] Germany and Russia mutually agree to waive their claims for compensation for expenditure incurred by either party on

behalf of prisoners of war. Furthermore the German Government agrees to forego compensation with regard to the expenditure incurred by it on behalf of members of the Red Army interned in Germany. The Russian Government agrees to forego the restitution of the proceeds of the sale carried out in Germany of the army stores brought into Germany by the interned members of the Red Army mentioned above.

Article 2 Germany waives all claims against Russia which may have arisen through the application, up to the present, of the laws and measures of the Russian Socialist Federal Soviet Republic to German nationals or their private rights and the rights of the German Reich and states, and also claims which may have arisen owing to any other measures taken by the Russian Socialist Federal Soviet Republic or by their agents against German nationals or the private rights, on condition that the government of the Russian Socialist Federal Soviet Republic does not satisfy claims for compensation of a similar nature made by a third Party.

Article 3 Diplomatic and consular relations between the German Reich and the Russian Socialist Federal Soviet Republic shall be resumed immediately. The conditions for the admission of the Consuls of both Parties shall be determined by means of a special agreement.

Article 4 Both Governments have furthermore agreed that the establishment of the legal status of those nationals of the one Party, which live within the territory of the other Party, and the general regulation of mutual, commercial and economic relations, shall be effected on the principle of the most favoured nation. This principle shall, however, not apply to the privileges and facilities which the Russian Socialist Federal Soviet Republic may grant to a Soviet Republic or to any State which in the past formed part of the former Russian Empire.

Article 5 The two Governments shall co-operate in a spirit of mutual goodwill in meeting the economic needs of both countries. In the event of a fundamental settlement of the above question on an international basis, an exchange of opinions shall previously take place between the two Governments. The German Government, having lately been informed of the proposed agreements of private firms, declares its readiness to give all possible support to these arrangements and to facilitate their being carried into effect.

Article 6 Articles 1[b] and 4 of this Agreement shall come into force on the day of ratification, and the remaining provisions shall come into force immediately.

While still at Genoa, Colonel Hasse sent a note to Maltzan, dated 17 April 1922, which gave a clear indication and example of how Sondergruppe R worked as a not-disinterested intermediary between German industry (in this instance, Junkers) and Soviet Russia, and how far the Reichswehr was willing to intervene in business affairs to ensure the success of their projects:

> With reference to our verbal conversations I inform you again of the ensuing developments concerning our desires with the matter of Junkers. We place the greatest of value on the quick conclusion of a contract between the Junkers firm and the Russian government over the establishment of an airplane production plant in Russia. The Junkers metal airplane is, from the military point of view, far superior from any other type. And the launching of this type in Russia is also of the greatest interest for us. The negotiations of the past months between Junkers and the Russian government have ended up being stalled. Junkers holds out for the possibility of using their constructed airplanes for the establishment of an air-link to Russia, as a necessary prerequisite for the conclusion of a contract, as otherwise no prospect exists for the possibility of training sufficient personnel and developing the aircraft, to meet the economic needs required by a thriving business. Military reasons leads to the same requirement, and furthermore to the wish, that the destination of an air-route serviced by Junkers airplanes lies preferably in Germany. The Russian government had until now given the impression that they would give such a transportation concession to Junkers. The recently come to light contract with Aero-Union gives however a total air-transport monopoly to this company. I am not able to assess if a conscious

deception against the Junkers firm occurred, or if the Russian negotiators knew nothing of the negotiations in Berlin with Aero-Union. We come to the point now, that the Junkers firm must secure the business of a transportation-concession despite the monopoly given to Aero-Union, or at least that they somehow become sufficiently involved along with them. This can happen, based on the official German position on Aero-Union which can be arrived at by comparing and observing the fact that the establishment of an air-traffic link to Germany infringes upon certain pre-existing rights of Junkers, which they acquired by virtue of being a member of the so-called Lloydostflug. Loydostflug is an air-traffic monopoly in Lithuania, which is underwritten by that country's government. The Lithuanian government believes that it can give Aero-Union the right of flight over Lithuanian air space, which it needs, without infracting upon the rights of Lloydostflug, in order to actually maintain a Russia–Germany air-link. Junkers disputes the right of the Lithuania to make such a concession to Aero-Union. The rights-question led to debate and was resolved with great difficulty. Apparently, Lithuania now requires that Aero-Union make a stopover in Kowno [Lithuania]. Thus the legal Lloydostflug concessions are undoubtedly guaranteed. It will therefore not be difficult to induce Aero-Union, in order to procure the required consent of Lloydostflug to allow the infringement upon their concession for the stopover, to deal with the wishes of Junkers. In Berlin I had a conversation with Mr Fiedt of the Reichsverkehrsministerium, in which I offered these same explanations of the situation.[22]

In essence, Sondergruppe R made it possible for Junkers to blackmail Aero-Union, in order to be certain of Junker's willingness to establish a factory with military uses, in Russia.

From the moment of Rapallo's signing, suspicions immediately existed that secret clauses were in existence. The British ambassador to Berlin, Lord D'Abernon, even saw fit to offer advice on how to deal with rumours circulating in the press. On 25 April 1922, a Foreign Ministry official (Staatssekretaer Haniel) reported D'Abernon's comments to Foreign Minister Rathenau:

Lord D'Abernon gave, in a detailed meeting, the following pieces of advice, which he of course asked to be considered private and strictly confidential:

Firstly. Repeated official denials of the 22 April Daily Mail's published 5 points of an alleged German–Russian secret treaty. It would be valuable if we [Germany] could disclaim in general, that never in our negotiations with Russia were military questions touched upon. In addition, however, it is urgent that we offer a refutation of each of the five points as well. The example offered was that Point 4 (Prevention of the transit of war material) seemed probable, because in actuality Russia had, as he knew, made similar proposals to other states. [fn 1: In telegram Nr 126 of 25 April, Haniel presented Wirth with a proposal for a denial of the press report. With telegram Nr 176 of the 26 April Maltzan answered: "For presentation by the Reichsminister. Telegram dealt with yesterday's solemn explanation of the Chancellor to the local German press, that the Russo-German agreement contained no secret military or political clauses. Reichminister therefore asks that further denials be refrained."] [...] Furthermore, the ambassador felt it important that it be forcefully stated that the Russian–German Treaty was to be considered only a conclusion of the questions left open between Russia and Germany since the cancellation of the Treaty of Brest-Litovsk, and not indicative of a new overall orientation of foreign policy. In Germany and in other interested circles the impression prevailed, that we were pursuing a new policy of keeping Russia away from the Allies. Such an understanding was damaging, among other issues, for the question of reparations. I already submitted, some days earlier, virtually all of our local material in order to convince him that the conclusion of the treaty did not have the sensationalized effect of fixing a closer relationship with Russia. His final remark was: "I am afraid your delegation got stampeded." Finally, he urgently recommended the acceptance of the recommendations of the Allies concerning the conversion of the Inter-Allied Military Control Commission. It was his opinion that this would also represent a domestic political success for the German government. This would be an occasion in which the German government for once did not give in to an ultimatum, but rather met with the Allies in a voluntary contractual agreement. I also hold a quick acceptance of the recommendations to be politically advisable. Perhaps this, if reported to Lloyd George, would also influence the atmosphere."[23]

Rumours continued onwards, and on 1 May 1922, Regierungsrat Schwartz (whom Radek had earlier attempted to discredit with the accusation that he sold secret documents to the English) in Genoa sent a note (bearing a handwritten acknowledgement by Maltzan), in which he stated that informants reported that

> Chicherin directed, on Sunday 30 April, a letter to Barthou, in which he again categorically declared that the German–Russian Treaty had no secret clauses of a political or military nature. Russia did not even consider proceeding with actions against France or any other power, or even to support such actions. The contract was to be understood as being the necessary final settling of accounts of the war, and as the first agreement of a series of treaties which should form a basis for true peace. Chicherin then briefly restated Russian policy toward France and pointed out that between the two countries there were many points of contact, which until the present France had been consistently hostile, and that an alteration of this attitude was very necessary.[24]

Despite continuing rumours that more than simply Rapallo was at play between Russia and Germany, the British ambassador Lord D'Abernon continued to give Germany the benefit of the doubt, even months later. As he wrote in a lengthy, anti-Semitic summary of his thoughts to London on 10 May 1922:

> I have always considered that the signature of the Treaty of Rapallo was certainly on the part of the Germans and possibly on the part of the Russians rather a provocatory or retaliatory demonstration than the outcome of any serious belief in a policy of lasting cooperation. [...] The signature of the Russo-German Agreement has produced an extraordinary crop of documents purporting to be military conventions between Russia and Germany, contracts for sale of arms by Germany to Russia, contracts for naval reorganization in Russia by German intermediary, contracts for the development of German trade in Russia, etc. The majority of these

documents are forgeries—some are genuine. Wherever there is a chance of a lucrative commercial deal without undue political risk, German firms will be found ready to enter upon it, but I am skeptical of any wide and general compact involving officially the German Government. The attitude of the military class in Germany and of German parties connected with the military class is too violently anti-communistic to allow much prolonged cooperation. Stories of German officers in Russia have been current for the last two years, but no solid foundation has ever been discovered for them, and so far as I know, nobody has yet seen a German officer in any authoritative position in the Russian army. During the Soviet attack on Poland in 1920, no German officers were found among the thousands of Russian troops who surrendered. Similarly, large official contracts for the delivery of war material by German firms must be viewed with suspicion if they involve direct violation of Germany's obligations under the Treaty of Peace. [...] it is obvious that any German having to choose between the destruction of old armaments by the Commission of Control and a possible sale to anybody—in Russia, Turkey, Afghanistan or India—will prefer to run a certain amount of risk in the hope of gain rather than lose his property and get no compensation. [...] Apart from ordinary considerations of gain, it must be constantly remembered that in Germany there are a large number of small Jewish traders, who are specialists and experts in second-hand dealing, and who are strongly attracted by the large profits obtainable on such transactions in arms. In a certain section of their complicated mentality these classes have more than a sneaking affection for the Bolsheviks. Many of them are inclined to regard their co-religionaries at Moscow as rather fine fellows who have done something to avenge the misfortunes of the Jewish race—they consider Trotsky and the Cheka somewhat as the apostolic successors to Judith and Deborah. The conjunction of this idealistic hero-worship with the possibility of a high percentage of gain, forms an almost irresistible temptation to such as happen not to be endued with an exceptional austerity in regard to international obligations. The German Government is cognizant of the folly of allowing operations of this kind to be carried on, but its police is not very efficient—its officials are ill-paid and open to bribery—its authority not very strong. Weakness is shown in high quarters rather than ill-will and many officials outside corrupt influences are politically recalcitrant. What I have said above regarding the non-probability of prolonged and close cooperation is subject to this reserve—that the two Governments are not driven together by external forces, and by exposure to a common danger.[25]

But of course, from the perspective of the German military and Soviet administration, the "external forces" driving them together had been in existence since virtually the time of the armistice which ended the First World War.

Another important impact of the Treaty of Rapallo, so far as Seeckt was concerned, was that by drawing closer attention on the two countries, it could create a new sense of hesitancy and fear in Germany. On 17 May, Seeckt described it to Hasse:

I see it not in its material contents, but in its moral effect. It is the first, but very essential strengthening of the German presence in the world. It follows therefore, that one suspects that there is more behind it than can actually be proven. No political-military agreements exist; however the possibility of their existence is believed. Is it in our interest to destroy this weak Nimbus? It is a by now convulsive addiction, to play upon the peaceable on all occasions. That Behnke [head of the navy] and I did not conclude any military agreement *with a written signature* [emphasis added], was something we knew we believed to be sensible. To help secure a Treaty in the future, must however be our goal. I will attempt anything, to reach it [...] The means at our disposal are small. The opinion of the enemies must magnify their appearance. If we repeatedly give our enemies the impression that we are weak and isolated, they we invite them to do with us as they please.

Seeckt was right to speak of a fear of the Treaty of Rapallo. The Social Democrats were not, apparently, enthusiastic about it, as it appeared possible that this would divert support away from the trade-unions. President Ebert, as well, was not happy that negotiations had apparently been conducted between the Chancellor and Radek, before Genoa. The President's attitude towards Seeckt, as well, was strained by the events.[26]

If D'Abernon in Berlin felt that not much of anything beyond the formal terms of the Treaty was happening, other reports reaching London indicated otherwise. In May 1920, a British representative in Finland sent a report to London listing some of the names of Germans who were apparently in Russian military service. They were supposedly 1700 in total, almost all military men, and were located, among other places, in the All-Russian General Headquarters, the topographical department of the Department of the General Staff, and at Kronstadt. As well, in the Seventh Department of the Russian General Staff, "[. . .] there are several German agents who are working on behalf of Russia and collecting information about Poland, Roumania and France". The British Admiralty was of the opinion, on 9 June 1922, that

> Though considerable German personnel will doubtless find its way into Russia by small instalments, it is assumed that the German Government will avoid a breach of Article 179 of the Treaty of Versailles. As regards the immediate naval result of the employment of Germans in the Russian Navy, German influence and ideas will appear in the various fleets and produce increased efficiency. The Russia-Baltic fleet can no longer be regarded as practically non-effective, but may become the most powerful force in the Baltic, greatly to the disadvantage of Finland and the Baltic States.[27]

A 20 May 1922 report to London commented on the trip to Russia of German Admiral Hintze, former Foreign Minister and one-time visitor of Radek, to help with military collaboration. The note referred to an earlier report of 2 May 1922, with increasing accuracy of the nature that the German–Soviet relationship had now assumed:

> [Hintze's] stay here was connected with negotiations which he had been conducting and which have as their object the reestablishment of the Russian war industry with German assistance. It has been arranged that various factories of munitions of war and artillery—among them the Molotilovka and Zlatoust Works—will be reorganised with German help. Two German aeroplane factories will also come under the arrangement. The output of the factories will, according to my information, be shared between the two countries. Weekly meetings are being held at the Kremlin under

the presidency of Trotsky to examine various projects arising in connection with the realization of this plan of operations.[28]

The rumours of Russo-German military cooperation thus continued, in reports filtering back to London:

> The truth is probably to be found halfway between the two extremes of a formal written agreement and no understanding at all, and that, while no definite convention has in fact been signed, the conversations and tacit arrangements between the Representatives of the German and the Representatives of the Soviet Governments did more than relate merely to the subject matter of the Treaty of Rapallo. [...] [I]t is difficult to resist the conclusion that all the evidence points to the non-existence of a formal document on the subject but rather to the fact that the new-born understanding between Germany and Russia implies that the former country will do all in its power to assist the latter, even in military matters, in the hope that it may somehow by these means improve its own position.[29]

As an example of what was appearing in the press, the *Daily Telegraph*, which had claimed at the time of Rapallo that a 5-point military convention had been signed between the Soviet Union and Germany, changed its story somewhat (like the British Foreign Office, towards a more accurate direction), in May 1922:

> [...] No signed document exists called the Russo-German military convention. [...] But there exists in Germany a powerful group of unemployed military leaders, allied to certain industrial interests which takes great interest in the military possibility of an agreement with Soviet Russia. They are in contact with the governing body of the Red army, and there is not the slightest doubt that co-operation has been fully discussed. It is known that the advances have come mostly from the Red side, where a thirst for Napoleonic adventure exists among the leaders produced by the Revolution. They dream about the Red troops repeating the exploits of the Russian troops of Alexander I in 1814: of entering Germany, of crossing the Rhine, and triumphantly entering Paris. The German militarists, in the despair of defeat, lend a willing

ear to Soviet Blandishments. The song of Moscow is sweet. By the Versailles Treaty Germany is deprived of the right to produce war material in sufficient quantities and of modern quality. But there is Russia, where munitions can be produced and stored, where fighting planes can be built and kept until the day of revenge. And there is the great mass of the Red army—splendid material in the hands of German experts. What Germany must not do, Russia, these German militarists think, will do for her. A Russo-German military alliance means the crushing of Poland some day and a secure rear in a future war with France. German interest in such plans, which all see at least ten years ahead, is stimulated by the dangerous fact that to-day the Red army and the Russian military industry are already under strong German influence. There are at least 400 officers, 5,000 NCO's and men, and more than 1,000 German munition and armaments experts in Russia. [...][30]

The German representation in London, in return, wrote (on 17 May 1922) that "As the author of the article in question reported, the British government seem to have come into the property of a report from Riga, which spoke of the migration of numerous skilled munitions-worker from Germany to Russia." The German embassy directly asked the correspondent to show his evidence for the accusations made in the article, claiming that much more was said in it than could justifiably be claimed. The German embassy believed that the information referred to by the article was furnished by British intelligence.[31]

The press in France was also reporting in a similar manner, to the concern of the German Foreign Office. In a report of 28 June 1922, an official in their embassy in Paris informed Berlin that the *Echo National* of 26 June "brings forth new information concerning a military treaty between Germany and Russia, and emphasized especially that the German army would reorganise the Russian fleet".[32]

On 26 May 1922, Colonel Hasse of Sondergruppe R inquired of Krestinsky "if the plans of the Soviet government and their relations with the special groups had been taken care of or not".[33] Yoffe, reporting to the Executive of the Central Committee at the start of June 1922, stated that in Berlin the Germans were still undecided whether or not they should sign the German-Russian treaty, but they decided to do so in Genoa in view of the attitude of the great powers. [...] the Treaty of between Russia and Germany is nothing further than a means to overcome the present difficulties and to avoid the danger of a war.

The implication was clear that the overall agreement between the two states amounted to more than simply the exchange of diplomatic recognition.[34]

By mid-summer, the United States' representative in Berlin was also being offered information about the Soviets, and their relations with Germany. In a report from the German Ministry of Public Order of 26 June, it was noted that:

A reliable source, with good relations to the Entente circles, reports, that he was told by the Intelligence Secretary of the American Legation in Berlin, Hamory, that that some days ago two Russians between the ages of 28 and 30 years old had offered information on the Soviet representative in Berlin. They went on to say that they were in the position to procure material on German–Soviet relations. Hamory noted it, and rejected the offer, since the American legation does not want to negotiate with Russian citizens about political affairs. The American government, he interjected here, was ambivalent as to what the German and Russian governments agree to with eachother, only Germany is to see that as soon as they are on their feet again the possibility exists that they will be popular with America and England. He believes certainly in an international loan for Germany as soon as its domestic policy is to some extent brought into order. In America one is of the option that in order for the health of Germany's finances to improve, the Rhineland must by 1923 at the latest be evacuated by inter-allied troops. An understanding between Germany and France is perfectly impossible, in his opinion, and therefore Germany must absolutely follow a large sea power. The American people are not averse to working with Germany, as soon as they see that Germany is seriously determined to bring order to its situation, and to take part in the reconstruction of Europe.[35]

At the end of May 1922, the German government finally appeared to have persuaded the Reparations Commission that the collapse of the mark was genuine and beyond its control, and that Germany was simply unable to continue to pay: despite French protests, the Commission granted Germany a moratorium of six months. A few weeks later, on 16 June, in response to direct pressure from the Allies, Germany formally accepted the cessation of eastern Upper Silesia. In the agreements leading to this decision, the economic interests of both Germany and Poland were protected, as well as the rights of minorities, based on the principle of reciprocity of treatment.

Communication between the German military and the ministry of foreign affairs was never on a particularly even level, even so late after Rapallo as 14 July 1922. In a response to a Foreign Office inquiry from earlier that month, the Reichswehrministerium stated that claims made concerning

> the activity of German officers in the Russian army and/or in the Russian general staff are based on tendentious invention. No active German officer is in any position of the Soviet army. Statements concerning the activity of former German officers in the Russian army have always proven wrong. News concerning German officers' participation in the military service of the Soviet-army appeared during the Polish–Russian war, and during the "Wrangel-struggle" of 1920 in the French, Polish, and francophile-Russian émigré press (for example, the "Obschtscheje Delo" of December 1920). Verification of the listed names proved, each time, the falsehood of the claims. Likewise, the Soviet government has formally denied the presence of German officers in Russian service [...] As evidence, the press often mentions the participation of a German officer named Bluecher in a leading position of the Soviet army [fn: meaning, the Soviet-Russian army commander W.K. Bluecher, which, it is erroneously claimed, is not a pseudonym]. This concerns the well-known communist Medwedjew (a metal-worker), who adopted the pseudonym Bluecher. [The German army's] position is that no Prussian officer is in the service of the Bolsheviks.[36]

On 17 July 1922, the British embassy in Paris wrote to London, concerning

German military and naval personnel believed to be in the employ of the Soviet Government and a report from the A[llied] M[ilitary] C[ommittee of] V[ersailles] on the export of war material by ex-enemy Powers [...] General Desticker, representing Marshal Foch, read a report from General Nollet [...] on the general question of military control in Germany. It was stated that General Nollet was of opinion that the present crisis in Berlin would render any representations now fruitless and that it would be better to wait for some three or four weeks. These two questions were therefore adjourned on the understanding that they would be embodied in the general representations which will eventually be addressed to the German Government.[37]

He followed this a few days later (24 July), by writing that

[...] I would like to avail myself of this opportunity to obtain your Lordship's views with regard to the action I am to take with regard to the enforcement of the military clauses of the Treaty of Versailles, which forbid the export of war material from Germany (article 170) and the employment of German officers by foreign Governments (article 179). In the War Office letter of the 13th June, the first of these questions appears in the category of outstanding questions "the complete execution of which the Army Council considers desirable, but which are actually of secondary importance only". The second of them appears in the category of questions "the complete execution of which is demanded by the French Government, but which the Army Council considers of no real importance". [...] I should be glad to know whether I am now to withdraw definitely these two questions from the agenda of the conference [of Ambassadors], on the ground that His Majesty's Government no longer consider them to be of sufficient importance to be taken up with the German Government in connection with the general representations which are to be made to them on the lines indicated in Lordship's despatch under reply.[38]

Bafour's reply on 1 August 1922, stated, among other things, that "[...] I do not consider it desirable that any further action should be taken [...] pending a definite decision of the [other] matters now under discussion"—meaning, general disarmament, and reorganization of the German police.[39]

The overall issue of reparations, and the problems they caused, were addressed in the British debt and reparations proposals made to the United States, on 1 August 1922. In it, the British attempted to link the two issues, with the proposal that a general settlement on war-debts and reparations be reached with America, in return for the abandonment of individual claims against individual states. The American government refused, arguing that debts and reparations were separate issues which should not be mixed.

In the aftermath of Rapallo, while rumours were rife in the capitals of Europe, the one main advantage gained for the supporters of a secret military relationship in Berlin and Moscow was that the activities could now more easily be camouflaged under the umbrella of normal diplomatic and economic relations. This would be possible if there was common agreement within each camp on the ability to conduct negotiations in this manner. From the Soviet side, there was no debate: secret and open diplomacy had been combined, and would continue to be combined, as a matter of course. But on the German side, the issue was less clear.

The German military viewed the civilian leadership and administration of the country as being in chaos and under the control of socialists, since the final days of the First World War. Since the start of the Weimar Republic, the German army's loyalty to the government was grudging at best. And throughout the evolution of the relationship with Soviet Russia, Seeckt saw no reason to trust or include the German Foreign Office in any of his calculations—Sondergruppe R was, in effect, a parallel, military foreign office department for relations with Russia. The decision to normalize relations through the Treaty of Rapallo was, in some ways, welcomed by the army, but not if it required surrendering control of the contacts and negotiations which had been begun three years earlier. Thus, the potential for conflict with the German Foreign Office existed, should the Foreign Office attempt to wrest control of the process from the Army.

In Brockdorff-Rantzau, Seeckt had a nemesis. The former foreign minister was not an individual who could be cowed or easily manipulated, and who was possessed with a sense of moral righteousness shared by few. When Brockdorff-Rantzau was proposed as the first official post-Rapallo Ambassador to Soviet Russia, it marked a crisis for the German army, over the future of the Russian relationship. In his attempt to prevent Brockdorff-Rantzau's appointment, Seeckt resorted to one of the most time-honoured traditions of bureaucratic infighting—character assassination. By August 1922, the rupture between the German Defence Ministry and Foreign Office was finally clear and in the open. Seeckt had protested vigorously to Chancellor Wirth against the appointment of Brockdorff-Rantzau to the position of German ambassador to Soviet Russia, and the latter learned that the ostensible grounds were that he was of "unpatriotic" character, given his behaviour as head of the German peace delegation at Versailles, in May 1919. Given that Brockdorff-Rantzau was the one who refused to sign the peace and returned to Berlin with Allied threats of war rather than a broken sense of his own honour, the accusation stung and outraged him.[40]

Brockdorff-Rantzau wrote an Aufzeichnung, or statement of record, on 1 August 1922, offering a direct insight into the intergovernmental manner in which the issue was dealt with, in Germany. He noted, for posterity, the conversation he had with the Chancellor, in which Brockdorff had informed Wirth that he would

> [...] regard any military agreements with the Russians as being extremely dangerous; we would make an internally weak Germany the battleground for the arguments between the East and the West. The task of the German Ambassador in Moscow can only consist, in my opinion, of restraining the Russians, after the failure of negotiations in the Hague, from pursuing the last policy of bankrupt governments—war; we should under no circumstances allow ourselves to be pulled into any trade; I would not take responsibility for the way in which Wirth dealt with the question, and asked whether the Reich President was informed of his plans. Wirth answered this in the negative, by noting the political responsibility which it carried; the question of constitutional responsibilities had already brought sharp differences between him and Mr. Ebert. I thereupon explained repeatedly, that Ambassadors, as representatives of the German people, and appointed by the Reich President, could not and would not conduct policies about which the Reich President is not informed. I would like to speak Mr. Ebert nevertheless about the affair. Wirth again urgently asked me not to do this. I continued, reminding him, as Wirth

> himself had agreed to earlier, that for my assumption of the position in Moscow [I had] placed as a condition [...] a program between the Reich President, the Reich Chancellor, and myself. This was a condition I could not abandon; if he, the Reich Chancellor, wanted with the military to take further responsibility, then that was his affair; I could not and would not as Ambassador burden myself with such things.

More tellingly, his statement then gave a clear indication of the fact that Brockdorff-Rantzau had no idea that the military had already developed a relationship with Soviet Russia years earlier:

> If the Treaty of Rapallo was to be extended politically with outside arrangements, then it would nevertheless be appropriate to have the Russians first send us suggestions; under no circumstances should the military know something of it; we could hear what the Russians really wanted, while at no point binding us in the present moment, particularly as the danger exists that the Russians would be likely to have indiscretions to the benefit of the Entente. I would have wanted to conclude a Rights Treaty, and as minister explained, that if a Rights Treaty was not signed, the seed of the revenge was already sown. With Versailles, the Entente dictated a forced-peace to us; I was thus always consistent as a politician, that I would therefore today be an apostle of revenge. [...] My point of view is [...] that haste would be criminal. Wirth asked again, that the Reich President not be informed and to leave matters as they were with reference to his relations with the military, thus attaching importance to maintaining these, because the military circles were ones which the President, in the rather tight current conditions, did not normally come into contact with. I noted that I understood this consideration, but advised however that the greatest of caution be exercised. In all other respects I did not leave a doubt to the Chancellor that I was not determined to support his policies through.[41]

Brockdorff-Rantzau followed this up a few days later (on 3 August 1922) with a cutting assessment of precisely why Chancellor Wirth's siding with the army was, in his view, so unwise, and of the dangers which there lay for Germany.[42]

For more than a month, the conflict between Seeckt and Brockdorff-Rantzau raged on. At first, Brockdorff-Rantzau believed that it was a matter of his honour being unjustly besmirched, and sought to clarify the record and defend his reputation. On 15 August 1922, in "Promemoria", he stated for the historical record (again) his version of the roots of the conflict with Seeckt (i.e. Versailles) surrounding his appointment to Moscow.[43]

On 26 August 1922, Brockdorff-Rantzau wrote that his suspicions of Seeckt had even been confirmed by a fellow military officer, and had learned that Seeckt had tried to open contacts with Trotsky already:

> [...] Captain Lohmann, quite uncommonly, spoke adversely the day before yesterday in the strictest confidence about Seeckt. Lohmann, who made an excellent impression upon me, to my direct question explained to me that he considered Seeckt as a character to be under the standing of Hintze and politically even more dangerous. Seeckt as well is extraordinarily jealous and has through him (Lohmann) obtained positive results in direct negotiations with Trotsky, already one year ago; it is in the last while in Russia that he [Lohmann] has met with distrust and passive resistance in all official places in Russia. This attitude of the Russian government was certainly due to Seeckt's agents.

Brockdorff-Rantzau's reaction was in the direction which was most feared by Seeckt:

> With this state of affairs I decided to go myself undersecretary of state Simons [...] I left no doubt [...] that I only would accept the post in Moscow, if I were absolutely and truly informed of everything which had been negotiated by the military with the Russians without the knowledge of our diplomatic mission.

But in response to his attempt to discern if the earlier conversations with Wirth had been passed along to the minister of foreign affairs, he was surprised to find out that the Chancellor had simply kept silent:

> [...] to my astonishment, he spoke of my "differences" with Seeckt. Simons was not informed about it. I communicated the

facts briefly to him and added, I naturally could not take the post, if someone like Seeckt, who had an extensive organization in Russia for years, was openly in working against me. I did not mention Seeckt's letter to Wirth. Simons answered very deliberately, that he shared my view completely; as far as he knew, Wirth was "cozy with Seeckt, but the customs of the Center do not correspondingly admit it that openly." I continued, that I must have clarity under all circumstances, and noted that it was literally more than a simple measure of confidence for me, in order to be able to take up my work effectively. Simons agreed with me and explained that he would speak with Wirth in the manner I wished. I asked him further, to have Seeckt informed by the Chancellor, informally but without any doubt, that I wanted to have clarity and put an absolute value on it, and to again explain to the chancellor my program in detail. Simons assured this readily and promised, to inform me soonest, as to when the Reichskanzler could.[44]

Thus, Brockdorff-Rantzau placed an ultimatum upon the outcome of the dispute. The closest which he was willing to go in finding a compromise, he wrote on 27 August, was to

> [...] treat what has happened to now in Russia officially and unofficially as behind closed curtains, to treat as facts. Since I did not participate, I am neither politically nor personally responsible for the agreements which were made before my assumption of office in Moscow. That means however by no means that I approve of these agreements identify with them or their consequences. I assume for me, rather, the right and necessity of, based on my personal observations in Moscow, making suggestions to modify the past agreement. With particular concern for the military questions [...] I would endorse for this price that large economic concessions be made [... but] I would absolutely reject any participation of the German government—the availability of official funds for military purposes. Require the Russians to provide the money for such purposes, and if we made sure that the guarantee was conveniently also in German interests, then the necessary amounts could be possibly supplied by unofficial channels to the Russians.[45]

In making his final points, Brockdorff-Rantzau was clear that he was not opposed *per se* to an unofficial and secret diplomacy—the point was simply that he did not trust General Seeckt and the army to be the ones to conduct it.

In early September 1922, Brockdorff-Rantzau finally, from his own sources, was able to piece together at least some of what had been going on between the German army and the Soviets, earlier. He wrote to the Minister of Foreign Affairs in Berlin with his discoveries:

> [...] the military had as early as 1920 entered into direct negotiations with Trotzky. At the end of 1920 Niedermayer was sent to Trotzky, and the end of 1920 saw discussions between Seeckt, Niedermayer and Kopp; later, according to my information, negotiations with Krupp took place. What role Admiral von Hintze played, is not known to me, likewise the task of Captain Fischer. For the building of airplanes and the establishment of armament factories in the Urals, amounts to the millions (100 or more) from the black fund (schwartz Fund) of the army command were placed at the disposal of the Russians.

Brockdorff-Rantzau was horrified both for the implications regarding public finance and for the potential for disaster should other countries find out. As important, from his perspective, was the belief that the Soviets (thanks to the bumbling efforts of Niedermayer) no longer wished to have any contact with Sondergruppe R:

> From where does this black fund come? Lloyd George knows of a secret letter of Niedermayer, which was intercepted. Also, the navy negotiated with Trotzky. The negotiations of the army administration and the navy disturbed themselves mutually. [...] Are you, Excellency, aware of these events? Were you informed of the negotiations with Trotsky and did you approve of the steps taken by the military. Is the Reich President informed? Is Cabinet informed? At the very least, was the Vice-Chancellor and the Reich Defence Minister? I find this procedure tremendously risky. Does your Excellency hold the Russians as being sufficient trustworthy for such steps? How does your Excellency think I can practically work, when I go to Moscow? Now I understand, why protest was raised against my appointment, from the military side. The gentlemen

know, that I carry the responsibility in Moscow, should their arbitrary actions be allowed. The Entente see in me that German politician who rejected the Diktat most sharply and fought against Versailles, and expect from me that I prepare revenge.[46]

By 14 September 1922, Brockdorff-Rantzau appeared to be under the impression that he at least had won his point with the Russians, and that Niedermayer and the rest of Sondergruppe R had overstayed their welcome in Moscow:

> Today I received Mr Waurick [Bernhard Waurick, of the German embassy]; he told me that he had spoken with Mr Chicherin in detail yesterday; this affects and has an impact on the activity our military in Russia; one does not wish to directly negotiate with these gentlemen any longer; in particular Niedermayer, made non fulfillable and impossible promises. (In Brockdorff Rantzau's statement of 5 Octobers (6812/E 517 927–28), it is written, among other things, that "Waurick reports to me today, Colonel Hasse of the Reich defence ministry told him, that he had a conversation with Chicherin, in the course of which Chicherin explained that the Soviet government, finally, rejects any direct communication with emissaries of the German military in the future. Under no circumstances does he wish to see Mr Niedermayer in Russia again; he promised too much and delivered nothing. Hasse had suggested to Chicherin that the Russian government might wish to reject me. Chicherin rejected this uncouth and impudent imposition.") Waurick maintained, that one is mainly annoyed in Moscow that confidence is placed in offices [i.e. the German army] which could be tempted to allow imprudent reports. Waurick has communicated Chicherin's statements to Major Schunke (or Tschunke?) of the local Wehrministerium and that this was included in a request letter sent to Seeckt; in the letter Schunke announces the Waurick's report and advises the general not to proceed in the future in working on his own in Russia, separately from the Foreign Office (with reference to the fact that it might give new food to the continual rumours concerning secret German-Russian military agreement [...] the exchange of military and naval attaches or experts should also be politely declined). Waurick told me furthermore, he personally received in the meantime an actual protest

from General Seeckt against my current appointment was sent to the Reich Chancellor. [. . .] The Reich Chancellor requested Seeckt to justify his protest.[47]

Although the German Foreign Ministry was clearly involved in the commercial negotiations of Junkers with the Soviets, Seeckt claimed, in his response to Brockdorff-Rantzau's Promemoria, that the conduct of negotiations and the future contacts were better off being directly conducted between the two armies, in order to limit political liabilities should embarrassing revelations come to public light. The army, in other words, was fulfilling its natural role in protecting the government and state against hostile repercussions. This was part of the reason for establishing Sondergruppe R and its Zentrale Moskau in the first place. According to Hilger, the government had, as a consequence of this line of reasoning, "lost not only control over German-Soviet military collaboration, but seems to have had only the sketchiest knowledge of the activities and deals of von Seeckt and his officers".[48]

Seeckt's attacks against Brockdorff-Rantzau, and consequently his attempt to maintain control over the negotiations with the Russians, continued unabated, to the extent that the foreign minister himself felt he had to intervene, in mid-October 1922, to take up the defence of Brockdorff-Rantzau; Simons further made a plea for peace to the army, directly to the Chancellor:

> I have myself as Minister time and time again commented upon the Russian question. You know that for me, this is the central question of Germany's future. Therefore I request that you permit me to attempt to provide a solution. I actively welcomed the appointment of the Count Brockdorff-Rantzau as the Ambassador in Moscow. [. . .] It is good that the most capable German diplomat be at the seat of the Soviet Government. And I still found, much to my surprise upon my return from Argentina to Berlin, and learned from a reliable source of the difficulties which his appointment is having, due to a protest of the Army command. The protest is based on the fact that Count Brockdorff-Rantzau personally lacks the necessary patriotic conviction, as was demonstrated by the results of the negotiations in Versailles. It is difficult for me to believe in the correctness of this report. I know the details of

Versailles better than possibly any other colleague of the Count, and I can assure that his patriotic attitude was if anything too rough rather than too soft. [...] [The current crisis between the two men would be] a misfortune for Germany, should it persist. [...] The mere fact of the dispute presents a grave danger for our policies, because if the Allies learned of them, they could exploit the distrust and lead to the most unwanted of conclusions. The continued resistance by the army command against the activity of the now-appointed Ambassador would limit not only his effectiveness, but could lead to unpredictable entangling of our overall policies. [...] Our representative in Moscow has a right to know, that he has not only the Reich Chancellor, but the entire office behind him. Otherwise the Fatherland, which we all serve, could come to ruin.[49]

From the Soviet side at the same time, the situation was simpler, and clearer. A report written by Radek in September 1922, entitled "From Brest-Litovsk to Genoa", stated that the inspiration behind everything to that point was to prevent the encirclement of the Soviet experiment by the imperialist powers. Further, Germany, despite its state, still had many things which were not a chimera, and which had to be considered: wealth, experience, organization, a desire to rule the world.[50]

Internationally, the situation was getting more difficult for Germany, but easier for Russia. During the London Conference of early 7–14 August 1922, the wisdom of the German turn to Russia appeared to be confirmed by France's increasingly assertive demands for expropriations from German mines in the Ruhr, and the appropriation of German property and capital throughout the left bank of the Rhine. The British disagreed with the French that such a course of action was the best way to entice cooperation from Germany, and rejected the demands. The French, in turn, refused the British proposal to grant a moratorium on reparations payments. Britain continued its approach of attempting to befriend rather than antagonize the outsider states of Europe; the Anglo-Russian Commercial treaty was signed a few weeks after the dispute with France, on 10 September; this was an attempt to open and thus normalize trade relations, despite the continued refusal of Russia to recognize foreign loans. The French response to the troubles in the Ruhr was to sign a 10-year military convention with Poland, on 13 September; a clear indication that they viewed German attempts to revise Versailles as bearing the potential for future military conflict. Germany would remain the main centre of international conflict after October, as on the 22nd of that month, Japan finally withdrew from Siberia, thus ending their participation in the Russian Civil War, and leaving the Soviets in control of the full extent of their territory.

A lengthy Soviet Foreign Office memorandum, dated 17 September 1922, offered a commentary and assessment of the overall relationship with Germany, and indicated that despite the existence of agreements, there were still grounds for dissatisfaction. The Soviets were apparently not very happy with the German interpretations of the accords made thus far, and referred specifically to a need for even closer military, diplomatic, and consultative relations than the Germans were apparently willing to embark upon.[51] Appended to the report was an undated French version of Rapallo, with a note written in English stating that Germany would undertake to tear up treaty if the others at Genoa gave Germany the same deal as the Russians did.[52]

Ultimately, in the face of a determined ambassador in Moscow who finally possessed the support of his minister, and who wielded the threat of going directly to the President for resolution of the question, the Chancellor had no choice but to apparently concede that the military contacts would henceforth fall under more concrete civilian control. In November 1922, Chancellor Wirth promised Brockdorff-Rantzau that the generals would be made to cooperate. The impact of this was not as decisive as Brockdorff-Rantzau might have hoped. The decision was simply made, at the end of the year, that all future negotiations with the Soviets should occur in Berlin—thus bypassing not only Niedermayer and the rest of Sondergruppe R's Zentrale Moskau, but Brockdorff-Rantzau and the German embassy as well. However, it was not an entirely lost cause either. When Chicherin, in the summer of 1923, sent Arkady Rosengolts to Berlin to continue and expand direct negotiations with the German cabinet, Brockdorff-Rantzau won a tactical victory, with the decision that Germany's execution of its agreements in Russia would be conducted through the embassy in Moscow, and not by agents operating independently of it. Thus, the deals were made in Berlin, but were carried out with at least some input of the Foreign Office.

Given the extent and nature of the later agreements, this served to extend the complicity for the activities to all reaches of the German government—both the military and civilian/foreign office leadership.[53]

By the end of the year, the details of the relationship between Germany and Russia were still effectively secret from others in Europe. In August 1922, D'Abernon again dismissed reports of Trotsky's involvement with Germans,[54] and in writing to London at the end of November, it was clear that D'Abernon had learned of nothing new to change his previous opinion:

> It is now abundantly evident that the Rapallo Treaty was really signed by German representatives in a moment of panic, and not as the result of a deliberate policy.[55]

He was simply wrong.

7
Conclusion

Within the history of the inter-war years, the Soviet–German relationship stands out as being decisive not only for Europe, but for the world. Well before Molotov and Ribbentrop had heard of each other, the German and Soviet armies had established a functional working relationship which would yield the tools later used in the Second World War. Safe from the prying eyes of the Allies, joint installations in Soviet Russia allowed for the German military air industry to develop and train pilots; armoured vehicle facilities at Kazan allowed for tactics and technology to improve from the rudimentary levels of the First World War to what would later be called Blitzkrieg; while in Berlin, the military expertise of the German War Academy polished many minds of officers of the Red Army, before Stalin later killed thousands in the Great Purges. The range of activities pursued by the two sides was restrained almost solely by available funds. Although there is no case to be made that the ultimate results in the Second World War were *intended* by the architects of the initial relationship, the historical fact remains that it had an impact on the later events and technologies.

Although much literature, both before the opening of the Soviet archives and after, has been devoted to the details of the concrete steps taken after the Treaty of Rapallo was signed in April 1922, little attention has been given to painting the picture of how this relationship came to be in the first place, rounding out the available access to archival material with a general context of the time, in a manner of use to specialists and relatively informed general readers.

The German army's willingness to deal with Bolsheviks went back at least to the decision to allow Lenin and his entourage safe conduct through Germany, to destabilize Tsarist Russia during the First World War. A short while after attaining power in the October Revolution, the Bolshevik leadership opened negotiations to end Russia's participation in the conflict, and it was here that Radek, as one of the participants in the negotiations alongside Trotsky, became known to the German military leadership. It was Radek's position and connections to the Soviet leadership which proved an irresistible lure to General Seeckt in early 1919, when Radek was arrested based on falsified evidence but probable guilt in Berlin.

Germany, whose army was hailed to be unvanquished in the field because the First World War was not brought directly home by the Allies, found in Soviet Russia a partner with whom it could attempt to avoid the restrictions on its military placed by a peace it never truly accepted. Soviet Russia, in the midst of armed struggle for survival against domestic and foreign foes, was only too happy to attempt to glean whatever advantage it could from the Entente-German split within the ranks of the capitalist states of Europe. Neither side was blind about the true intentions and aims of the other—the German military demonstrated its opinion of Bolshevism with brutality when called upon to calm the domestic scene, and the Soviets continued to try to negotiate as a state while still exporting the ideology of Revolution through the Comintern for as long as it could.

The German military, viewing itself as the defender of the German people in a chaotic post-war world, clearly placed itself above the weak civilian controls of the Weimar Republic. Under General Seeckt, it continued its traditional habit of considering military affairs and foreign policy to be two sides of one coin. The main difference in the post-war years was that this had to be done carefully and in secret, not only from the Entente, but from other branches of the German government as well.

The German army showed presence of mind and foresight, given the revolutionary situation in the country as a whole, to make the first attempts at opening a wire to the Soviets at the start of 1919, using Enver Pasha as a conduit. Whether this was amoral or immoral may be open to debate, but the speed with which they decided to act and take advantage of Radek's imprisonment was impressive: despite indications of the distinct possibility that a Wilsonian peace might not be the one which would be presented, the Allies were nonetheless still haggling among themselves at the time of the first attempts to reach the Soviets, who in turn were working to bring about a revolution in Germany. Though many sectors of German opinion may have been shocked and dismayed at the "un-Wilsonian" outcome of the Paris Peace Conference, the German army had clearly decided to brace itself for the worst, and had begun to make contingency plans accordingly.

The contacts took a while before yielding increasingly tangible results. This was the result of both the physical difficulties involved in trying to open a line of communication (as Enver Pasha's adventures demonstrated), as well as the incredible sways and fluxes in the domestic and foreign political scenes for both Germany and Russia in 1919 and 1920. For Russia, Civil War (with the Whites, but also involving the Allied powers) combined with conflicts with both its Baltic neighbours and, more critically, Poland. Trotsky was so involved in directing the military needs of the fledgling Soviet state that he played no direct role in the evolution of the relationship with his counterparts in Berlin. Although the channels were encouraged at the start by his ally Radek, at best he was kept informed of the process through Victor Kopp for most of these years, a matter of note given that the contacts were being explored by the Reichswehr and the importance from the Soviet side of maintaining the military as well as civilian industrial interest of the German firms involved. Neither did Lenin play a significant role; in terms of early Soviet decision-making, it is clear that for the most part, the matters from the Russia end were led by Chicherin and his assistants. While in Germany the army negotiated while the Foreign Ministry was kept in the background, the opposite was the case in Soviet Russia. The main split in the Soviet camp came with trying to tame the impact of the revolutionary fervour of the Comintern. The debate and ultimate decision was a bureaucratic precursor to the debate over "Socialism in One Country", in that the pragmatic needs of strengthening the state were given precedence over ideological objectives of global revolution.

The German Foreign Office was slow to gain knowledge of what Seeckt's men were doing in Russia, and proved powerless to do anything about it until after full diplomatic relations were established between the two states. Even then, the victory was at best hollow, as the negotiations for how best to secretly violate the peace terms of the war were simply transferred to Berlin, leaving the Foreign Office once again somewhat out of the picture. Brockdorff-Rantzau may have won an important battle (and at the very least salvaged his reputation from a major attack on his patriotism), but lost the greater bureaucratic war. Ultimately, what played out between the German army and foreign ministry was a conflict of means rather than ends; Brockdorff-Rantzau made his position clear in Paris in May 1919. This was not a conflict between "good" and "bad" Germans; it was simply a question of how best to survive and preserve the strengths of the German state until the time came when the structure imposed by Versailles could be undermined without disasterous consequences from abroad. This was demonstrated by the fact that Gustav Stresemann (briefly Chancellor, and Foreign Minister until his death in 1929), who would be hailed as the German with whom a peaceful Europe could be constructed, at the same time encouraged and allowed the military cooperation with the Soviets blossom to truly significant levels in the post-Rapallo years.

The Entente powers themselves, while suspicious from an early date, were unable to confirm the ongoing process enough to do anything about it. The French did not appear to know more than general trends and rumours, while the British seemed consistently better informed of what was likely transpiring, despite the often wilder tales which accompanied the occasionally accurate reports. Within their sources of information, however, an important caveat needs to be noted: the man closest to the centre of German decision-making, Ambassador D'Abernon in Berlin, was blinded by his proximity and reliance upon the German Foreign Office for information. In a manner which mirrored the later experiences of Neville Henderson during the critical years leading to the Second World War, the British diplomatic representation in Berlin could not see the forest for the trees. Until the end of 1922 at least, D'Abernon was still convinced that nothing too unusual was afoot, and his influence upon British policy towards the Continent given this is one aspect of the history which needs further exploration.

Ultimately, well before the Treaty of Rapallo provided the necessary diplomatic camouflage which would allow for the German–Soviet relationship to truly take off, the momentum of the early contacts ensured its success. The two pariah states of the First World War had indeed, as the Italian Prime Minister Nitti feared, made common cause against the West, with implications to be felt in the decades to come.

Notes

1 Introduction

1. DBFP. I/7/Doc. 22.
2. ADAP. Serie A, Band IV, Nr. 255.
3. ADAP. Serie A, Band I, Nr. 18.
4. See Klemperer.
5. Hilger, p. 194.
6. Hilger, pp. 198–199.
7. The most thorough of these is Zeidler, but see also Gorlov's 1990 article, "Soviet-German Military Cooperation, 1920–1930", and Nekrich.
8. Carsten, pp. 135–136. Cites Tschunke to Rabenau, 13 February 1939.
9. The general contextual information and narrative can be found in many sources. Readers are referred to the following, for more on the inter-war years: Marks, *Illusion* (the best introduction to the topic, with a useful bibliography); Marks, *Ebbing*; Macmillan; and Gatzke, *European*.
10. In some instances, archival findings noted in this study have been cited as well in other studies. In cases where the earlier work provided the direction to the archival material, both the archival reference and the other author were cited: thus, "AVPRF. 028/1/6/76; Linke, p. 60" refers the reader to a point drawn from a specific file at the Russian foreign ministry archives in Moscow, which had been previously cited by Linke. Where the information was arrived at independently, only the archival reference was cited.
11. As well, the published documentary collections on foreign policy for Germany, France, Great Britain, the United States, and the Soviet Union were consulted. Of these, by far the most useful were the German and the British collections. The Soviet-era collection was incomplete, obsolete, and superfluous when compared to what was available in the Russian archives, and so the Russian archival citations were used instead. The American collection was little of direct use, with the exception of material on the Paris Peace Conference itself; the *Documents diplomatiques français* contained a few references to the relationship, but given the ties with Poland, there was surprisingly little more. Where material from the German archives also appeared in the *Akten zur deutschen auswärtigen Politik*, the published citation was generally used. The *Documents on British Foreign Policy* provided a plethora of examples of the rumours reaching London concerning the Germans and the Russians.

2 Historical Background: End of War and Start of "Peace"

1. On the domestic scene in Russia during the First World War, see Gatrell.
2. On Wilson and the Fourteen Points, see Czernin.
3. For Soviet policy at this time, see Debo, *Revolution*.
4. See Baumgart, *Von Brest-Litovsk*.
5. On the Civil War, see Mawdsley.
6. Of the 6 billion, Russia had sent a shipment of 260 million marks in gold roubles before the 11 November 1918 armistice put a halt to future shipments; the Russian gold was subsequently confiscated by the Allies, and placed in the Bank of France for safe keeping. For this and other details on the transfer of gold from Russia to Germany, see Smele, "White Gold".
7. For more details on what follows on Germany during the chaotic early months, see Eyck; Mommsen; and Kolb.
8. On Eisner, see Grau.
9. For the details of the precise impact of the naval blockade of Germany, see Vincent.
10. For this and the following quotes from the German leaders of the time, see Pinson, pp. 350 ff.
11. On the reparations issue, see Weill-Raynal; and Schuker.
12. On Poland as well as details on the problems in central and eastern Europe, see Cienciala and Komarnicki; Lundgreen-Nielsen Jan Karski; Olivova; Wandycz; and Rothschild.
13. Philip Gibbs, article reproduced in Horne, vol. VI.
14. The most complete and recent biography of Radek is by Fayet.
15. Karl Radek, "Noyabr" *Krasnaya Nov* October 1926, pp. 139–175. A lengthy (and the most significant) portion of this article was translated by E. H. Carr in the early 1950s. Although the full original (i.e. Russian-language) article was used for this study, unless otherwise noted the English translations which I offer are from the previously published (and excellently translated) version: E. H. Carr, "From Soviet Publications: Radek's 'Political Salon' in Berlin 1919". Reprint of extracts from this article is with the kind permission of Taylor and Francis Journals, http://www.tandf.co.uk.
16. See Broué.
17. See Broué; and Waldman.
18. On the activities of the Freikorps, see Koch; and Thoms.
19. On the Conference, see MacMillan; and Sharp. For the details concerning American involvement, see *FRUS (The Paris Peace Conference, 1919)*.
20. PA-AA. R 2042.
21. NARA. Seeckt Nachlass, Reel 21: 22 March 1919.
22. Hilger, p. 190.

3 Exploring the Options: 1919

1. BA-MA. Nachlass Friedrich von Rabenau (N 62/7).
2. Hilger, p. 191.

3. PA-AA. R 2044.
4. See Goltz; and Popov.
5. See McDermott and Agnew.
6. Carr, pp. 419–420.
7. Yamauchi, whose account of Enver's career is by far the most thorough and thoroughly documented, only places Talaat's first visit to Radek as coming in the late summer, based on a reference to the encounter written in December 1919. Yamauchi does not state that this was Enver's first visit as well, but otherwise agrees with Carr's implication that Enver likely visited Radek "at the suggestion of the Reichswehr officers". Yamauchi, pp. 14–15.
8. NARA. Seeckt Nachlass, Reel 20. Report by Tschunke, Befreiung Enver Paschas aus litauischer Gefangenschaft im Februar [handwritten correction to April] 1919: no date. See also Yamauchi, p. 16.
9. NARA. Seeckt Nachlass, Reel 20.
10. As Marks points out (*Illusion*, p. 169, fn. 7), the United States did offer a warning to Germany on 8 March 1919 that the German interpretation of Wilson's Fourteen Points was unacceptable, and that they had in fact lost the war.
11. NARA. Seeckt Nachlass, Reel 20.
12. Ibid.
13. Yamauchi, p. 16, citing a letter written by Enver to a Turkish colleague, Cavit, dated 18 November 1919.
14. Rabenau, p. 306.
15. NARA. Seeckt Nachlass, Reel 1: 12 July 1919.
16. In Radek's memoir, for instance, he writes that "[d]*uring one of the visits* of Talaat Pasha and Enver Pasha, Harden came. I had very little love for this brilliant publicist of the Wilheimine era [...]" [emphasis added]. Carr, op. cit.
17. See Luckau.
18. See Horne, vol. VII.
19. DBFP. I/3/Doc. 236.
20. Quoted in Rosenbaum, p. 8.
21. DBFP. I/3/Doc. 244.
22. DBFP. I/3/Doc. 497.
23. ADAP. Serie A, Band II, Nr. 67.
24. ADAP. Serie A, Band II, Nr. 86.
25. ADAP. Serie A, Band II, Nr. 101.
26. See Oppenheimer.
27. See Ratenhof; and Causey.
28. NARA. Seeckt Nachlass, Reel 1: 19 September 1919.
29. See also ADAP. Serie A, Band III, Nr. 8.
30. ADAP. Serie A, Band III, Nr. 8.
31. Hilger, p. 191.
32. AVPRF. 82/1/6/76; Linke, "Der Weg nach Rapallo", p. 60.
33. On Curzon and British policy under his reign, see Bennett.

34. ADAP. Serie A, Band II, Nr. 216.
35. Carr, p. 412.
36. Karl Radek, "Noyabr", pp. 139–175; Carr, pp. 411–430.
37. DBFP. I/3/Doc. 552.
38. DBFP. I/3/Doc. 602.
39. PA-AA. R 2044.
40. AVPRF. 82/2/2/3.
41. Ibid.
42. At one point, Radek was supposed to have travelled with Enver to Russia: "The delay in the departure began to worry me. We ordered a plane, and I was to fly together with Enver Pasha. But upon receipt of a telegram from Captain Ignat Berner, the Chief of the Polish military intelligence, fixing the time for my transit through Poland, I gave up the journey by plane." Carr, op. cit.

4 Opening the Door Wider, Amid Rumours and Chaos

1. See Sutterlin.
2. See Hallgarten.
3. BA-MA. Nachlass Friedrich von Rabenau (N 62/7).
4. NARA. Seeckt Nachlass, Reel 1: 19 January 1920.
5. AVPRF. 82/3/3/3.
6. AVPRF. 82/3/3/5.
7. AVPRF. 82/3/3/3.
8. PA-AA. R 2044.
9. Linke, p. 63.
10. On Schleswig-Holstein, see Scharff.
11. DBFP. I/7/Doc. 17.
12. DBFP. I/7/Doc. 22.
13. DDF, 1920, I, Nr. 394.
14. GARF. 1703/1/441.
15. DBFP. I/9/Doc. 27.
16. DBFP. I/9/Doc. 30.
17. DBFP. I/9/Doc. 36.
18. DBFP. I/9/Doc. 45.
19. DBFP. I/9/Doc. 51.
20. DBFP. I/9/Doc. 57.
21. DBFP. I/9/Doc. 86.
22. DBFP. I/9/Doc. 73.
23. DBFP. I/9/Doc. 85.
24. DBFP. I/9/Doc. 437.
25. DBFP. I/9/Docs. 448, 453, and 491.
26. On the Putsch, see especially Koennemann and Schulze; and Rhefus.
27. See Koennemann and Schulze.
28. BA-MA. Seeckt Nachlass, 212; Linke, p. 62.
29. PA-AA. R 83656.

30. DDF, 1920, III, Nr. 376. In a foonote to the document, the editors refer to an earlier report making reference to a "supposed treaty" of military alliance signed in Berlin between Maltzan, Kopp, and Radek, on 17 July 1920.
31. AVPRF. 82/4/4/7.
32. DBFP. I/9/Doc. 533.
33. PA-AA. R 83377.
34. Ibid.
35. DBFP. I/10/Doc. 260.
36. The details of the Spa Conference can be found in DBFP, I, VII.
37. DDF, 1920, II, Nr. 235.
38. PA-AA. R 31488k.
39. PA-AA. R 83377.
40. AVPRF. 4/52/340/55237; Linke, p. 64.
41. AVPRF. 82/3/3/1 and 4/52/340/55237; Linke, p. 64.
42. DBFP. I/10/Doc. 265.
43. Reprinted as document 117 in Huerten, p. 212.
44. Ibid.
45. Reprinted as document 135 in Huerten, p. 244.
46. ADAP. Serie A, Band III, Nr. 223, 31 July 1920.
47. Ibid.
48. Article 117 stated, "Germany undertakes to recognize the full force of all treaties or agreements which may be entered into by the Allied and Associated Powers with States now existing or coming into existence in future in the whole or part of the former Empire of Russia as it existed on August 1, 1914, and to recognize the frontiers of any such States as determined therein."
49. ADAP. Serie A, Band III, Nr. 223, 31 July 1920.
50. See Wandycz, *Soviet-Polish Relation*; and Davies.
51. RTsKhIDNI. 76/3/106; and Gorlov, *Sovershenno sekretno*, p. 39.
52. RTsKhIDNI. 17/84/119 and 17/3/102, and AVPRF. 4/3/12/3; Gorlov, *Sovershenno sekretno*, p. 40.
53. AVPRF. 4/52/340/55237, and 4/3/12/3/192. Cited also in Gorlow, Sergei A. "Geheimsache Moskau-Berlin", pp. 134–135.
54. AVPRF. 4/52/340/55237.
55. Ibid.
56. Gorlov, *Sovershenno sekretno*, p. 33, referring to Agabekov G. C. *Sekretnii terror: zapiski razvedchika*. Moscow, 1996, p. 56.
57. NARA. Seeckt Nachlass, Reel 24: 25 August 1920; reprinted in Rabenau, pp. 306–307.
58. Ibid.
59. NARA. Seeckt Nachlass, Reel 24: 26 August 1920; reprinted in Rabenau, p. 307.
60. Nachlass Seeckt, box 15, no. 202 f. Translation of Carsten, *Reichswehr*, pp. 70–71.
61. Carsten, p. 71.

62. DBFP. I/10/Doc. 197.
63. DBFP. I/10/Doc. 279.
64. AVPRF. 4/52/340/55237; Linke, "Der Weg nach Rapallo", p. 64.
65. PA-AA. Abt.IV/Ru/2/1.
66. RGVA. 33987/3/52. Cited also in D'iakov, p. 32.
67. DBFP. I/10/Doc. 205.
68. AVPRF. 82/3/3/3.
69. PA-AA. R 83377; DBFP. I/10/Doc. 287.
70. PA-AA. R 83377.
71. PA-AA. R 83378.
72. AVPRF. 4/13/73/1038.
73. DBFP. I/10/Doc. 289.
74. PA-AA. R 83378.
75. AVPRF. 4/13/73/1038. Cited in Gorlow, "Geheimsache Moskau-Berlin", p. 135.
76. RGASPI. 5/1/2056.
77. PA-AA. R 83378.
78. PA-AA. R 83379.
79. Ibid.
80. ADAP. Serie A, Band IV, Nr. 20.
81. PA-AA. R 83643.
82. Linke, "Der Weg nach Rapallo", p. 68.
83. AVPRF. 0165/101/7, and 0165/101/10; Linke, "Der Weg nach Rapallo", p. 78.
84. AVPRF. 82/4/4/7.
85. PA-AA. R 83656.
86. DBFP. I/10/Docs. 229 and 232.
87. ADAP. Serie A, Band IV, Nr. 51 and Nr. 65.
88. DBFP. I/10/Doc. 235.
89. DBFP. I/10/Doc. 248.
90. ADAP. Serie A, Band IV, Nr. 129.
91. DBFP. I/10/Doc. 237.
92. DDF, 1921, II, Nr. 283.
93. AVPRF. 4/13/73/1038; reprinted in full in Gorlov, *Sovershenno sekretno*.
94. AVPRF. 82/74/1051; Linke, p. 78.
95. PA-AA. R 83380.
96. DDF, 1920, I, Nr. 162.

5 Confirming the Contacts, Building a Framework

1. AVPRF. 82/74/1049.
2. Ibid.
3. Ibid.; Linke, "Der Weg nach Rapallo", p. 78.
4. AVPRF. 82/4/5/18.
5. AVPRF. 82/4/4/8.
6. AVPRF. 82/4/4/8 and 165/1/101/3.

7. AVPRF. 82/4/4/8.
8. Ibid.
9. AVPRF. NKID 4/4/4; Linke, "Der Weg nach Rapallo", p. 75.
10. See Bariéty.
11. AVPRF. 82/74/1051/1.
12. AVPRF. 82/4/4/8.
13. Ibid.
14. PA-AA. Buero RM/9/3; Linke, "Der Weg nach Rapallo", p. 74.
15. RGASPI. 326-c/1/17a.
16. RGVA. 4/3/611.
17. RGVA. 4/3/1727.
18. AVPRF. 82/4/4/2.
19. NARA. Seeckt Nachlass, Reel 24; reprinted in Rabenau, p. 307.
20. NARA. Seeckt Nachlass, Reel 24.
21. RGASPI. 5/1/2056.
22. AVPRF. 82/4/4/8.
23. ADAP. Serie A, Band IV, Nr. 255.
24. ADAP. Serie A, Band IV, Nr. 257.
25. RGASPI. 5/1/2057.
26. Hilger, p. 195.
27. Hilger, pp. 195, 197.
28. DBFP. I/20/Doc. 481.
29. DBFP. I/20/Doc. 495.
30. See Adam.
31. See Allied Powers. Reparation Commission.
32. See Sigmund Karski.
33. AVPRF. 82/4/4/4.
34. AVPRF. 82/4/4/9.
35. PA-AA. Abt. IV/Ru/2/3; Linke, "Der Weg nach Rapallo", p. 76.
36. RGVA. 4/3/611.
37. RGVA. 4/3/1727.
38. AVPRF. 82/4/4/2.
39. AVPRF. 82/4/4/9; Linke, "Der Weg nach Rapallo", pp. 79–80.
40. AVPRF. 82/74/1049.
41. AVPRF. 418/1/1/2 and 82/4/101/1; Linke, "Der Weg nach Rapallo", p. 70.
42. Their output was impressive, and the collection of much of their work is found at the former-Comintern archives, RGASPI: 504/1/141 and 504/1/142.
43. RTsKhIDNI. 17/3/175; Gorlov, *Sovershenno sekretno*, p. 52.
44. AVPRF. 82/4/4/8.
45. Ibid.
46. AVPRF. 82/102/59460 and 82/4/4/8; Linke, "Der Weg nach Rapallo", p. 82.
47. AVPRF. 4/13/74/1066; Linke, "Der Weg nach Rapallo", p. 85.
48. AVPRF. 82/4/4/8.

49. Carsten, p. 137. Cites Nachlass Mentzel, no. 5, Koblenz.
50. Hilger, p. 193.
51. DBFP. I/20/Doc. 370.
52. RGVA. 33987/1/460.
53. AVPRF. 82/4/4/8.
54. Ibid.
55. AVPRF. 82/4/4/2.
56. Ibid.
57. Ibid.
58. AVPRF. 82/74/1049.
59. Ibid.; Linke, "Der Weg nach Rapallo", p. 78.
60. RGVA. 33988/1/431.
61. AVPRF. 82/442.
62. AVPRF. 4/13/74/1055.
63. Ibid.
64. AVPRF. 4/52/341/55262; Linke, "Der Weg nach Rapallo", p. 86.
65. AVPRF. 82/4/4/8.
66. Rabenau, pp. 308–309.
67. Ibid.
68. AVPRF. 82/4/4/8. Also: Nachlass Seeckt, box 19, no. 278. Notes of General Lieber "Seeckt als Chef der Heeresleitung", p. 38, with extracts from Hasse's diary, under 24, 26, 29 September, 2, 18 October, 3 and 8 December 1921. Cited as well in Carsten, pp. 135–137.
69. AVPRF. 82/4/4/8.
70. Ibid.
71. AVPRF. 4/13/74/1066.
72. ADAP. Serie A, Band V, Nr. 132.
73. PA-AA. R 31490.
74. Ibid.
75. Ibid. Reprinted in ADAP. Serie A, Band V, Nr. 146.
76. PA-AA. R 31490.
77. AVPRF. 4/13/74/1066; see also Linke, "Der Weg nach Rapallo", p. 87; and Gorlov, *Sovershenno sekretno*, p. 56.
78. PA-AA Nachlass Brockdorff-Rantzau 10/3.
79. DDF, 1921, II, Nr. 283.
80. RTsKhIDNI. 17/3/219; Gorlov, *Sovershenno sekretno*, p. 57.
81. AVPRF. 82/3/3/1.
82. AVPRF. 165/1/101/2.
83. AVPRF. 82/4/47/1049; Linke, "Der Weg nach Rapallo", pp. 89–90.
84. Carsten, p. 137. Cites Nachlass Mentzel, no. 5, Koblenz.
85. PA-AA. R 315657.
86. DDF, 1921, II, Nr. 386. In a footnote to this document, the editors make reference to a report in a German journal *Ost-Dienst*, in which it claimed that many specialized technicians and workers, among them officers and NCOs of various branches of the German military, had gone to Russia of late to serve as instructors to the Red Army.

87. DDF, 1921, II, Nr. 391.
88. RGASPI. 5/1/2376.
89. AVPRF. 82/4/4/8.
90. Carsten, p. 137. Cites Tschunke to Rabenau of 13 February 1939, as well as Anlage 12 to letter of Mueller and Wels to Gessler, 6 December 1926: Reichskanzlei, Akten betr. Reichswehr etc., vol. v, R 43 I 686, BA.
91. AVPRF. 165/1/101/3.
92. Rabenau, pp. 308–309.
93. AVPRF. 0165/1/101/10; Gorlov, *Sovershenno sekretno*, p. 58.
94. Rabenau, pp. 308–309.
95. AVPRF. 82/4/7/4.
96. Article 116: "Germany acknowledges and agrees to respect as permanent and inalienable the independence of all the territories which were part of the former Russian Empire on August 1, 1914.

    In accordance with the provisions of Article 259 of Part IX (Financial Clauses) and Article 292 of Part X (Economic Clauses), Germany accepts definitely the abrogation of the Brest-Litovsk Treaties and of all other treaties, conventions and agreements entered into by her with the Maximalist Government in Russia.

    The Allied and Associated Powers formally reserve the rights of Russia to obtain from Germany restitution and reparation based on the principles of the present Treaty."
97. RGASPI. 5/1/2060.
98. PA-AA. R 31695.

6 Under the Umbrella of Rapallo

1. AVPRF. 418/1/11/40.
2. Radek, *Karl Radek in Deutschland* (Dietrich Moeller, ed.), pp. 33–34.
3. PA-AA Nachlass Brockdorff-Rantzau 10/1.
4. RGASPI. 5/1/2376.
5. RGVA. 4/1/37/Reel 2.
6. RGVA. 33988/3/56.
7. Carsten, p. 138. Cites General Lieber's notes, pp. 50–51 in the Nachlass Seeckt, box 19, no. 278.
8. Rabenau, p. 309.
9. AVPRF. 4/76/1101.
10. Rabenau, p. 309.
11. PA-AA. R 94272.
12. AVPRF. 4/13/76/1101.
13. AVPRF. 4/13/74/1101.
14. AVPRF. 165/1/101/1.
15. AVPRF. 82/4/4/8.
16. AVPRF. 165/1/101/2.
17. Carsten, p. 138. Cites Nachlass Mentzel, no. 5, pp. 63 ff: a copy of the contract, signed for the Sondergruppe by "Neumann".

18. RGVA. 33988/2/433.
19. AVPRF. 82/5/8/11.
20. Rabenau, pp. 309–310; Carsten, p. 139, citing General Lieber's notes, pp. 51–53, 59 in the Nachlass Seeckt, box 19, no. 278.
21. PA-AA. Nachlass Brockdorff-Rantzau 9/5.
22. ADAP. Serie A, Band VI, Nr. 58.
23. ADAP. Serie A, Band VI, Nr. 71.
24. ADAP. Serie A, Band VI, Nr. 80.
25. DBFP. I/20/Doc. 497.
26. Rabenau, p. 313.
27. DBFP. I/20/Doc. 501.
28. DBFP. I/20/Doc. 502.
29. DBFP. I/20/Doc. 505.
30. The newspaper clip was copied whole into the German Foreign Office files: PA-AA. R 83382.
31. PA-AA. R 83382.
32. PA-AA. R 83825.
33. AVPRF. 0165/1/101/10; Linke, p. 88.
34. PA-AA. R 31695.
35. PA-AA. R 31696.
36. ADAP. Serie A, Band VI, Nr. 151.
37. DBFP. I/20/Doc. 249.
38. DBFP. I/20/Doc. 253.
39. DBFP. I/20/Doc. 260.
40. PA-AA. Nachlass Brockdorff-Rantzau 11/2. A full series of letters exchanged from October 1922 and onwards between Brockdorff-Rantzau and Maltzan, Simons, Gessler, and others, on the conflict with Seeckt, are in the Nachlass Brockdorff-Rantzau 10/4. They are numerous, and the selections quoted from in the main text provide an overview of their essence.
41. ADAP. Serie A, Band VI, Nr. 167.
42. ADAP. Serie A, Band VI, Nr. 171.
43. ADAP. Serie A, Band VI, Nr. 176.
44. ADAP. Serie A, Band VI, Nr. 182.
45. ADAP. Serie A, Band VI, Nr. 185.
46. PA-AA. Nachlass Brockdorff-Rantzau 11/2. In the ADAP version, a footnote is entered, in which Brockdorff-Rantzau argued that centralization of the overall representation in Moscow was required, and the current diplomatic situation was untenable. Wiedenfeld was a hard worker, but viewed as a German professor by the Soviets, who in contrast viewed Brockdorff-Rantzau as Germany's first "real" representative in the country. ADAP. Serie A, Band VI, Nr. 191.
47. ADAP. Serie A, Band VI, Nr. 199.
48. Hilger, p. 199.
49. PA-AA. Nachlass Brockdorff-Rantzau 9/5.
50. RGASPI. 326-c/1/17a.

51. AVPRF. 82/5/8/22.
52. Ibid.
53. Hilger, p. 201.
54. DBFP. I/20/Doc. 537.
55. D'Abernon, vol. II, pp. 134–135.

Bibliography

Archives

Germany
PA-AA. Politisches Archiv des Auswaertigen Amts. Foreign Ministry Archives, Berlin.
BA. Bundesarchiv. Federal Archives, Berlin.
BA-MA. Bundesarchiv-Militaerarchiv. Federal Military Archives, Freiburg im Breisgau.

Russia
AVPRF. Arkhiv vneshnei politiki Rossiiskoi Federatsii. Archive of Foreign Policy of the Russian Federation [Historico-Documentary Department of the Ministry of Foreign Affairs], Moscow.
GARF. Gosudarstvennyia arkhiv Rossiiskoi Federatsii. State Archive of the Russian Federation, Moscow.
RGVA. Rossiiskii gosudarstvennyi voennyi arkhiv. Russian State Military Archive, Moscow.
RGASPI [formerly: RTsKhIDNI]. Rossiiskii gosudarstvennyi arkhiv sotsial'no-politicheskoi istorii [formerly: Rossissiiskii tsentr khraneniia i izucheniia dokumentov noveishei istorii]. Russian State Archive of Socio-Political History [formerly Russian Center for Preservation and Study of Records of Modern History], Moscow.

United States
NARA. National Archives and Record Administration, Washington DC.

Published government documents

ADAP. *Akten zur deutschen auswärtigen Politik.*
DBFP. *Documents on British Foreign Policy.*
DDF. *Documents diplomatiques français.*
DVPSSSR. *Dokumenti vneshnei politiki SSSR.*
FRUS. *Foreign Relations of the United States.*

Articles

Carr, E. H. "From Soviet Publications: Radek's 'Political Salon' in Berlin 1919". *Soviet Studies* 3/4 (1952), pp. 411–430.

Fraenkel, Ernst. "German-Russian Relations Since 1918: From Brest-Litovsk to Moscow". *The Review of Politics* 2/1 (1940), pp. 34-62.
Gatzke, Hans. "Russo-German Military Collaboration during the Weimar Republic". *The American Historical Review* 63/3 (1958), pp. 565-597.
Gorlov, Sergei A. "Soviet-German Military Cooperation, 1920-1930". *International Affairs* (Moscow) (1990), pp. 95-112.
Gorlow, Sergei A. "Geheimsache Moskau-Berlin. Die militaerpolitische zusammenarbeit zwischen der Sowjetunion und dem Deutschen Reich 1920-1933". *Vierteljahreshefte fuer Zeitgeschichte* 1 (1996), pp. 133-165.
Hallgarten, G. W. F. "General Hans von Seeckt and Russia, 1920-1922". *Journal of Modern History* 21 (1949), pp. 28-34.
Himmer, Robert. "Soviet Policy Toward Germany during the Russo-Polish War, 1920". *Slavic Review* 35/4 (1976), pp. 665-682.
Klemperer, Klemens von. "Towards a Fourth Reich? The History of National Bolshevism in Germany". *The Review of Politics* 13/2 (1951), pp. 191-210.
Kochan, Lionel. "The Russian Road to Rapallo". *Soviet Studies* 2/2 (1950), pp. 109-122.
Linke, Horst Guenther. "Der Weg nach Rapallo". *Historische Zeitschrift*. Bd. 264 (1997), pp. 55-109.
Mueller, Gordon H. "Rapallo Reexamined: A New Look at Germany's Secret Military Collaboration with Russia in 1922". *Military Affairs* 40/3 (1976), pp. 109-117.
Radek, Karl. "Noyabr". *Krasnaya Nov*. (October 1926), pp. 139-175.
Schuddekopf, Otto-Ernst. "German Foreign Policy between Compiegne and Versailles". *Journal of Contemporary History* 4/2 (1969), pp. 181-197.
Smele, J. D. "White Gold: The Imperial Russian Gold Reserve in the Anti-Bolshevik East, 1918-?—An Unconcluded Chapter in the History of the Russian Civil War". *Europe-Asia Studies, Soviet and East European History*. 46/8 (December 1994), pp. 1317-1347.
Smith, Arthur L. "The German General Staff and Russia, 1919-1926". *Soviet Studies* 8/2 (1956), pp. 125-133.
Tucker, Robert C. "The Emergence of Stalin's Foreign Policy". *Slavic Review* 36/4 (1977), pp. 563-589.

Books and dissertations

Adam, Magda. *The Little Entente and Europe (1920-1929)*. Budapest, 1993.
Akhtamzian, A. A. *Rapall'skaia politika: sov.-germ. diplomat. otnosheniia v 1922-1932 gg*. Moskva, 1974.
Akhtamzian, A. A. *Ot Bresta do Kilia; proval antisovetskoi politiki germanskogo imperializma v 1918 gody*. Moskva, 1963.
Aleksandrov, Vladimir Viktorovich. *Ob"edinenie Germanii i proval germanskoi politiki sovetskogo rukovodstva*. Moskva, 1995.
Allied Powers. Reparation Commission. *Reparation Papers of the Allied Powers Reparation Commission*. [microform] Arlington, VA, 1975.

Anderle, Alfred. *Die deutsche Rapallo-Politik; deutschsowjetische Beziehungen, 1922–1929*. Veroffentlichungen des Instituts fur Geschichte der Volker der UdSSR an der Martin-Luther-Universitat Halle-Wittenberg. Reihe B: Abhandlungen, Bd. 4. Berlin, 1962.
Anderle, A., ed. *Nauchnaia sessiia posviashchennaia sorokaletiiu Rapall'skogo dogovora (1962: Moscow). Rapall'skii dogovor i problema mirnogo sosushchestvovaniia; materialy Nauchnoi sessii, posviashchennoi 40-letiiu Rapall'skogo dogovora (25–28 aprelia 1962 goda)*. Moskva, 1963.
Aust, Hans Walter, ed. *50 Jahre deutsch-sowjetischer Beziehungen, 1917–1967. Deutsche Aussenpolitik*. Sonderheft, 1967; Berlin, 1967.
Bariéty, Jacques. *Les relations franco-allemandes après la Première Guerre mondiale: 10 novembre 1918–10 janvier 1925: de lexécution à la négociation*. Paris, 1977.
Bauer Max. *Das Land der roten Zaren*. Hamburg, 1925.
Baumgart, Winfried. *Deutsche Ostpolitik 1918*. Wien, Muenchen, Oldenbourg, 1966.
Baumgart, Winfried, ed. *Von Brest-Litovsk zur deutschen November-Revolution*. Goettingen, 1971.
Bennett, G. H. *British Foreign Policy during the Curzon Period, 1919–1924*. New York, 1995.
Biermann, Rafael. *Zwischen Kreml und Kanzleramt: wie Moskau mit der deutschen Einheit rang*. Studien zur Politik; Bd. 30. Paderborn, 1997.
Bluecher, Wipert von. *Deutschlands Weg nach Rapallo; Erinnerungen eines Mannes aus dem zweiten Gliede*. Wiesbaden, 1951.
Bothmer, Karl Graf von. *Mit Graf Mirbach in Moskau; Tagebuchaufzeichnungen und Aktenstucke vom 19. April bis 24. August 1918*. Tuebingen, 1922.
Bournazel, Renata. *Rapallo, naissance d'un mythe: la politique de la peur dans la France du bloc national*. Travaux et recherches de science politique, no. 28. Paris, 1974.
Bradley, John. *Allied Intervention in Russia, 1917–1920*. New York, 1968.
Broué, Pierre. *The German Revolution, 1917–1923*. Boston, 2005.
Brüning, Heinrich. *Memoiren. 1918–1934*. Stuttgart, 1970.
Carr, E. H. *German-Soviet Relations Between the Two World Wars, 1919–1939*. Johns Hopkins University Press reprints, New York, 1951.
Carsten, F. L. *The Reichswehr and Politics, 1918–1933* Oxford, 1966.
Causey, Beverley Douglas. *German Policy towards China, 1918–1941*. Ph.D. Dissertation, Harvard, 1942.
Centre d' études anticommunist. *L'Allemagne et le bolchevisme*. Paris, 1938.
Cienciala, Anna M. and Titus Komarnicki. *From Versailles to Locarno, Keys to Polish Foreign Policy, 1919–1925*. Lawrence, KS, 1984.
Cleinow, Georg. *Die deutsch-russischen Rechts- und Wirtschaftsvertrage nebst Konsularvertrag vom 12. Oktober 1925*. Deutsche Wirtschafts-gesetze. Bd. 5. Berlin, 1926.
Curtius, Julius. *Sechs Jahre Minister der deutschen Republik*. Heidelberg, 1948.
Czernin, Ferdinand. *Versailles, 1919*. New York, 1965.
D'Abernon, Viscont Edgar Vincent. *An Ambassador of Peace*. London, 1929–1930.

Davies, Norman. *White Eagle Red Star. The Polish-Soviet War, 1919–1920.* London, 1972.
Debo, Richard. *Revolution and Survival.* Toronto, 1979.
Debo, Richard. *Survival and Consolidation.* Buffalo, NY, 1994.
Deutsches Institut fur Zeitgeschichte. *Dokumente zur Deutschlandpolitik der Sowjetunion.* Berlin, 1957.
D'iakov, IU. L. *Fashistskii mech kovalsia v SSSR: Krasnaia armiia i Reikhsver: tainoe sotrudnichestvo, 1922–1933: neizvestnye dokumenty.* Rossiia v litsakh, dokumentakh, dnevnikakh. Moskva, 1992. [Published in English as: *The Red Army and the Wehrmacht: How the Soviets Militarized Germany, 1922–33, and Paved the Way for Fascism. From the secret archives of the former Soviet Union.* Russian studies series. Amherst, NY, 1995.]
Dirksen, Herbert von. *Moskau Tokio London. Erinnerungen und Betrachtungen zu 20 Jahren deutscher Außenpolitik 1919–1939.* Stuttgart, 1949.
Dollinger, Hans. *Von Lenin bis Gorbatschow: die deutsch-sowjetischen Beziehungen.* Geschichte live. Recklinghausen, 1991.
Dreetz, Dieter. *Bewaffnete Kampfe in Deutschland 1918–1923. Kleine Militargeschichte. Bewaffnete revolutionare Kampfe.* Schriften des Militargeschichtlichen Instituts der DDR. 1. Aufl. Berlin, 1988.
Dyck, Harvey Leonard. *Weimar Germany & Soviet Russia, 1926–1933; A Study in Diplomatic Instability.* Studies of the Russian Institute, Columbia University. New York, 1966.
Elias, Rolf, ed. *Die Deutsch-sowjetischen Beziehungen: e. Ausw. von Vertragen, Erklarungen u. Reden.* Berlin (West), 1979.
Eschenburg, Theodor. *Also horen Sie mal zu: Geschichte und Geschichten, 1904 bis 1933.* 1. Aufl. Berlin, 1995.
Eyck, Erich. *Geschichte der Weimarer Republik.* Erlenbach-Zurich, 1954–1956.
Fayet, Jean-François. *Karl Radek (1885–1939): biographie politique.* Bern, 2004.
Feigina, L. *B'orskoe soglashenie iz istorii russko-germanskikh otnoshenii.* Moskva, 1928.
Feiler, Oswald. *Moskau und die Deutsche Frage.* Edition D; 8. Krefeld, 1984.
Fink, Carole. *The Genoa Conference: European Diplomacy, 1921–1922.* Chapel Hill, NC, 1984.
Fink, Carole, Axel Frohn, and Juergen Heideking, eds. *Genoa, Rapallo, and European Reconstruction in 1922.* Publications of the German Historical Institute, Washington, DC: German Historical Institute. New York, 1991.
Fink, Woldemar. *Ostideologie und Ostpolitik; die Ostideologie ein Gefahrenmoment in der deutschen Aussenpolitik.* Berlin, 1936.
Foerster, Juergen et al., eds. *Deutschland und das bolschewistische Russland von Brest-Litowsk bis 1941.* Abhandlungen des Gottinger Arbeitskreises, Bd. 8. Berlin, 1991.
Forsthoff, Ernst, ed. *Deutsche geschichte von 1918 bis 1938 in dokumenten.* Kroners taschenausgabe. Bd. 113. Stuttgart, 1943.
Frank, Alexandra. *Die Entwicklung der ostelbischen Gutswirtschaften im Deutschen Kaiserreich und in den Anfangsjahren der Weimarer Republik.* Beitrage zur Wirtschafts- und Sozialgeschichte; Bd. 6. Weiden, 1994.

Freund, Gerald. *Unholy Alliance; Russian-German Relations from the Treaty of Brest-Litovsk to the Treaty of Berlin*. New York, 1957.
Fritsch-Bournazel, Renata. *De Rapallo a Zavidovo: reflexions sur le devenir des relations germano-russes*. Les cahiers du CREST, 11. Paris, 1993.
Gackenholz, Hermann. *Das Diktat von Versailles und seine Auswirkungen: gemeinverstandliche Darstellung*. Reclams Universal-Bibliothek; Nr. 7248. Leipzig, 1934.
Ganetskii, IA. S. *Sovetsko-germanskii torgovyi dogovor*. Moskva, 1926.
Gatrell, Peter. *Russia's First World War. A Social and Economic History*. Harlow, UK, 2005.
Gatzke, Hans. *European Diplomacy between Two World Wars*. Chicago, 1972.
Gehl, Walther. *Der deutsche Aufbruch, 9. November 1918 bis 31. Dezember 1940*. Hirts deutsche Sammlung. Sachkundliche Abt.: Geschichte und Staatsburgerkunde. Gruppe II: Ereignisse; Bd. 9. 4. Breslau, 1941.
Germany. *Soglasheniia s germaniei, zakliuchennye v Berline 6 maia 1921 goda*. Moskva, 1921.
Germany. Auswartiges Amt. *Germany and the Revolution in Russia, 1915–1918; documents from the Archives of the German Foreign Ministry*. London, New York, 1958.
Gessler, Otto. *Reichswehrpolitik in der Weimarer Zeit*. Hrsg: Kurt Sendtner. Stuttgart, 1958.
Goldbach, Marie-Luise. *Karl Radek und die deutsch-sowjetischen Beziehungen 1918–1923*. Schriftenreihe des Forschungsinstituts der Friedrich-Ebert-Stiftung, Bd. 97. Bonn-Bad Godesberg, 1973.
Goltz, Ruediger von der. *Meine Sendung in Finnland und in Baltikum*. Leipzig, 1920.
Gorlov, Sergei A. *Sovershenno sekretno, Moskva-Berlin, 1920–1933: voenno-politicheskie otnosheniia mezhdu SSSR i Germaniei*. Moskva, 1999.
Gradmann, Christoph and Oliver von Mengersen, eds. *Das Ende der Weimarer Republik und die nationalsozialistische Machtergreifung: Vortrage Heidelberger Historiker in der Reichsprasident Friedrich Ebert-Gedenkstatte*. Heidelberg, 1994.
Grau, Bernhard. *Kurt Eisner, 1867–1919: eine Biographie*. Muenchen, 2001.
Grieser, Helmut. *Die Sowjetpresse uber Deutschland in Europa. 1922–1932. Revision von Versailles und Rapallo-Politik in sowjetischer Sicht*. Kieler historische Studien, Bd. 10. Stuttgart, 1970.
Groehler, Olaf. *Selbstmorderische Allianz: deutsch-russische Militarbeziehungen 1920–1941*. Berlin, 1992.
Haffner, Sebastian. *Die Teufelspakt: die deutsch-russischen Beziehungen vom Ersten zum Zweiten Weltkrieg*. Manesse Bucherei; 11. 3. Aufl. Zurich, 1988.
Haigh, R. H. *German-Soviet Relations in the Weimar Era: Friendship from Necessity*. Aldershot, Hants, England, 1985.
Haller, Johannes. *Die russische Gefahr im deutschen Hause*. Russische Gefahr; 6. Stuttgart, 1917.
Haupts, Leo. *Deutsche Friedenspolitik, 1918–19: eine Alternative zur Machtpolitik des Ersten Weltkrieges*. Duesseldorf, 1976.
Helbig, Herbert. *Die Trager der Rapallo-Politik*. Veroffentlichungen des Max-Planck-Instituts fur Geschichte, 3. Goettingen, 1958.

Heuss, Theodor. *Friedrich Naumann; der Mann, das Werk, die Zeit.* Siebenstern-Taschenbuch, 121/123. Hrsg. von Alfred Milatz. Muenchen, 1968.

Hildebrand, Klaus. *Das Deutsche Reich und die Sowjetunion im internationalen System: 1918–1932: Legitimitat oder Revolution?* Frankfurter historische Vortrage; Heft 4. Wiesbaden, 1977.

Hilger, Gustav. *Wir und der Kreml. Deutsch-sowjetische Beziehungen, 1918–1941. Erinnerungen eines deutschen Diplomaten.* Frankfurt am Main, Berlin, 1964.

Hilger, Gustav and Alfred G. Meyer. *The Incompatible Allies. A Memoir-History of German-Soviet Relations 1918–1941.* New York, 1953.

Hilger, Gustav and G. Rosenfeld, *Sowjetunion und Deutschland, 1922–1933.* Berlin, 1984.

Hillgruber, Andreas. *Deutschlands Rolle in der Vorgeschichte der beiden Weltkriege.* Die Deutsche Frage in der Welt, Bd. 7. Goettingen, 1967.

Hoeffkes, Karl, ed. *Deutsch-sowjetische Geheimverbindungen: unveroffentlichte diplomatische Depeschen zwischen Berlin und Moskau im Vorfeld des Zweiten Weltkriegs.* Veroffentlichungen des Institutes fur Deutsche Nachkriegsgeschichte; Bd. 15. Tuebingen, 1988.

Horne, Charles F., ed. *Source Records of the Great War.* New York, 1923.

Huck, Walter. *Russland spielt wieder die deutsche Karte: eine politisch-historische Analyse der deutsch-russischen Beziehungen.* Brennpunkt Politik. Muenchen, 1991.

Huerten, Heinz, ed. *Die Anfaenge der Aera Seeckt. Militaer und Innenpolitik 1920–1922.* Duesseldorf, 1979.

Joachim, Hermann. *Vom Bundnisprojekt Moskaus zur neutralen Ausgestaltung des Rapalloverhaltnisses unter Stresemann.* Dissertation, Mainz, 1964.

Joost, Wilhelm. "Botschafter bei den roten Zaren". *Die deutschen Missionschefs in Moskau, 1918 bis 1941. Nach Geheimakten und personlichen Aufzeichnungen.* Wien, 1967.

Karski, Jan. *The Great Powers and Poland, 1919–1945.* Lanham, MD, 1985.

Karski, Sigmund. *Albert (Wojciech) Korfanty: eine Biographie.* Duelmen, 1990.

Khvostov, Vladimir Mikhailovich et al., eds. *Deutsch-sowjetische Beziehungen von den Verhandlungen in Brest-Litowsk bis zum Abschluss des Rapallovertrages; Dokumentensammlung.* Berlin, 1967.

Kent, George P. *Realpolitik or revpolitik: the influence of two contrasting elements in Soviet policy towards the Communist Party of Germany, 1925–33.* Thesis, Harvard, 1989.

Klein, Fritz. *Die diplomatischen Beziehungen Deutschlands zur Sowjetunion, 1917–1932.* Berlin, 1952.

Klumpen, Heinrich. *Deutsche Aussenpolitik zwischen Versailles und Rapallo: Revisionismus oder Neuorientierung?* Studien zur Geschichte der Weimarer Republik, Bd. 1. Munster, 1992.

Kobliakov, I. K. *Ot Bresta do Rapallo; ocherki istorii sovetsko-germanskikh otnoshenii s 1918 po 1922 g.* Moskva, 1954.

Kobliakov, I. K. *Von Brest bis Rapallo; geschichtlicher Abriss der sowjetisch-deutschen Beziehungen von 1918 bis 1922.* Berlin, 1956.

Koch, H. W. *Der deutsche Bürgerkrieg: eine Geschichte der deutschen und österreichischen Freikorps, 1918–1923.* Dresden, 2002.

Kochan, Lionel. *Russia and the Weimar Republic*. Westport, CT, 1978.
Koenen, Gerd and Lew Kopelew, eds. *Deutschland un die Russische Revolution 1917–1924*. Muenchen, 1998.
Kohler, Henning. *Geschichte der Weimarer Republik*. Beitrage zur Zeitgeschichte, Bd. 4. Berlin, 1981.
Kolb, Eberhard. *The Weimar Republic*. London, 1998.
Kolb, Eberhard and Walter Muelhausen, eds. *Demokratie in der Krise: Parteien im Verfassungssystem der Weimarer Republik*. Schriftenreihe der Stiftung Reichsprasident-Friedrich-Ebert-Gedenkstatte; Bd. 5. Muenchen, 1997.
Koennemann, E. and G. Schulze, eds. *Der Kapp-Luettwitz-Ludendorff Putsch: Dokumente*. Muenchen, 2002.
Köstring, General Ernst. *Der militärische Mittler zwischen dem Deutschen Reich und der Sowjetunion 1921–1941*. Bearb. von Hermann Teske. Frankfurt am Main, 1965.
Krassin, Lyubov B. *Leonid Krassin*. London, 1929.
Krummacher, F. A. *Krieg und Frieden; Geschichte der deutsch-sowjetischen Beziehungen*. Muenchen, 1970.
Kul'bakin, V. D. *Germaniia v 1918–1939 gg.: lektsii*. Moskva, 1952.
Lang, Gordon. *Die Polen verprugeln: sowjetische Kriegstreibereien bei der deutschen Fuhrung, 1920 bis 1941*. Askania-Weissbuch-Reihe, Ed. 3–4. Lindhorst, 1988.
Linke, Horst Guenther. *Deutsch-sowjetische Beziehungen bis Rapallo*. Abhandlungen des Bundesinstituts fur ostwissenschaftliche und internationale Studien, Bd. 22. Koeln, 1970.
Linke, Horst Guenther, ed. *Quellen zu den Deutsch-Sowjetischen Beziehungen 1917–1945*. Darmstadt, 1998.
Liszkowski, Uwe, ed. *Russland und Deutschland*. Kieler historische Studien; Bd. 22. Stuttgart, 1974.
Loser, Jochen. *Revolution der Sicherheit: Dialog uber die deutsch-sowjetische Annaherung*. Muenchen, 1991.
Luckau, Alma. *The German Delegation at the Paris Peace Conference*. New York, 1941.
Luckwaldt, Friedrich. *Deutschland, Russland, Polen: die geschichtliche Entwicklung der Ostprobleme: zwei Vortrage*. Gedanken und Gestalten; Heft 2. Danzig, 1929.
Lundgreen-Nielsen, Kay. *The Polish Problem at the Paris Peace Conference*. Odense, Denmark, 1979.
MacMillan, Margaret. *Paris 1919*. New York, 2003.
Manteuffel, Karl. *Deutschland und der Osten*. Muenchen, 1926.
Marks, Sally. *The Ebbing of European Ascendancy: An International History of the World, 1914–1945*. London, 2002.
Marks, Sally. *The Illusion of Peace: International Relations in Europe, 1918–1933*. 2nd edition. London, 2003.
Martini, Johannes. *Mit oder gegen Moskau? Eine Mahnung an das Deutsche Volk*. Dresden, 1927.
Mawdsley, Evan. *The Russian Civil War*. Boston, 1987.
McDermott, Kevin and Jeremy Agnew. *The Comintern: A History of Interntional Communism from Lenin to Stalin*. New York, 1997.

Melville, Cecil Frank. *The Russian Face of Germany, An Account of the Secret Military Relations Between the German and Soviet-Russian Governments.* London, 1932.

Meissner, Boris and Alfred Eisfeld, eds. *50 Jahre sowjetische und russische Deutschlandpolitik sowie ihre Auswirkungen auf das gegenseitige Verhaltnis.* Studien zur Deutschlandfrage; Bd. 14. Veroffentlichung/Gottinger Arbeitskreis; Nr. 467. Berlin, 1999.

Meissner, Otto. *Staatssekretär unter Ebert, Hindenburg, Hitler.* Hamburg, 1950.

Merz, Kai-Uwe. *Das Schreckbild: Deutschland und der Bolschewismus, 1917–1921.* Berlin, 1995.

Mielcke, Karl. *Geschichte der Weimarer Republik.* Beitrage zur Geschichtsunterricht; Heft 23. Braunschweig, 1951.

Mommsen, Hans. *The Rise and Fall of Weimar Democracy.* Chapel Hill, NC, 1996.

Morgan, J. H. *Assize of Arms, Being the Story of the Disarmament of Germany and Her Rearmament (1919–1939).* London, 1945.

Mueller, Gordon H. *The Road to Rapallo: Germany's Relations with Russia, 1919–1922.* Thesis, University of North Carolina, 1970.

Muller, Rolf-Dieter. *Das Tor zur Weltmacht: die Bedeutung der Sowjetunion fur die deutsche Wirtschafts- und Rustungspolitik zwischen den Weltkriegen.* Wehrwissenschaftliche Forschungen. Abteilung Militargeschichtliche Studien; 32. Boppard am Rhein, 1984.

Narochnitskaia, L. I. *Rossiia i voiny Prussii v 60-kh godakh XIX v. Za obedinenie Germanii "sverkhu".* Moskva, 1960.

Nekrich, A. M. *Pariahs, Partners, Predators: German-Soviet Relations, 1922–1941.* New York, 1997.

Norden, Albert. *Zwischen Berlin und Moskau; zur Geschichte der deutschsowjetischen Beziehungen.* Berlin, 1954.

Oertzen, Friedrich Wilhelm von. *Die deutschen Freikorps, 1918–1923.* Muenchen, 1939.

Olivova, Vera. *The Doomed Democracy: Czechoslovakia in a Disrupted Europe, 1914–1938.* London, 1972.

Oppenheimer, Heinrich. *The Constitution of the German Republic.* London, 1923.

Orlow Alexander. *Kreml-Geheimnisse.* Wuerzburg, 1953.

Orth, Wilhelm. *Rathenau, Rapallo, Koexistenz.* Schriften der LDPD; Heft 24. Berlin, 1982.

Osthoff, Hans Werner. *Die deutsch-russischen Vertragsbeziehungen im Spiegel ihrer Zeit: 1878–1978.* Bern, 1980.

Pavlov, N. *Ob"edinenie, ili, Rasskaz o reshenii germanskogo voprosa s kommentariiami i otstupleniiami.* Moskva, 1992.

Pavlov, N. *Die deutsche Vereinigung aus sowjet-russischer Perspektive: ein Bericht zur Losung der deutschen Frage, versehen mit Kommentaren und historischen Ruckblicken.* Frankfurt am Main, 1996.

Perry, Hans-Juergen. *Der Russlandasusschuss der deutschen Wirtschaft. Die deutsch-sowjetischen Wirtschaftsbeziehungen in der Zwischenkriegszeit.* Muenchen, 1985.

Philbin, Tobias R. *The Lure of Neptune: German-Soviet Naval Collaboration and Ambitions, 1919–1941.* Studies in Maritime History. Columbia, SC, 1994.
Pinson, Koppel S. *Modern Germany: Its History and Civilization.* London, 1966.
Poertner, Rudolf, ed. *Alltag in der Weimarer Republik: Erinnerungen an eine unruhige Zeit.* Dusseldorf, 1990.
Popov, G. K. *Sowjetherrschaft in Europa; Die Rigaer Kommunistenzeit und ihre Lehren. Mit einem Geleitwort des Grafen Rüdiger von der Goltz.* Bern, 1935.
Posser, Diether. *Die deutsch-sowjetischen Beziehungen seit 1917.* Frankfurt am Main, 1963.
Potemkin, V. P. *Politika umirotvoreniia agressorov i borba Sovetskogo Soiuza za mir.* 2-e izd. Moskva, 1946.
Rabenau, Friedrich. *Seeckt. Aus seinem Leben, 1918–1936.* Berlin, 1940.
Radek, Karl. *Karl Radek in Deutschland: Revolutionar, Intrigant, Diplomat.* Hrsg: Dietrich Moeller. Koeln, 1976.
Ratenhof, Udo. *Die Chinapolitik des Deutschen Reiches 1871–1945: Wirtschaft, Ruestung, Militaer.* Boppard am Rhein, 1987.
Rauch, Georg von. *Die deutsch-sowjetischen Beziehungen von 1917 bis 1967.* Der Gottinger Arbeitskreis. Veroffentlichung, Nr. 367. Wuerzburg, 1967.
Rhefus, Reiner. *Spurensicherung 1920: der Arbeiteraufstand gegen den Kapp-Putsch und die damalige Arbeiterkultur im Bergischen Land.* Essen, 2000.
Roques, P. *Le controle militaire interallie en Allemagne septembre 1919-janvier 1927.* Paris, 1927.
Rosenbaum, Kurt. *Community of Fate; German-Soviet Diplomatic Relations, 1922–1928.* Syracuse, NY, 1965.
Rosenfeld, Gunter. *Sowjetrussland und Deutschland, 1917–1922.* Koeln, 1984.
Rosenfeld, Gunter. *Sowjetunion und Deutschland, 1922–1933.* Koeln, 1984.
Rosenko, I. A. *Sovetsko-germanskie otnosheniia, 1921–1922 gg.* Leningrad, 1965.
Rothschild, Joseph. *East Central Europe between the Two World Wars.* Seattle, WA, 1974.
Ruge, Wolfgang. *Die Stellungnahme der Sowjetunion gegen die Besetzung des Ruhrgebietes; zur Geschichte der deutsch-sowjetischen Beziehungen von Januar bis September 1923.* Deutsche Akademie der Wissenschaften zu Berlin. Schriften des Instituts fur Geschichte. Reihe 1: Allgemeine und deutsche Geschichte; Bd. 12. Berlin, 1962.
Sauer, Eberhard. *Osteuropa und wir das Problem Russland.* Neuwerk Bucherei; Bd. 2. Schluchtern, 1921.
Scharff, Alexander. *Schleswig-Holsteinische Geschichte.* Wuerzburg, 1984.
Scheidemann, Philipp. *Memoiren eines Sozialdemokraten.* 2 Bde. Dresden, 1928.
Schieder, Theodor. *Die Probleme des Rapallo-Vertrags eine Studie ueber die deutsch-russischen Beziehungen 1922–1926.* Arbeitsgemeinschaft fuer Forschung des Landes Nordrhein-Westfalen. Geisteswissenschaften, Hft. 43. Koeln, 1956.
Schieder, Theodor, ed. *Beitrage zur Geschichte der Weimarer Republik.* Historische Zeitschrift. Beiheft 1. Muenchen, 1971.
Schiesser, Gerhard. *Russisch Roulette: das deutsche Geld und die Oktoberrevolution.* Berlin, 1998.
Schlesinger, Moritz. *Erinnerungen eines Außenseiters im diplomatischen Dienst.* Koeln, Verlag Wissenschaft und Politik, c.1977.

Schlochauer, Hans Jurgen. *Der deutsch-russische ruckversicherungsvertrag; eine historisch-volkerrechtliche untersuchung.* Frankfurter abhandlungen zum modernen volkerrecht. Hft. 22. Leipzig, 1931.
Schueddekopf, Otto-Ernst. *Das Heer und die Republik. Quellen zur Politik der Reichswehrfuehrung 1918 bis 1933.* Hannover, 1955.
Schueddekopf, Otto-Ernst. *Nationalbolschewismus in Deutschland 1918–1933.* Frankfurt am Main, 1973.
Schuker, Stephen. *American "Reparations" to Germany, 1919–1933.* Princeton, NJ, 1988.
Schwertfeger, Bernhard Heinrich. *Deutschland und Russland im Wandel der europaischen Bundnisse.* 2. Aufl. Hannover, 1939.
Seeckt, Hans von. *Die Zukunft des Reiches.* Berlin, 1929.
Seeckt, Hans von. *Gedanken eines Soldaten.* Berlin, 1929.
Seeckt, Hans von. *Deutschland zwischen West und Ost.* Hamburg, 1933.
Seeckt, Hans von. *Die Reichswehr.* Leipzig, 1933.
Seeckt, Hans von. *Aus meinem Leben 1866–1917.* Leipzig, 1938.
Seraphim, Ernst. *Deutsch-Russische Beziehungen, 1918–1925.* Berlin, 1925.
Sharp, Alan. *The Versailles Settlement.* London, 1991.
Sievers, Leo. *Deutsche und Russen: Tausend Jahre gemeinsame Geschichte.* Hamburg, 1980.
Sobolev, D. A. *Nemetskii sled v istorii sovetskoi aviatsii: ob uchastii nemetskikh spetsialistov v razvitii aviastroeniia v SSSR.* Moskva, 1996.
Sommer, Erich F. *Geboren in Moskau: Erinnerungen eines baltendeutschen Diplomaten 1912–1955.* Muenchen, 1997.
Soviet Union. Ministerstvo inostrannykh del. *Sovetsko-germanskie otnosheniia ot peregovorov v Brest-Litovske do podpisaniia Rapall'skogo dogovora. [Sbornik dokumentov].* Moskva, 1968.
Soviet Union. Ministerstvo inostrannykh del SSSR, Ministerstvo inostrannykh del GDR. *Sovetsko-germanskie otnosheniia, 1922–1925 gg.: Dokumenty i materialy.* Moskva, 1977.
Stegemann, Wolf. *Dorsten zwischen Kaiserreich und Hakenkreuz: die Krisenjahre der Weimarer Republik 1918–1933. Eine Dokumentation zur Zeitgeschichte;* Bd. 5. Dorsten, 1987.
Sukhorukov, Sergei Romanovich. *Zapadnogermanskaia burzhuaznaia istoriografiia sovetsko-germanskikh otnoshenii 1917–1932.* Moskva, 1976.
Sundermann, Helmut. *Das Erbe des falschen Propheten; Moskaus Kampf um Deutschland, von Lenin bis heute—und morgen?* Leoni am Starnberger See, 1958.
Sutterlin, Ingmar. *Die "Russische Abteilung" des Auswartigen Amtes in der Weimarer Republik.* Historische Forschungen; Bd. 51. Berlin, 1994.
Thoms, Robert. *Handbuch zur Geschichte der deutschen Freikorps.* Muenchen, 2001.
Tiedemann, Helmut. *Sowjetrussland und die revolutionierung Deutschlands 1917–1919.* Historische studien. Hrsg. von dr. Emil Ebering. Hft. 296. Berlin, 1936.
Trubaichuk, Anatolii. *Brudershaft dvokh dyktatoriv: XX storichchia, politika v portretakh.* Kyiv, 1993.

Trukhnov, G. M. *Iz istorii sovetsko-germanskikh otnoshenii: (1920–1922 gg.)*. Minsk, 1974.
Trukhnov, G. M. *Pouchitel'nye uroki istorii: tri sovetsko-germanskikh dogovora (1922–1926 gg.)*. Minsk, 1979.
Trukhnov, G. M. *Rapallo v deistvii: iz istorii sovetsko-germanskikh otnoshenii, 1926–1929 gg*. Minsk, 1982.
Verpasst eure Chancen nicht: Aspekte der deutsch-russichien Beziehungen im 20. Jahrhundert: Beitrage. Schriften der Muhlheimer Initiative. Mainz, 1992.
Vincent, C. Paul. *The Politics of Hunger: The Allied Blockade of Germany, 1915–1919*. London, 1985.
Volkov, F. D. *Tainoe stanovitsia iavnym: deiatel'nost' diplomatii i razvedki zapadnykh derzhav v gody vtoroi mirovoi voiny*. Moskva, 1989.
Wagner, Armin. *Das Bild Sowjetrusslands in den Memoiren deutscher Diplomaten der Weimarer Republik*. Studien zur Weimarer Geschichte; Bd. 2. Munster, 1995.
Wagner, Gerhard. *Deutschland und der polnisch-sowjetische Krieg 1920*. Veroffentlichungen des Instituts fur Europaische Geschichte Mainz; Bd. 93. Wiesbaden, 1979.
Waldman, Eric. *The Spartacist Uprising of 1919 and the Crisis of the German Socialist Movement*. Milwaukee, 1958.
Walsdorff, Martin. *Westorientierung und Ostpolitik. Stresemanns Russlandpolitik in d. Locarno-Ara*. Bremen, 1971.
Wandycz, Piotr. *France and Her Eastern Allies, 1919–1925*. Minneapolis, MN, 1962.
Wandycz, Piotr. *Soviet-Polish Relations, 1917–1921*. Cambridge, MA, 1969.
Weill-Raynard, Etienne. *Les Reparations allemandes et la France*. Paris, 1947.
Wyss, Roger de. *L'Allemagne et la paix; documents de 15 annees*. Paris, 1932.
Yamauchi, Masayuki. *The Green Crescent Under the Red Star: Enver Pasha in Soviet Russia, 1919–1922*. Tokyo, 1991.
Zarusky, Jurgen. *Die deutschen Sozialdemokraten und das sowjetische Modell: ideologische Auseinandersetzung und aussenpolitische Konzeptionen 1917–1933*. Studien zur Zeitgeschichte; Bd. 39. Muenchen, 1992.
Zeidler, Manfred. *Reichswehr und Rote Armee, 1920–1933: Wege und Stationen einer ungewohnlichen Zusammenarbeit*. Beitrage zur Militargeschichte; Bd. 36. Muenchen, 1993.
Zitelmann, Franz Carl. *Russland im Friedensvertrag von Versailles (Artikel 116, 117, 292, 293, 433 des Friedensvertrags)*. Berlin, 1920.
Zsigmond, Laszlo. *Zur deutschen Frage, 1918–1923; die wirtschaftlichen und internationalen Faktoren der Wiederbelebung des deutschen Imperialismus und Militarismus*. Studia historica Academiae Scientiarum Hungaricae, 55. Budapest, 1964.
Zug, Josef. *Versuche der Wiederannaherung an Russland unter Reichskanzler Furst Chlodwig zu Hohenlohe-Schillingsfurst*. Dissertation,Tuebingen, 1934.

Index

AEG, 55, 71, 81, 130
Aero-Union, 147
Allenstein, 47, 83, 89
Alsace-Lorraine, 10, 45, 47
Anglo-Russian Trade Agreement, 109
Armenia, 79, 80
Ataturk, 36, 40
Ausamt, 108, 112
Avalov-Bermondt, 43, 56, 69, 95

Baden, 73
Baku, 14
Balfour, 157
Bauer, 46, 69, 72, 73
Bauer, Colonel, 36, 58, 70
Bavaria, 3, 16, 17, 18, 20, 55, 73, 74
Behrendt, 131
Behrens, Herr, 81
Bela Kun, 33, 39, 52
Belgium, 46, 47
Belorussia, 14, 25, 79
Berklund, 132
Bersol, 5, 63
Bismarck, 2, 35
Blitzkrieg, 4
blockade of Germany, 18, 47, 48
Bogdanov, 128
Bolshevik Revolution, 8, 16
Boxer Rebellion, 53
Breen, Captain, 71
Briande, Aristide, 130
Brockdorff-Rantzau, 1, 44, 50, 92, 113, 114, 126, 129, 130, 137, 138, 143, 144, 158, 159, 160, 161, 162, 163, 164, 165, 167, 172
Brygkov, 100, 101
Bukharin, 26, 86, 119
Bulgaria, 30

Cannes Conference, 137
Carr, E. H., 36, 41, 58
Carsten, F. L., 6, 92
Center Party, 14, 20
Chicherin, 2, 25, 69, 80, 84, 85, 90, 91, 94, 95, 97, 101, 104, 106, 107, 108, 109, 111, 112, 113, 114, 119, 121, 122, 124, 125, 126, 128, 129, 132, 134, 136, 138, 141, 142, 144, 149, 164, 167, 171
China, 52, 53
Churchill, Winston, 28
Clemenceau, Georges, 39, 44, 47, 63
Cologne, 22
Comintern, 2, 5, 38, 56, 58, 64, 76, 99, 101, 106, 111, 112, 113, 114, 119, 120, 121, 124, 125, 135
Conference of Ambassadors, 105
Curzon, 57, 69, 70, 71
Czech Legion, 12, 13
Czechoslovakia, 13, 37, 39, 112, 116

D'Abernon, 103, 124, 147, 148, 149, 152, 168, 172
Danzig, 89
Dardanelles, 10
de Gaulle, Charles, 93
Denikin, 28, 29, 38, 52, 57, 79
Denmark, 66, 67
Derby, Earl of, 71
Deschanel, Paul, 63
Desticker, 157
Deutsch, 55, 81, 130
Deutsche Offizierbund, 81
Djemal Pasha, 71
Dzerzhinskii, 90

East Prussia, 42, 73
Ebert, 14, 19, 20, 22, 26, 27, 30, 31, 32, 72, 73, 151, 159
Eckhardstein, Baron, 71
Ehrhardt brigade, 73
Eisner, Kurt, 3, 16, 17, 32, 34
Ekaterinburg, 13, 28
Entente, 2
Enver Pasha, 36, 40, 41, 42, 43, 44, 50, 53, 54, 55, 57, 61, 64, 65, 71, 90, 91, 92, 95, 96, 98, 113, 170, 171
Erzberger, Matthias, 15, 18, 20, 23, 69
Estonia, 11, 12, 14, 22, 28, 43, 66
Eupen, 47, 97

February Revolution, 8, 9
Fehrenbach, 119
Finland, 12, 14, 21, 49, 98, 152
Fischer, 139, 140, 163
Foch, Marshal, 75, 103, 157
Fourteen Points, 9, 15, 16, 18, 28, 30, 31, 51
Franco-Polish Mutual Assistance Treaty, 107
Freikorps, 30, 33, 36, 38, 43, 72, 73
Freiwillige Russische Westarmee, 56

Galle, 112
Genoa conference, 21, 137, 140, 141, 143
Georgia, 14
German colonies, 47, 49
Gesellschaft zur Foerderung gewerblicher Unternehmungen (GEFU), 5, 62, 63
Gilan, Soviet Republic of, 79
Goltz, Ruediger von der, 38, 43, 53, 54, 56
Gorbynov, 133, 138
Gorlov, Sergei A., 7
Great Purges, 23
Groener, 19, 33

Haase, Hugo, 2, 24, 25, 26, 32, 127, 128, 132, 134, 140, 143, 146, 151, 154, 164
Haniel, 147, 148
Hedley, 70, 71
Heinrich of Prussia, 15
Henderson, Neville, 172
Hilger, Gustav, 55, 114, 115, 120, 129, 165
Hindenburg, 19, 96
Hintze, 59, 152, 163
Hitler, 4, 5
Hoffmann, 11, 24, 103, 107
Hoover, Herbert, 48
Humann, 41, 43, 53, 54
Hungary, 39

Independent Socialists, 15, 16, 17, 18, 19, 27, 29, 32, 33, 100
Inter Allied Aeronautical Committee of Control (IAACC), 96
Iron Division, 38
Italian Socialist Congress, 56

Japan, 13, 49, 53, 66
Junkers, 63, 127, 132, 134, 136, 142, 147, 165

Kapp Putsch, 72, 73, 76, 79, 87
Kapp, Wolfgang, 72, 74, 75
Karakhan, 115, 133, 142
Kazan, 4, 169
Kerensky, 9, 12
Kiel mutiny, 15, 20, 32
Kiev, 37, 50
Kilmarnock, 69, 70, 71, 80
Kolchak, 22, 28, 56, 57
Kopp, 55, 57, 58, 60, 68, 70, 71, 80, 81, 84, 93, 94, 95, 97, 100, 101, 102, 104, 106, 107, 108, 111, 112, 113, 114, 115, 119, 120, 121, 122, 125, 126, 127, 128, 129, 133, 134, 135, 163, 171
Korfanty, 117, 118
Kowno, 41, 42

KPD (German Communist Party), 29, 30, 31, 58, 59, 74, 75, 111, 112, 114
Krasin, 66, 100, 107, 127, 128, 140
Krestinsky, Nikolai, 131, 133, 134, 138, 140, 141
Krupp, 101, 102, 113, 121, 122, 123, 136, 138, 139

Lange, 64
Latvia, 11, 12, 29, 38, 43, 56, 66, 84
Laurent, Charles, 130, 133
Le Rond, Henri, 118
League of Nations, 31, 45, 63, 67, 97, 118, 119, 130, 133, 141
Lebedev, 134
Lejava, 94
Lenin, 3, 9, 12, 27, 37, 38, 61, 69, 90, 91, 95, 97, 113, 119, 120, 121, 126, 131, 133, 136, 138, 171
Leningrad, 5
Levine, Eugen, 33
Liebknecht, Karl, 20, 24, 27, 30, 33
Linke, Horst Guenther, 7
Lithuania, 11, 12, 21, 25, 29, 41, 42, 43, 56, 57, 60, 83, 84, 93, 95, 97, 147
Little Entente, 122
Litvinov, Maxim, 121, 131, 132, 134, 141, 142
Livonia, 14
Lloyd George, David, 9, 39, 47, 49, 67, 93, 118, 149
Lloydostflug, 147
Lohmann, 161
London Conference, 67, 166
Ludendorff, 3, 21, 36, 59, 69, 80, 96, 102, 103, 104, 107, 129, 130
Luettwitz, 72
Luftwaffe, 4
Lutovinov, 112, 119, 121, 126
Luxemburg, Rosa, 27, 29, 30, 58

Majority Socialists, 17, 18, 19, 27
Malcolm, Neill, 69, 70, 102
Malmedy, 47, 97

Maltzan, 66, 71, 84, 101, 124, 130, 131, 133, 138, 146, 148
March Action, 111
Marienwerder, 83, 89
Marx, Karl, 8, 54
Maximilian of Baden, 15, 19
Memel, 47, 67
Mirbach, 95
Mohammed VI, Sultan, 36
Molotilovka and Zlatoust Works, 152
Molotov, 125, 169
Molotov–Ribbentrop Pact, 4, 35
Moor, Karl, 41
Moresnet, 47
Moscow, Treaty of, 84
Mueller, Gordon H., 57, 71, 74, 76

National Bolshevism, 4, 36
National Constituent Assembly, 22, 27, 29, 31, 50
Neumann, Herr, 5
Niedermayer, Oskar Ritter von, 5, 62, 100, 101, 104, 106, 114, 115, 120, 124, 126, 127, 128, 129, 134, 139, 140, 163
Niessel, 103, 104
Nitti, Signor, 1, 67, 173
Nollet, 157
Noske, Gustav, 15, 32, 38, 69, 73

Odessa, 37, 50
Omsk, 56
Ostpolitik (Eastern Policy), 35, 106
Ottoman Empire, 10

Paris Conference, 107
Paris Peace Conference, 30, 31, 39, 48, 61, 171
Petrograd, 5
Pilsudski, 16, 21, 28, 39, 60, 93
Poland, 4, 5, 10, 11, 12, 16, 21, 28, 32, 36, 37, 39, 44, 45, 51, 52, 57, 60, 67, 68, 69, 76, 77, 78, 79, 82, 83, 84, 85, 88, 89, 90, 91, 93, 96, 97, 103, 108, 110, 118, 119, 127, 139, 141, 171

Pomerania, 73
Posen, 4, 28, 47, 89
Provisional Government, 9

Rabenau, 35
Radek, Karl, 23, 29, 30, 32, 33, 34, 36, 37, 40, 41, 44, 50, 54, 55, 58, 60, 61, 64, 65, 102, 112, 124, 132, 133, 134, 135, 138, 139, 140, 141, 142, 149, 151, 166, 170, 171
Rakovsky, 26, 140
Rathenau, Walther, 54, 55, 125, 130, 142, 143, 144, 147
Red Army, 4, 5, 28, 33, 37, 52, 56, 61, 69, 78, 80, 84, 84, 95, 98, 113, 120, 124, 136, 141, 156, 169
Reibnitz, 36, 58
Reichstag, 14, 45, 47, 50, 51
reparations, 82, 107, 110, 117, 120, 156, 158
Reparations Commission, 45
Revolutionary Shop Stewards, 15
Rhineland, 74, 75
Rhineland Republic, 49
Ribbentrop, 169
Riga, 38, 43
Romania, 39, 116
Rosengolts, 167
Royal Navy, 22
Rumania, 27
Russian Civil War, 2, 4, 12, 13, 18, 28, 31, 49, 52, 56, 59, 61, 66, 98, 143, 167, 171
Russo-Polish war, 36, 65, 79, 80, 83, 84, 85, 88, 90, 93, 95, 109, 140, 156
Rykov, Alexey, 107, 138

Saar region, 67
Sabbatnig, 112
Said Emin Effendi, 53, 54
St Petersburg, 5
Salzburg, 120
Samara, 5

San Remo, 76
Saxony, 73
Scapa Flow, 46
Scheidemann, 19, 32, 46, 113
Schering, 139
Schlesinger, 70, 102
Schleswig, 47, 66, 67
Schlieffen, 134
Schmidt, Gustav, 59
Schubert, 62, 128
Schuler, Geheimrat, 81
Schwartz, Regierungsrat, 149
Seeckt, Hans von, 35, 36, 40, 41, 42, 43, 44, 47, 50, 53, 61, 62, 64, 72, 76, 77, 78, 79, 85, 86, 87, 88, 90, 91, 92, 93, 102, 103, 104, 106, 113, 124, 126, 127, 129, 130, 132, 134, 137, 139, 140, 141, 142, 143, 151, 158, 159, 161, 162, 163, 165, 170, 171
Semenov, Nikolai, 56
Senegalese troops, 75
Serbia, 10
Shantung, 53
Shoeneberg, Dr, 70
Silesia, 38, 47, 73
Simons, 55, 94, 95, 100, 103, 107, 108, 112, 161, 165
Sklyansky, 92, 142
SMS Markgraf, 15
Soblatnik, 133
Social Democrats, 3, 14, 22, 30, 31, 32, 151
Sondergruppe R., Wirth, 5, 62, 63, 101, 106, 114, 115, 124, 128, 131, 134, 135, 139, 142, 143, 146, 147, 154, 158, 164, 167
Spa, 19
Spa Conference, 82
Spanish influenza, 20, 27, 48
Spartacists, 18, 20, 27, 29, 30, 31, 32, 74
Stalin, 5
Stinnes, 101, 127, 131, 133
Stomonyakov, 139
Strasbourg, 21

Stresemann, Gustav, 172
Switzerland, 33

Talaat Pasha, 40, 71
Tallents, Colonel, 93
Tartu, Treaty of, 66
Tashkent, 71
Teschen, 37
Thomsen, 140
Tilsit, 42
Tirpitz, Admiral, 72
Treaty of Brest-Litovsk, 2, 4, 8, 12, 13, 14, 18, 21, 23, 34, 148
Treaty of Dorpat, 98
Treaty of Rapallo, 4, 6, 21, 106, 137, 143, 144, 151, 160, 168, 169
Treaty of Riga, 84, 93, 98, 109
Treaty of Versailles, 2, 4, 6, 41, 46, 47, 48, 50, 52, 56, 58, 61, 63, 74, 75, 76, 82, 85, 89, 97, 100, 108, 110, 117, 118, 134, 138, 152
Trotsky, 11, 13, 23, 34, 38, 69, 92, 94, 95, 100, 107, 119, 124, 128, 131, 132, 133, 134, 136, 139, 153, 161, 163, 170, 171
Tschunke, 41, 42, 128, 164
Tukhachevsky, 80, 83, 90, 93, 94
Tula, 5
Turkey, 30

Ukraine, 11, 12, 14, 27, 37, 38, 50, 53, 79, 98, 131
United States, 12
Unshlikht, 94
Upper Silesia, 51, 67, 108, 110, 111, 117, 118, 119, 125, 127, 130, 133, 141

Varga Bureau, 121
Vemach, 139
Vickers, 102
Vilna, 29, 84, 97
Vilnus, 83
Vladivostok, 66

Warsaw, 4, 36
Weimar Constitution, 50, 51
Weimar Republic, 3
Werchoski, 78
West Prussia, 4, 47, 74, 88, 90
Weygand, Charles de Gaulle, 93
White Russians, 2, 12, 13, 22, 28, 29, 31, 38, 43, 52, 56, 61, 79, 81, 98, 109, 171
Wiedefeld, 129, 134, 138, 142
Wilhelm II, Kaiser, 2, 15, 19, 63
William, King of Lithuania, 21
Wilson, 15, 16, 25, 31, 39, 45, 47, 48, 51, 61, 89
Wirth, Sondergruppe R., 63, 92, 119, 127, 130, 142, 143, 159, 160, 161, 167
Wrangel, 79, 98
Wuerttemburg, 73, 74
Wurtzbacher, 132

Yoffe, 23, 24, 25, 55, 56, 76, 93, 154
Young Turks, 36, 40
Yudenich, 28, 52, 57

Zentrale Moskau, 5, 115, 165, 167
Zinoviev, 98
Zlatoust, 5